T0293276

The Changing C-Suite

The Changing C-Suite

Executive Power in Transformation

José Luis Alvarez
Silviya Svejenova

OXFORD
UNIVERSITY PRESS

OXFORD
UNIVERSITY PRESS

Great Clarendon Street, Oxford, OX2 6DP,
United Kingdom

Oxford University Press is a department of the University of Oxford.
It furthers the University's objective of excellence in research, scholarship,
and education by publishing worldwide. Oxford is a registered trade mark of
Oxford University Press in the UK and in certain other countries

Impression: 1

Published in the United States of America by Oxford University Press
198 Madison Avenue, New York, NY 10016, United States of America

British Library Cataloguing in Publication Data
Data available

Library of Congress Control Number: 2021939897

ISBN 978-0-19-872842-9

DOI: 10.1093/oso/9780198728429.001.0001

Printed and bound by
CPI Group (UK) Ltd, Croydon, CR0 4YY

Hilma af Klint, *The Ten Largest, No. 3, Youth,* 1907.

To Camila and Adrian

To Isabel, Emil, and Johanne

Contents

List of Figures and Tables

Figures

Tables

1
The Changing C-Suite

> The serendipity pattern refers to the fairly common experience of observing an *unanticipated, anomalous and strategic* datum which becomes the occasion for developing a new theory or for extending an existing theory. . . . it stimulates the investigator to 'make sense of the datum', to fit it into a broader frame of knowledge.
>
> **Merton (1948: 506, emphasis in original)**

This book is about changing corporate power structures, and as such, is concerned with formal organization mechanisms and elites. Specifically, we examine the evolving ways in which power at the apex of complex organizations is structured through roles and relationships in anticipation of and in response to diverse forces and interests. Our attention was drawn to the changing C-suite, a term denoting the most important senior executives in an organization, by the variation in and proliferation of new Chief X Officer (CXO) roles, in which X stands for a specific domain (e.g. sustainability, communication, data, innovation, human resources, etc.).

The choice of Swedish artist Hilma af Klint's painting 'Youth' (The Ten Largest, No. 3, Group IV, 1907) as the cover image of the book is not accidental. It goes beyond the fascination we harbour for the artist's pioneering spirit and powerful work. It has to do with this painting's force to capture 'a present mood of restless searching' (Schjeldahl, 2018). We believe af Klint's lively, dynamic, and colourful forms encapsulate and aptly convey the main quest of this book: to enable a better understanding of the restless organizational search for new executive roles, and overall, more generally, of executive power in transformation.

By exploring the multiple forces and entangled interests involved in the emergence and evolution of these CXO roles and the ongoing transformation of the C-suite they constitute, we seek to understand these elites' new 'command posts' and forms of expertise (Zald and Lounsbury, 2010).

The Changing C-Suite. José Luis Alvarez and Silviya Svejenova, Oxford University Press.
© José Luis Alvarez and Silviya Svejenova (2022). DOI: 10.1093/oso/9780198728429.003.0001

By advancing this understanding, we aim to extend the political perspective of organization (March, 1962; Weber and Waeger, 2017; Waeger and Weber, 2019), which has largely overlooked the changing design of executive power and its implications for organization. We think that the current moment is particularly timely for such an investigation, as it is in moments of environmental change as well as strategic and structural transformation, such as the ongoing introduction of a plethora of new CXO roles, that the political model of organizations is better revealed and assessed (Ocasio, 1994). Our aim is to develop a theoretical account (combined with numerous empirical illustrations) of the C-suite's transformation over the last two decades: its magnitude and meaning, its co-construction by different interests, and its potential significance for organizational control, executive expertise and identity, and dynamics of top management teams (TMTs).

There is growing interest among practitioners in the evolution of the C-suite and different CXO roles in TMTs. It is visible in a wealth of 'how-tos', 'tool boxes', or 'playbooks' with 'confessions' of successful CXOs, as well as insights into their work realities and future needs (among a lengthy list of possibilities, see for example, Carruthers and Jackson, 2018 on the Chief Data Officer; Roberts and Watson, 2014 on the Chief Information Officer; Elkeles and Phillips, 2011 and Elkeles, Phillips, and Phillips, 2017 on the Chief Learning Officer and its transition into Chief Talent Officer; Wright et al., 2011 on the Chief Human Resource Officer; McCracken, 2009 on the Chief Culture Officer; Bottger, 2008 on leading as a member of the top team and the challenges confronted by CXOs, and Bennett and Miles, 2006a on the COO).

Moreover, sustained media attention has highlighted the emergence, proliferation, and obsolescence of CXO roles; zoomed in on distinguished role occupants (e.g. the appointment of Sir Jonathan Paul (Jony) Ive as Apple's first Chief Design Officer, etc.); and provided interpretations of this phenomenon for both business audiences and the general public. For example, an article in *The Economist* (30 January 2021: digital edition) suggested that 'fresh executive roles' are 'a convenient tool' for chief executive officers.

A *Financial Times* article (Jacobs, 2021; online edition) zoomed in on the recent Covid-19-related expansion of Chief Medical or Chief Health Officers (typically former doctors) from 'healthcare, science, sport and pharmaceuticals' where the focus originally was 'on helping to create and market products and services for customers' to the likes of Google, BP, or

Ford of Britain where the emphasis is on 'work[ing] with human resources and senior executives to develop and implement strategies to take care of employees' physical and mental health, as well as overseeing workplace safety' and well-being (Jacobs, 2021).

Media articles have also voiced concerns regarding title inflation and the associated 'uptitling' and 'title-fluffing' vocabulary, cautioning that in some cases, 'C is for Silly' (Goudreau, 2012). An article 'Shallow Impact' (*The Economist*, 10 April 2021, p. 52) featured a mocking 'leaked memo from a chief impact officer', in which he ('a white male on a six-figure salary') addresses the organization for the first time since his appointment, justifying his title:

> The job title may seem odd, but with a change of one letter in the title, think of me as a 'champo', championing the things our organisation cares about. I will be flying round the world to promote our focus on combating climate change. Along with the chief happiness officer, I will be trying to maintain employee morale. Expect to receive regular weekly surveys about your physical and mental health, and on whether you are able to get on with your work or feel bogged down by corporate bureaucracy. Remember, there is no 'I' in team but there are three in chief impact officer. I will be using them to watch over you all.

The fictitious chief impact officer also clarifies that his 'plan is to invest in high-quality impact data to ensure we are at the leading edge of impact measurement' (*The Economist*, 10 April 2021, p. 52). An article in *The Economist* (24 June 2010: digital edition) titled 'Too many chiefs', which includes an illustration of a diligently working Chief Stationery Officer who also holds a number of other titles, affirms that, if left unchecked, this trend has the potential to bring about 'a bull market in chief safety officers and chief apology officers'. Yet, as Power (2004: 52) reminds us, one should 'be wary, but not entirely dismissive of new roles with fancy titles who talk up the value-adding potential' of certain functions and activities.

Additionally, as we show in this book, the C-suite, with its army of classic and contemporary CXO titles, has been (since the late 1990s) at the centre of a continuously developing interest and practice area for global professional services, management consultancies and executive search firms. Firms such as Accenture, Bain & Company, Boston Consulting Group (BCG), Deloitte, Egon Zehnder, Ernst & Young (EY), IBM, Heidrick &

Struggles, Korn Ferry, KPMG, and McKinsey & Company, among others, have surveyed, interviewed, and engaged in deep-dive conversations with CEOs (Chief Executive Officers) and other CXOs to provide and publish advice on the evolution of different roles in reports, white papers, and articles. These publications have continuously affirmed which roles are critical at a given point in time, whether they are 'rising' or 'falling', and what the hurdles and opportunities are for the future. Because they draw on and quote from a wealth of interviews and in-depth conversations with CEOs and CXOs, such publications offer insights not only into the provided consulting advice, but also into executives' changing views and priorities.

Last, scholars have begun to examine the adoption and evolution of a variety of C-suite roles (Menz, 2012; Guadalupe, Li, and Wulf, 2014; Radek and Menz, 2020) and the diffusion and legitimation of specific roles, among which Chief Financial Officer (CFO; Fligstein, 1987; Zorn, 2004), Chief Operations Officer (COO; Dobbin et al., 2001; Hambrick and Cannella, 2004), and knowledge chiefs such as the Chief Knowledge Officer, Chief Learning Officer, Chief Privacy Officer (Bontis, 2001; Awazu and Desouza, 2004); Chief Risk Officer (Power, 2007; Pernell, Jung, and Dobbin, 2017), Chief Strategy Officer (Delmar, 2003; Menz et al., 2013; Menz and Scheef, 2014), Chief External Officer (Doh et al., 2014), Chief Sustainability Officer (Miller and Serafeim, 2014), and Chief Digital Officer (Kunisch, Menz, and Langan, 2020).

Yet, despite this growing interest in CXOs, academic research into executive power structures is still lacking, as Menz (2012) and Radek and Menz (2020) recognized in their reviews, which are the most exhaustive to date. Scholars have not sufficiently researched CXO roles in terms of their macro- and micro-dynamics, nor have they delved into incumbents' shared expertise, identity, and style; their dynamic interactions with other C-suite executives; and their potential to change how TMTs function. Above all, there is a need for a comprehensive theoretical articulation and understanding of the different aspects of the CXO phenomenon: the macro, mezzo, and micro processes associated with it, and not least, its significance and implications for formal organization and organizational elites. We seek to address this need in this book.

This is our second co-authored book on the topic of executive power. In our first book, *Sharing Executive Power: Roles and Relationships at the Top* (Alvarez and Svejenova, 2005), we began with the assumption that

in large, complex organizations which are embedded in highly differentiated environments, a single executive leader—no matter how exceptionally
gifted, and regardless of personality or competencies—cannot cope with
the increasing and variegated demands of the top role. We centred on a particular solution to that executive challenge, which we called 'small numbers
at the top', that is, duos and trios collectively fulfilling the top executive's
responsibilities, which was a rarely recognized and undertheorized phenomenon at the time. Doing so enabled us to take a deep dive into the
significance of power sharing roles and relationships in the unfolding of
executive action. It also allowed us to question the individualism that pre-
dominates in conceptions of organizational power, reveal a plurality of
alternative power structures, and explore important contingencies affecting
them. In that book, we focused mainly on Chief Executive Officers (CEOs),
CFOs, and COOs. However, as noted in Merton's (1948) opening quote,
that endeavour made us aware of a 'strategic datum'—the growing ecology
of CXOs which continued to expand and change its status ordering before
our eyes as we began to study the changing C-suite—thereby prompting the
current theorizing.

In this book, we build on these insights into power design, redirect-
ing our focus to a universal element of complex organizations' vertical
structures: the TMT. This unit is responsible for formulating and implementing a firm's strategy, and redefining and re-shaping its horizontal
structures by making decisions about the division and coordination of
labour and organizational systems (e.g. information, control, compensation, etc.). Drucker (1973: 603) discussed top management as a distinctive
kind of work under the 'organizational roof', defining it as 'the directing,
vision-setting, standard-setting organ' and recognizing the 'challenges of
structure and strategy with respect to size and complexity, diversity and diversification, growth, change, and innovation'. In a later interview (Harris,
1993: 122), Drucker acknowledged his discomfort with the term 'manager'
because it implied subordinates, and his preference for the term 'executive' as it indicated responsibility for a specific functional area. If one
goes back to Barnard (1938: 215; italics in original), executive work is
defined as 'the specialized work of *maintaining* the organization in operation'. As such, it ensures the maintenance of 'a system of cooperative effort'
(Barnard, 1938: 216).

Hence, this is a book about the changing executive team, which Selznick
(2005) termed 'private government'. In line with this metaphor, Selznick

(2005: 37) used the term 'governors' to refer to members of TMTs due to the important impacts they have on the well-being of organizational stakeholders and members and 'much else that goes on in the life of a large enterprise'. As such, we do not deal with the structure of governance bodies and actors, such as boards of directors and shareholder groups, although we do take them into account in discussing the complexities that must be addressed by the top executive group, as boards are part of CEOs' and executive committees' external environment.

1.1 Theoretical opportunity

There is a major academic opportunity to study executive teams in terms of the division of labour across different CXO roles. As Strang and Baron (1990) noted in relation to the structure of job titles, research that views the division of labour as problematic is scant, leading to overlooking essential aspects of organizational inequalities and politics. This observation is especially pertinent in relation to the division of labour in executive teams. Mintzberg's (1979) assertion decades ago that the 'strategic apex' is a black box that must be opened and explored largely remains true today.

Two main perspectives inform the understanding of TMTs: strategic leadership and organizational demography (Beckman and Burton, 2011). Strategic leadership (Finkelstein and Hambrick, 1996), also known as the 'upper echelons' perspective (Hambrick and Mason, 1984), emphasizes the critical role of CEOs and TMTs in explaining phenomena ranging from firms' strategies to their social and political orientations. However, even the academic leader of this approach, Donald Hambrick (2007: 337), recognizes that 'there needs to be much more attention paid to the structure of TMTs, to complement—and improve—our understanding of TMT composition and processes'. Another stream of work on strategic leadership has emphasized its collective character and has focused on the process through which it unfolds, as well as on how roles and influences evolve; it has also examined it 'as a supraorganizational phenomenon in which leadership roles and influences on them can extend beyond focal organizational boundaries' (Denis, Lamothe and Langley, 2001: 810). The top management demography perspective, informed by sociology and organization studies, has sought to capture the structural conditions that influence top team interactions. However, since the mid-1990s, the study of senior teams' structures has become dominated by the strategic leadership perspective and lost sight of structure and dynamics (Beckman and Burton, 2011). More recently, Guadalupe et al. (2014: 824) also affirmed that 'we know less about the 'structure' and the 'allocation of roles' among the positions reporting directly to the CEO, and how these have changed over time'.

We recognize the contributions of the strategic leadership and organizational demography literatures to the understanding of executive power structures, and focus on the very same unit of analysis. Yet, we adopt a different approach in the direction proposed by Beckman and Burton (2011) in their critique of research on TMTs. Their research agenda emphasizes delving deeper into TMT structures by focusing on roles and exploring how these roles and teams transform over time, something which also resonates with research by Denis et al. (2001). Beckman and Burton (2011) acknowledged:

> Given the known game of musical chairs in the executive suite as people come and go, and the extensive changes in organizational structures that change the chairs drawn up to the table, it is surprising that most scholarship on top management team (TMT) demography is cross-sectional in nature and implicitly treats the TMT as a stable entity.
>
> (Beckman and Burton, 2011: 49)

Our approach to advancing the theoretical understanding of CXO roles and executive teams involves examining the theorizing, expansion, identity, expertise, and style of top executives' roles and titles, and implications for executive team dynamics. Our line of reasoning can be understood in the context of recent calls for scholars to revisit formal organization and its management (Greenwood, Hinings, and Whetten, 2014; du Gay and Vikkelsø, 2017) wherein job definitions are central (Strang and Baron, 1990), and to delve into organizational microstructures (Puranam, 2018).

Our arguments draw on different theories. First, we not only borrow insights from institutional and neo-institutional theories of organization, but seek to contribute to them, particularly by enabling a better understanding of the overall structuring and management of organizations (Greenwood et al., 2014). We build on research on organizational and strategic responses to institutional complexity resulting from exposure to and ambivalent interpretations of multiple and conflicting pressures (Greenwood et al., 2011; Raynard, 2016; Vermeulen et al., 2016). As incompatible prescriptions and conflicting demands increase, new CXO roles are being designed and established to address them. Thus, additional attention needs to be directed to 'the way jobs are defined, related and coordinated at different levels in the organization' (Vermeulen et al., 2016: 283), particularly in the C-suite as the private government (Selznick, 2005), as organizations seek to ensure legitimacy, competitiveness, and survival.

Moreover, neo-institutionalists have rather prominently studied the diffusion of practices and symbols across organizations (DiMaggio and Powell, 1983; Tolbert and Zucker, 1983; Fligstein, 1985; Baron, Dobbin, and Jennings, 1986; Meyer, 2002; Boxenbaum and Jonsson, 2017), providing useful insights for the diffusion of CXO roles in a context of global expansion of organizations and management (Bromley and Meyer, 2015, 2021). In addition, early and subsequent institutional accounts have been foundational to the understanding and theorization of roles. For example, acknowledging how organizational roles 'share in the controlling character of institutionalization', Berger and Luckmann (1966[1991]: 74) recognized that 'the construction of role typologies is a necessary correlate of the institutionalization of conduct' and 'roles, objectified linguistically, are an essential ingredient of the objectively available world of any society'. We complement the institutional insights on roles and role identities at the field level (Meyer and Hammerschmid, 2006; Goodrick and Reay, 2010) with work on roles as political resources at the organizational level (Baker and Faulkner, 1991; Callero, 1994).

Second, we rely on contingency theory, which—despite claims of its obsolescence—remains a relevant lens for understanding the structural design of organizations, particularly in terms of how they are managed and coordinated (Greenwood et al., 2014) in their specific organizational and environmental contexts. Lawrence and Lorsch's (1967a) work on the differentiation of organizational units in response to the complex and changing environment and the need for subsequent integration through different devices continues to be a lens for understanding power design, as it provides a useful set of concepts to depict organizational management (Van de Ven, Ganco, and Hinings, 2013). Moreover, as Chandler (1962: 299) affirmed, design decisions typically are part of the top job:

> Complexity in itself, it should be emphasized, did not assure innovation or change; some responsible administrator had to become aware of the new conditions. Furthermore, awareness had to be translated into a plan

for meeting the new conditions, and then the plan had to accepted by most of the senior executives.

Third, we connect with and contribute to political theories of organizations (March, 1962; Tushman, 1977a), which conceptualize organizations as open polities and focus on management elites (Weber and Waeger, 2017). As Joseph, Ocasio, and McDonnell (2014: 1835) astutely pointed out: 'Powerful organizational elites strategically respond to new logics, seeking to adopt structures that ostensibly conform, but which function in practice to promote the elites' own interests.' In their review of the current state of political theories, Weber and Waeger (2017) affirmed their key premise that internal political processes interface with external contingencies via boundary processes. Waeger and Weber (2019) also argued that organizational responses to institutional complexity can be accounted for by attending to the historical imprinting of political features. As we show in the chapters that follow, CXOs operating at the hierarchical apexes of organizations are the ones performing that boundary work. They are also design manifestations of this historical imprinting.

In this book, we bring these theoretical streams together to advance conceptual ideas about how the management 'category' of CXOs expands in nomenclature and adoption, as well as how the meaning of CXO labels and roles is constructed and reconstructed in terms of expertise, identities, style, and interactions with the CEO and other CXOs in the top team. As Menz (2012: 46) acknowledged, research on changes in the power structures of organizations' top decision-making teams is a relatively young area with great potential where 'there is a need to integrate dispersed insights and approaches upon which future studies can build'. The integrated theorizing of this phenomenon is the main ambition and pursued contribution of this work.

1.2 Empirical phenomenon

This book is motivated by and delves into a significant empirical phenomenon: the new realities of executive roles (i.e. CXOs) in terms of their expansion, expertise, identity, style, and relationships (which involve both competition and collaboration), and how they are changing organizational power structures and dynamics in the C-suite. At the end of the twentieth century, Rivero and Spencer (1998: 60) observed that the C-suite was changing: 'Over the past twenty years there has been a shift in the strategic distribution of leadership roles at the top of corporate organizations'. Nearly a decade and a half later, Guadalupe et al. (2014) noted that the size of the C-suite had doubled since the mid-1980s. Here, we highlight some aspects of the phenomenon in very broad strokes; we delve into specificities and provide potential theoretical explanations in the chapters to come.

The C-suite is a relatively recent phenomenon and alternative accounts exist about when, where, and how it originated. Here, we present two such accounts—Drucker's (1973) and Chandler's (1976)—without seeking to reconcile them, as they describe developments in Europe and the United States at different points in time.

Drucker (1973) situated the origins of the top team in Germany in relation to the development of the institution of the 'universal bank'— specifically, Deutsche Bank and the work of Georg Siemens between 1870 and 1880. Drucker (1973: 606–7) clarified that Siemens had built 'a top management [team]—the first such organ in economic and business history'—which 'transformed this partnership of co-owners into a top management team of professionals'. Drucker (1973) described Siemens's work in detail:

> He analysed the key activities of the bank and made sure that each of them was an assigned responsibility of one member of the team. He analysed the key relations of the bank, with major investments and major customers or with such major outside factors as governments, and again made sure that one member of the top management team was responsible for each of them. There was, of course, a captain of the management team—Siemens himself for many years.
>
> (Drucker, 1973: 607)

Drucker (1973: 609) concluded, 'the story of the Deutsche Bank under Georg Siemens demonstrates that top management requires a specific structure. It is a different organ from any other organ of management and has to have a different design'.

In the United States, top management developed in what Chandler (1976) called 'managerial enterprises' that had resulted from several mergers. Such companies established collegial and collective top management groups, which met as executive committees. However, hierarchies of managers appeared before the top team took shape. Chandler (1984) provides a comparative analysis of what he labelled 'managerial capitalism' across the United States, Great Britain, Germany, and Japan, positing that:

> it differed from traditional personal capitalism in that basic decisions concerning the production and distribution of goods and services were made by teams, or hierarchies, of salaried managers who had little or no equity ownership in the enterprises they operated.
>
> (Chandler, 1984: 473)

Chandler (1977, 1984) dated the establishment of the first managerial hierarchies to the 1850s and 1860s in relation to the coordination needs of railroad and telegraph operators, and later, companies engaged in the mass distribution of goods.

In his foundational book *Strategy and Structure*, Chandler (1962) discussed a number of issues that arose with the (re)structuring of executive committees of large industrial enterprises in the United States, as they were changing their strategies and fashioning their organizational structures during a period of 'creative innovation' in the 1920s and early 1930s. His description of du Pont's acceptance of the multidivisional structure in the wake of the economic crisis provides insights into the challenges experienced by the executive committee. For example, one of the company's department managers (H. Fletcher Brown) had suggested that 'the executive committee should not be made up of operating executives', as 'its members were unable to get an overall picture of the company's needs and problems' (Chandler, 1962: 105).

Along with Drucker's (1973) account of the creation of Deutsche Bank's top management, Chandler's (1962) account is among the early depictions of the dynamics of executive teams. As Chandler (1962) summarized on the basis of the four cases he examined, early changes in the C-suite arose as follows:

> The inherent weakness in the centralized, functionally departmentalized operating company and in the loosely held, decentralized holding company became critical only when the administrative load on the senior executive officers increased to such an extent that they were unable to handle their entrepreneurial responsibilities efficiently. This situation arose when the operations of the enterprise became too complex and

the problems of coordination, appraisal, and policy formulation too intricate for a small number of top officers to handle both long-run, entrepreneurial, and short-run, operational administrative activities. To meet these new needs, the innovators built the multidivisional structure with a general office whose executives would concentrate on entrepreneurial activities and with autonomous, fairly self-contained operating divisions whose managers would handle operational ones.

(Chandler, 1962: 299)

Discussing the significance of the organizational innovation, Chandler explains (1962: 10) that 'the new structure left the broad strategic decisions as to the allocation of existing resources and the acquisition of new ones in the hands of a top team of generalists'.

It could be argued that the new realities driving the proliferation and rapid diffusion of CXO roles across very different organizations are prompted by a highly complex, interconnected, and unpredictable environment characterized by globalization; information and communication technologies (ICTs); technological, economic, and social changes; and continuously shifting regulatory landscapes. These complexities are driven by forces such as a stronger 'audit society' (Power, 1997) and increasing demands to respond to the new era of 'surveillance capitalism' in order to secure a fair digital future (Zuboff, 2019). The interest in corporate actions increasingly goes beyond shareholder value, demanding increased transparency and accountability in multiple domains and along different dimensions, such as ensuring diversity, sustainability, social responsibility, a liveable climate, a democratic digital future, etc. Such an environment magnifies and gives new meaning to traditional organizational design dilemmas and tensions, such as differentiation versus integration, autonomy versus interdependence and coordination, centralization versus delegation, and local adaptation versus global responsiveness. It also offers new insights into professionalization and career opportunities in top management, the content and status evolution of CXO roles (Groysberg, Kelly, and MacDonald, 2011), and the growing importance of an international background for CEOs and other CXO incumbents (Kunisch, Menz, and Cannella Jr., 2019).

Since the introduction of the CEO, many C-level roles have been added to the executive team, such as the CFO, COO, Chief Marketing Officer,

Chief Information Officer, Chief Human Resources Officer, and many others. Adoption of these roles has been expanding across organizations. For example, by 1989, 40 per cent of Business Week 1000 companies had a Chief Information Officer (Gupta, 1991); by 2002, 25 per cent of Fortune 500 companies had a Chief Knowledge Officer (Bontis, 2002); and by 2015, 25 per cent of the organizations studied by Gartner (2015) had a Chief Digital Officer. Although these data points are difficult to compare and even to properly interpret, they do reveal the expansion of these roles. Other roles such as Chief Sustainability Officer, Chief Risk Officer, or Chief Compliance Officer are expanding as well. At the same time, some traditional C-level positions, such as the COO, have been losing status and influence in recent times, with an overall steady decline in the number of companies with a COO on the leadership team (Leahey, 2011; Miles, Bennett, and Shill, 2012; Neilson, 2015). In contrast, other positions such as the CFO have assumed more strategic responsibility and operational centrality (Accenture, 2014).

New CXO titles are spreading not only across large corporations, but also among start-ups to signal potential to investors and prospective employees. Even public and non-profit organizations are increasingly adopting them as a sign of growing managerialism. For example, organizations as diverse as the City of New York, Harvard University, the Metropolitan Museum of Art, and McDonald's have appointed a Chief Digital Officer. Many CXO roles have dedicated associations and professional forums, some of which are industry-specific, indicating attempts to engage in legitimation and professionalization.

Some CXO roles are established to address special challenges in a given industry or sector. For example, media conglomerates, advertising agencies, and design firms, such as the Walt Disney Company, Ogilvy, and Frog, which compete on creativity, have Chief Creative Officers. Global healthcare and biopharmaceutical companies, such as Pfizer or Bayer HealthCare have Chief Medical Officers, a hybrid role 'driving the clinical development and CRO [contract research organization] management while meeting the needs of investors and positioning for an appropriate exit' (Chief Medical Officers Summit, 2020). Other roles reflect current social dynamics (e.g. Chief Global Diversity and Engagement Officer). Furthermore, these label variations are compounded in plurality by terminological differences among different business systems, for instance between the United States and Europe. But even within a single business system and country, as a comparison of the executive leadership of the Coca-Cola Company and Pepsi Co. reveals, ways of accomplishing the same tasks and activities vary greatly.

The labelling of these new executive roles as 'officers' provides them with distinctive seriousness and 'officialdom' (Power, 2004), whereas their 'chief'-ing adds an air of grandiosity (Alvesson, 2013). Over time, these titles and associated meanings have mutated. In a number of companies, the top personnel role (which since the 1990s has had the Chief Human Resources Officer title in many organizations) is undergoing a 'karyokinesis' as it is being deconstructed, partially or fully, into a variety of roles. These roles, for example Chief Talent Officer, Chief Leadership Officer, and Chief Learning Officer, which tend to be lower in the hierarchy, have organizational and personnel development responsibilities that are not clearly differentiated.

Finally, as organizational processes become more complex and interdependent than ever before, many are calling for even closer collaboration among the executives at the top, because collective goals and joint responsibilities enable alignment of diverse projects and priorities into a coherent organizational whole (Ibarra and Hansen, 2011). For example, the Chief Marketing Officer has increasing involvement in and dependence on technology, requiring coordination with the Chief Information Officer, sometimes channelled via a new CXO role, the Chief Marketing Technology Officer (Brinker and McLelland, 2014).

1.3 Main argument

Our main argument unfolds in the form of a theoretical essay over the course of the following six chapters, in which conceptual arguments are put forward and illustrated with examples from the collected data. First, we provide an overview of perspectives on roles as resources that can change social structures (Baker and Faulkner, 1991; Callero, 1994) and professional role identities (Meyer and Hammerschmid, 2006; Goodrick and Reay, 2010), suggesting how labelling (Grodal and Kahl, 2017) and meaning making are political processes that contribute to creating, legitimating, and changing organizational roles. We then examine research contributions to the understanding of both classic (CEO and CFO) and contemporary CXO roles. We argue that while the study of 'classic' executive roles from an organizational perspective has been a fruitful arena for developing an understanding of the changing nature of the external control of organizations (e.g. Fligstein, 1990; Dobbin et al., 2001; Zorn et al., 2004), systematic knowledge of the plethora of contemporary CXO roles and the executive power structures in which they are introduced and operate is scant and in need of development. To understand the ongoing production of CXOs, we then introduce the network of diverse actors, which collectively constitute the 'fast fashion industry' of CXOs. We also acknowledge how connections across multiple interests drive the continuous and rapid (re)fashioning of the vocabularies of organizing (Ocasio and Joseph, 2005) associated with CXO roles, which contribute towards the constructing of organizational life (Lawrence and Phillips, 2019).

Second, we unravel macro processes influencing the worldwide expansion of CXO roles and provide three possible inter-related theoretical explanations grounded in institutional and contingency theory approaches: category extension (Delmestri and Greenwood, 2016), the global expansion of organizations (Bromley and Meyer, 2015) and the strategic and structural responses of organizations to different types of complexity (Greenwood et al., 2011). We acknowledge both the more functional value of new executive roles, which are established to respond to complexities, and their symbolic currency, not only as signals of executive attention (Ocasio, 1997) but also as forms of 'symbolic inflation' or even title 'vulgarization' (Boltanski, 1987), 'window dressing' in search for legitimacy, and 'scapegoating' (Power, 2007).

Third, we consider CXOs as a group—a management category—of executive roles, and seek to unravel the group's distinctive characteristics. We argue that unlike other categories of globally mobile professionals (e.g. transnational professionals; Harrington and Seabrooke, 2020), the common denominator of CXO roles is not so much an abstract body of knowledge as it is their orientation to action, focused on the distinctive arenas depicted by the 'X' in their titles (e.g. innovation, information, diversity), and a specific, boundary-crossing, integrative way of doing (i.e. a particular executive style and psychology profile). This is where we touch upon some micro-dynamics. We make the argument that what is shared across a variety of CXOs is a new form of executive expertise, devoid of an abstract knowledge base and grounded in action-oriented tasks related to value, strategy, and transformation, as well as their volatile, ever-evolving role identities based on shifting, externally-posed expectations to these roles. We posit that the sources of executive expertise and these ever-evolving identity expectations, along with the CXOs' distinctive style (based on networking, politics, and boundary spanning) make it difficult to professionalize CXO roles as a distinctive management category. Much like the 'fabricated' category of 'cadres' in French society examined insightfully by Boltanski (1987), the CXO category remains rather fuzzy and its identity remains an enigma, albeit for different reasons; thus, those who fulfil such roles must continuously cope with uncertainty and anxiety.

The final part of our argument is that executive expertise, identity, and style come into play in the C-suite by providing a top team with a distinctive structure, composition, and processes, and defining the 'arena' and 'game' in which CXOs' 'orbits' (Raskino, 2015) encounter each other. Their interactions pave the way for collaboration across overlapping and/or interdependent responsibility domains and for competition over areas of responsibility, seats at the executive table, status, and privileged access to and communication with the CEO. Zooming in on this ambivalent cooperation-competition dynamic within the TMT enables us to explore how it influences the functioning of TMTs and the executive power structures in organizations, with possible change in the C-suite model and implications for the nature of organizational control, suggesting a shift to a wider constellation of actors who influence the design of organizations. Overall, both the organizational level we study (i.e. TMTs) and the power-seeking moves of different actors in organizations and the field justify drawing on political theories to explore C-suite organizing. We seek to contribute to these political theories by offering insights into the micro- and macro-dynamics of CXOs and these executive roles' resourcefulness. This resourcefulness, we argue, has multiple layers: from the politics of labelling these roles as chiefs and officers, through their usefulness as political, governance, and strategic resources in and across organizations as well as means for creativity in designing and changing organizational structures, to their potential as developmental resources for executive talent and means for expressing status and identity. We show how this executive roles' resourcefulness contributes not only to changing the C-suite but also to transforming executive power, bringing fresh possibilities for action in response to ever-changing interests, demands, and temporal horizons in and around organizations.

1.4 Research journey

Writing this book has been a long and winding journey, continuously branching into new paths and directions, yet also one of ongoing fascination with the empirical phenomenon and theoretical possibilities to explore and give sense to it. In the years following the publication of our previous book (Alvarez and Svejenova, 2005), our attention was captured and captivated by an *'unanticipated, anomalous and strategic* datum' (Merton, 1948: 605; italics in original): the changing C-suite and the ever-expanding nomenclature of CXO titles. After identifying academic sources focused primarily on specific roles and documenting their numerous manifestations, meanings, and evolution with a wealth of sources over time, we began to develop and articulate theoretical insights which we discussed with colleagues in different forums and private conversations. Whereas our ambition is theoretical, throughout this book we illustrate and connect these conceptual ideas with an extensive collection of empirical material. Below, we briefly describe our data sources and analytical approach, which have informed our insights and writing.

Data sources. As part of the research for this book, we collected data from different sources, such as databases, role-centred papers and reports, websites (of role-based professional forums and associations, consultancies, and executive search firms), organizational press releases introducing and justifying the need for new CXO roles, and other sources (e.g. public video interviews with CXOs, practitioner books on CXOs, 'how-to' advice, LinkedIn searches to assess the pervasiveness of CXO positions, meetings with senior executives from executive search firms). Here, we provide a brief overview of the databases and reports constituting the core empirical data from which we derived our insights.

To understand the evolution in media coverage of CXO titles, we drew on Factiva, an international news database produced by Dow Jones. In particular, we traced media references of forty CXO roles in addition to the terms 'CEO', 'CXOs', and 'C-suite', from their first mentions in the database until September 2018, when the search was conducted (subsequently, we updated these records until December 2020, and focused on roles from the four complexity clusters we had identified and which we introduce in Chapter 3). Appendix 1 provides a comparative overview of Factiva mentions in the period 2000–2020 related to the C-suite and CXOs as collective labels for the phenomenon under study, as well as of selected roles from the different complexity clusters, including the CEO, CFO, and COO as roles occupying what we call the core. We also used The Official Board database in 2015 and then again in 2020 to identify the most frequently used CXO titles in companies featured in the database. The Official Board (https://www.theofficialboard.com/) is a global data boutique, providing real-time data on corporate organizational charts and executive moves; it covered 77,426 companies in 89 industries and 244 countries as of March 2020. As noted on its website, 'Beyond the CEO, the board members and a few key officers, we display the N-1 to the CEOs and the N-2 to the CEOs, providing a real-time understanding of a company priorities and personnel strategies'. Appendix 2 provides an overview of the top forty titles in 2020 with their distribution by geography and industry, as well as their role domain, responsibility level, and if they are found in a 'mother' firm or in 'daughter' firms. Finally, we drew on the 2015 S&P100 Index, which measures the performance of large-cap companies in the United States, using data from The Official Board to understand the spread of CXO titles and their variations (the tables in Chapter 3 draw partly on this data).

We performed several waves of searches, tracing CXO-related papers and reports produced by fifteen renowned consultancies and executive search firms between 2000 and February 2020 (Appendix 3 presents a breakdown of sources by period and firm). We collected and reviewed a total of 560 papers and reports on CXO roles, which are based on surveys or interviews with role holders. We also explored how professional service firms define their C-suite practices. For example, Deloitte's 2020 C-suite publications target the roles of CEO, CFO, Chief Information Officer, Chief Legal Officer, and Chief Marketing Officer. In addition to publishing papers and reports on these roles, Deloitte offers programmes for CXOs. For example, its CFO programme consists of a range of specific offerings for CFOs at different career stages, its mission being to inform, develop, connect, and empower members of the CFO community. IBM's Institute for Business Value has published twenty editions of its global C-suite study; the study published in 2020 is based on a survey of 13,000 C-suite executives. In addition, the institute publishes role-specific studies on the CEO, CFO, Chief Operations Officer, Chief HR Officer, Chief Information Officer, and Chief Marketing Officer.

Analytical approach. By following the phenomenon in real time from the mid-2000s until the present and collecting data from a vast range of sources, we have developed a deep, holistic understanding of its different aspects and dynamics, and rich insights into its evolution. Our holistic understanding is complemented by an analysis of extant organizational perspectives on CXOs (Chapter 2); role frequencies and clustering (Chapter 3); media interest in specific CXO roles (Chapter 4); an analysis of vocabulary (Chapters 4 and 6); and a 'CXO rhetoric reading' approach (Chapter 5). We identified the vocabulary of CXO roles by examining common themes in strategy texts, such as consulting and executive search reports and articles on roles, which we considered to have textual agency (Vaara, Sorsa, and Pålli, 2010) in defining CXO roles and sustaining their proliferation. Whereas these analyses are neither meant nor able to provide a proper quantification of what is a rather dispersed and highly diverse phenomenon, they do enable us to offer some insights into its magnitude and meaning, as well as to provide illustrations of the theoretical issues we surface with regard to the changing C-suite. Chapter 7 brings these insights together into a discussion of the transformation of executive power structures and its significance for the political perspectives on organization.

Acknowledgements. As a long and complex enterprise, this book would have remained a mere fantasy without the support and patience of institutions, colleagues, friends, editors, and family. The Research Division of INSEAD and the Department of Organization (IOA) at Copenhagen Business School (CBS) provided generous support, both economic and otherwise, and our colleagues at INSEAD and CBS created an inspiring intellectual context for writing. The INSEAD Corporate Governance Centre, of which José Luis Alvarez is Director and the Mubadala Chaired Professor in Corporate Governance and Strategy, provided a strong platform that enabled him to develop important insights on the studied phenomenon. The CBS OT@IOA Group, which Silviya Svejenova co-leads with Eva Boxenbaum and Renate Meyer, and the CBS Centre for Organization and Time (COT), offered an inspiring community for the development and theorizing of novel ideas in the domain of organization studies. Silviya's stints as a visiting scholar at Harvard University's Weatherhead Center for International Affairs, guest professor at the Institute for Organization Studies at Vienna University of Economics and Business, and adjunct professor at the Department of Leadership and Organizational Behavior at BI Norwegian Business School provided a stimulating environment that helped her unfold the book's ideas. Throughout the data collection and analysis stages, research assistance was competently provided by Brian Henry and

Valerio Incerti at INSEAD, and by Laura Fischerova, Julia Kozcorowska, Jeppe Nygaard Johansen, and Giuliano Tosto at CBS.

We explored and advanced the initial insights of this book at several academic and practitioner events, where we received new leads, supportive comments, as well as necessary criticism and questions that pushed us to clarify our thinking. We presented early ideas for the book at the Workshop on 'Organizational Change in Democratic Societies' hosted by the Department of Sociology and Human Geography at the University of Oslo in 2012. Attendees of the Competition(s) Workshop at CBS in 2016, and the EGOS Colloquia—in particular, participants in sub-theme 34 'Something to Talk about: Building Bridges to Understand the Power of Words and Vocabularies in Organising' in Naples in 2016, and sub-theme 51 'Top Managers and Strategizing' in Copenhagen in 2017—helped us develop and refine our ideas. We published the first insights from our research on the C-suite in a chapter (Svejenova and Alvarez, 2017) in the New Institutional Workshop's edited volume titled *New Themes in Institutional Analysis: Topics and Issues from European Research* (Kruecken et al., 2017). Feedback from presentations at BI Norwegian Business School in 2017, the 2020 CIONET gala in Warsaw, Poland, HR and Top Executive events at the Centre for Leadership (CFL) in Copenhagen in 2018, the 15th International Human Resource Management (IHRM) Conference in Madrid in 2018, the SCAN-COR Public Lecture at Vienna University of Economics and Business in 2018, sessions at the CBS EBA MSc programme in Strategy, Organization, and Leadership (SOL) in 2019 and 2020, and the Weatherhead Center for International Affairs' SCANCOR-Weatherhead seminar at Harvard University in 2020 enabled us to crystalize, elaborate, and strengthen our initial insights.

In developing our thinking and deepening our theorizing of the phenomenon, we also enjoyed and benefited greatly from occasional encounters and informal conversations held across geographies. Generous colleagues provided inspiration and suggested fruitful directions for further exploring the phenomenon and strengthening our organizational theorizing. In particular, we would like to thank Eva Boxenbaum, Patricia Bromley, Haldor Byrkjeflot, Arne Carlson, Guoli Chen, Neil Fligstein, Paul du Gay, Frédéric Godart, Stine Grodal, Heather Haveman, Tor Hernes, Torben Iversen, Øyvind Kvalnes, Carmelo Mazza, Wolf Meixner, Renate Meyer, Louise Mors, Woody Powell, Majken Schultz, Mark Ventresca, Signe Vikkelsø, Luis Vives, and Andrea Whittle. Over the years, as we continued to explore the changing landscape of CXO roles, colleagues and students continued to send us relevant theoretical references or news clippings on new CXO titles that they encountered.

When we began entertaining the idea of writing this book, David Musson from Oxford University Press was receptive to our ideas and requested changes that significantly strengthened our work; we value him as a true intellectual colleague. Subsequently, Adam Swallow and Jenny King from the publishing house exhibited the same professional and timely engagement, for which we are grateful. Kara Stephenson Gehman has been an exceptional English editor, professionally improving the clarity and consistency of the manuscript. At earlier stages of our writing, we also appreciated the editing help of Justin Peterson.

Finally, we extend a very important acknowledgement to our families, who have patiently provided invaluable support and understanding throughout our busy days of researching and writing, and have served as vital sources of inspiration, energy, and joy: Jacqui, Camila, and Adria for José Luis, and Haldor, Isabel, and Johanne for Silviya. We are immensely fortunate and grateful.

All of these people and experiences have influenced the book's journey, enriching and enhancing our ideas in different ways. Responsibility for any outstanding errors is ours alone and shared. We have contributed equally to the book, listing our names in an alphabetical order.

1.5 Book structure and content

The remainder of the book unfolds over six chapters. Here, we briefly introduce these chapters and the topics they cover.

In *Chapter 2, 'Theorizing CXO Roles'*, we delve into extant organizational research on roles, focusing on two perspectives with relevance to our argument: roles as resources (Baker and Faulkner, 1991; Callero, 1994) and professional role identities (Meyer and Hammerschmid, 2006; Goodrick and Reay, 2010). We also discuss how labelling and the politics of meaning shape executive roles. We then review organizational scholarship on the 'classic' C-suite roles (i.e. CEO and CFO) that have sustained their centrality in the TMT and current theorization of the panoply of new CXO roles. Subsequently, we unravel the 'fast fashion industry' involved in theorizing executive roles, legitimating and diffusing them, as well as shaping ideas about their executive expertise, identity, and style. In particular, we explore the role of experts (consulting companies and executive search firms), the media, and CXO networks that bring professionals together and support the visibility and legitimation of specific roles, as well as the connections among them. We conclude the chapter by suggesting how this labelling of and collective meaning making in relation to an ever-expanding range of CXO roles could be indicative of a changing model of organizational control driven by an extra-organizational network of stakeholders that is wider and more diverse than ever before.

In *Chapter 3, 'CXO Expansion'*, we document and reflect on the significance of the proliferation and spread of CXO roles. The chapter outlines some significant characteristics of CXO expansion as an organizational phenomenon: the panoply of CXO roles in TMTs; the spread of CXOs across sectors, geographies, and types of organizations; as well as status differences and the ongoing morphing of titles and mandates. In exploring the expansion of chiefs theoretically, we pursue three directions, grounded in institutional theory and contingency theory: category extension (Delmestri and Greenwood, 2016), hyper-organization and the related notion of hyper-management (Bromley and Meyer, 2015, 2021), and strategic responses to complexity (Greenwood et al., 2011). Pursuing the first theoretical direction, we conceive CXOs as a management category of executive roles and explore both its horizontal and vertical dimensions. Following the second direction, hyper-organization, we connect the rampant inflation of chiefs to the claimed professionalization and myths of management, and argue that the establishment of CXO roles is an important aspect of the elaboration of an organization into a hyper-organization and of management into hyper-management, as depicted by Bromley and Meyer (2015, 2021). Delving into the third direction, strategic responses to complexity, we interpret CXO expansion through organizations' strategic (substantial and/or symbolic) responses to four domains of complexity (i.e. institutional, information, primary task, and administrative) and outline respective clusters of chief officer roles.

In *Chapter 4, 'Executive Expertise and Identity'*, we focus on the professionalization of CXO roles and examine the foundation of their ability to accomplish tasks, that is, their executive expertise and role identity. We theorize CXOs' expertise and identity along two dimensions. First, we delve into the shared action orientation of executive expertise. As elaborated in reports produced by consultancies and executive search firms, at the heart of this action orientation is the theorized ability of professionalized managers not only to respond to rules and pressure, but also to 'define and provide solutions for newly constructed problems not fully specifiable by legal and accounting rules' (Bromley and Meyer, 2015: 94). We illustrate this action orientation by highlighting three main aspects of the 'vocabulary' used in reports on CXO roles: value, strategy, and transformation. Second, we discuss the volatility of CXOs' role identity, distinguishing its evolving nature as a shared feature and its distinctive aspects (assertiveness and endurance). We then zoom in on executive roles that are perpetually seeking identity, with particular focus on Chief Human Resource Officers (CHROs). We conclude the chapter by discussing how the shared action orientation of executive expertise is countered by differences in the volatility of executive role identities, creating a tension that contributes to weak professionalization of executive roles.

In *Chapter 5, 'The Style of Executive Power'*, we delve into the 'how' of executive roles (i.e. the style with which CXOs perform their tasks) which, along with executive expertise and role identity (Chapter 4), shapes their occupational essence. In exploring executive style, we derive insights on expectations about role occupants' abilities to put their action-based expertise to work. In particular, we discuss the importance of networking and social skill, the latter associated with the ability to motivate and mobilize cooperation, and establish and maintain political coalitions (Fligstein, 1997; Fligstein and McAdam, 2012a, 2012b) and theorize the inherently relational style of CXOs, which involves high behavioural abilities. First, we suggest how a return to political perspectives of organization could not only enhance understanding of executive roles in general and the style of executive power in particular, but can also help extend the power and leadership agenda of neo-institutional research, which has not paid sufficient attention to the upper echelons of organizations. We then provide numerous examples of what CXO styles are and what they should be according to professional services firms in consulting and executive search by engaging in 'CXO rhetoric reading'. We argue that the most distinct components of CXO styles are the incessant building of social capital via networking and of political capital via reputation, and the use of these resources to exert the influence required to successfully perform internal and external interfacing tasks. Next, we relate networking and influencing to academic research on boundary spanning and integration, as we find substantial analogies between these and CXOs. Finally, we argue that the most robust psychological profile for CXOs is a scarce resource that limits the pool of candidates for these roles.

In Chapter 6, '*Top Team Dynamics*', we draw attention to the dynamic interplay of different roles in their shared playing field, the C-suite. We explore framings of competition and collaboration between different CXOs, as well as struggles for status and influence in relation to the CEO. We theorize these dynamics by drawing on research on TMT structure, composition, and processes to provide a foundation for readers who may be less familiar with them, as well as contingency theory and political theories. On the one hand, drawing insights from early contingency theorists, we suggest that such competitions tend to be won by those who solve the most pertinent organizational problems (i.e. those who are most relevant to organizational survival). However, in the context of ever-increasing complexity, with multiple interests at play, these organizational problems change continuously, generating constant volatility between CXO winners and losers.

In Chapter 6, we also consider the different CXO roles in interaction, particularly in terms of their involvement in and contributions to the senior leadership team. In doing so, we shift the lens from CXOs' expertise, identity, and style to their relationships and how they work with one another and with the CEO as part of a team. To explore these collective dynamics and the inherent challenges associated with them, we return to the vocabulary approach introduced in Chapter 4 and explore the vocabulary of competition and collaboration among CXOs on TMTs, thereby revealing tensions and possible organizational solutions to them. We also overview the changing model of the C-suite, concluding with some reflections on the importance of and suggestions for conceiving, theorizing, and empirically investigating TMTs and their dynamics as a nexus of possible futures.

In *Chapter 7, 'Executive Power in Transformation'*, we bring together observed and theorized aspects of C-suite dynamics, and consider possible implications for the nature of organizational control and the political perspective of organizations. In particular, we review the main manifestations of the clustering of CXOs studied in Chapter 3, reflect on the lure of the CXO label, and highlight some theoretical consequences from the jurisdictional battles between senior executive roles. We propose 'why' the CXO phenomenon appeared and proliferated, 'what' its essential nature is, 'where' in organizations it is promoted, 'how' it operates, and 'who' CXOs are psychologically. We conclude by arguing that studying the expansion of CXO roles reveals a more nuanced understanding of what it means to be a CXO, and thus the core of what it means to be an executive. Specifically, the CEO is the quintessential chief officer: the ideal type of CXO.

We now proceed to the first part of our argument, revealing main aspects of the theorizing of CXO roles and elaborating on the theoretical ideas that can help explain it.

2
Theorizing CXO Roles

One of the most important strategies for gaining influence and exercising power is to use roles as a resource for altering social structure . . . chief executive officers or presidents of formal organizations can use their roles to restructure a bureaucracy by creating new roles and eliminating others.

Callero (1994: 240)

Do CXO roles matter organizationally and, if so, how and why? How and by whom is their meaning constructed? Moreover, how has research on CXO roles evolved in the field of organization and management studies, and what are the theoretical opportunities for new insights on these roles? As the opening quote from Callero (1994) affirms, certain roles—particularly those at the top of organizational hierarchies—carry the potential to introduce, develop, or eliminate roles, altering the social structures of their organizations and shifting them in new directions. At the same time, these roles and associated role identities are themselves subject to framing and labelling by experts, professional networks, and media that have different interests in their fortunes. They are also an important area of organizational research.

A Spencer Stuart report (Alexander et al., 2015), for example, suggests that CXO roles are organizational resources in at least two senses: strategic (for the organization) and developmental (for the top team). In the report, it is argued that a newly created CXO role 'can serve as a lightning rod for a new strategic priority', helping the organization focus attention on, progress against, or develop capabilities to realize a specific agenda (Alexander et al., 2015: 3). At the same time, the report also points out that by articulating CXO roles' areas of responsibility, the CEO—an organization's chief designer or architect—can foster the development of competences and perspectives among members of the TMT. As Alexander et al. (2015) emphasize:

The Changing C-Suite. José Luis Alvarez and Silviya Svejenova, Oxford University Press.
© José Luis Alvarez and Silviya Svejenova (2022). DOI: 10.1093/oso/9780198728429.003.0002

A larger role with an expanded set of responsibilities can help executives gain a broader, enterprise-wide perspective on the business and help them to develop new skills. For example, we have seen CEOs combine the responsibilities of the chief marketing officer and chief sales officer to create a single, larger chief commercial officer role overseeing both functional areas.

(Alexander et al., 2015: 3)

Reports such as the one published by Spencer Stuart are a currency in a vibrant 'fast fashion industry' of experts, professional networks, and media, occupied with advancing the meaning and sustaining these roles, while also securing customers and audiences.

This 'fast fashion industry', together with academic research, contributes to the theorizing of CXO roles in several ways. Theorization, as defined by Strang and Meyer (1993: 492), is 'the self-conscious development and specification of abstract categories and the formulation of patterned relationships such as chains of cause and effect'. It is a 'discursive process by which concrete forms or practices are turned into types' (Meyer, 2014: 80). As we discuss later in this book, the theorizing of CXO roles involves skilful, interested, and authoritative theorists (Strang and Meyer, 1993) who label and frame the meaning of these executive roles, shape them into a recognizable management category, and convert them into 'panaceas' with general appeal, independent of context (Mazza and Strandgaard Pedersen, 2015).

In this chapter, we outline different aspects of the theorizing of CXO roles. First, we delve into the organizing power of roles, overviewing selected theoretical contributions and singling out two perspectives: roles as resources and professional role identities. Next, we delve into the framing and labelling of roles as processes essential for theorizing CXO roles. We then review organizational research on CXO roles, which has examined classic roles—CEO and CFO—as well as those that have emerged more recently. Last, we outline the main theorists in the 'fast fashion industry' of CXOs, highlighting the roles of experts, professional networks, and media, and discussing how they separately and collectively contribute to the theorizing of CXO roles. We conclude by arguing for more systematic attention to top executive roles to develop a better understanding of the changing nature of executive power and, by extension, corporate control.

2.1 Organizing power of roles

Understanding of the organizing power of roles has been advanced under what has come to be known as role theory (Biddle, 1986), as well as in relation to other, wider perspectives, such as formal organization (Brown, 1965; Du Gay and Vikkelsø, 2017) and institutional theory (Berger and Luckmann, 1966; DiMaggio, 1991). Role theory has enjoyed a wealth of interest and contributions during the 1960s and 1970s, yet interest in it has waxed and waned since then. Some scholars such as Biddle (1986) have sought to synthesize diverse and diverging contributions by distinguishing five main perspectives—functional, symbolic interactionist, structural, organizational, and cognitive role theory—and charting some common ground between them.

Relatedly, the delineation of roles and role relationships has been considered part and parcel of the formalization of organization (Brown, 1965; Smircich and Morgan, 1982) and an important aspect in the study of formal organization as a core task of organization and management theory (Du Gay and Vikkelsø, 2017). Wilfred Brown (1960: 33), for example, argued that 'the nature and function of each role can be studied and made a subject of explicit statements. The relationship of one role to another can be understood and regulated.' He also noted that 'the system exists irrespective of people'. As noted by Gordon (1976), roles are 'basic structural components' or building blocks of social and personal systems, which connect person to culture (through the roles' value aspects), motivate and structure social action (through their normative aspects), and enable 'sense-making' (through their interpretive aspects). Roles 'formalize' in that they are sets of activities or expected behaviour (Katz and Kahn, 1978). At the same time, they are subject to different degrees of formalization, from specific to loosely defined discretionary boundaries (Hickson, 1966).

Roles also have distinctive meaning in institutional theory (Berger and Luckmann, 1966; DiMaggio, 1991). They are considered to represent 'the institutional order. ... First, performance of the role represents itself. ... Second, the role represents an entire institutional nexus of conduct', and thus 'stands in relationship to other roles' (Berger and Luckmann, 1966: 74). Roles 'institutionalize the interactions and definitions that shape the reality of organizational life' (Smircich and Morgan, 1982: 259) and are associated with legitimating accounts, which convert them into 'powerful sources of standardization and order' (DiMaggio, 1991: 81). Roles reveal 'the mediations between the macroscopic universes of meaning objectivated in a society and the ways by which these universes are subjectively real to individuals' (Berger and Luckmann, 1966: 79).

Two distinctive perspectives on the organizing power of roles, both of which stem from dissatisfaction with role theory explanations, are of particular relevance to our inquiry into CXO roles and the changing C-suite. The first is *roles as resources* in organizations (Baker and Faulkner, 1991; Callero, 1994; Alvarez and Svejenova, 2005), on which we build further in Chapter 3 in relation to roles as strategic responses to institutional complexity. The second is *professional role identities* in professional fields (Meyer and Hammerschmid, 2006; Goodrick and Reay, 2010), with which we engage in Chapter 4 when delving into executive expertise and identity. We briefly discuss each of these approaches here.

Roles as resources. Baker and Faulkner (1991) first outlined this perspective in a study of roles in the Hollywood film industry, and it was subsequently reviewed and elaborated by Callero (1994: 230), who explained that it developed out of dissatisfaction with role theory's 'inability to explain the dynamics of power and for its tacit acceptance of inequitable structures'. This perspective reverses previous structural accounts of roles, suggesting instead that roles influence social structures, as they are used to create positions and their relationships (Baker and Faulkner, 1991). Baker and Faulkner defined roles as a nexus of resources as well as keys to controlling and unlocking these resources, which serves organizational interests and shapes the directions organizations take. Roles are thus considered political resources employed 'to achieve political ends'; Callero (1994: 240) further explained that 'by acquiring a legitimate claim to a role, one gains entry into a network of interaction' which 'not only facilitates the securing of symbolic, cultural, and material capital, but also establishes a platform for exercising control and power'. Understood as resources, roles are considered important for adaptation and coordination, as they are communicative and attention-focusing devices (Shepherd, McMullen, and Ocasio, 2017) that influence an organizational system's capacity for regulation and persistence in the face of disturbances (Ashby, 1968).

Related to this political function, roles are resources of particular relevance to TMT dynamics. Beckman and Burton (2011: 50), for example, advocated the importance of 'explicitly treating roles as entities worthy of study independent of the executive who holds the role' and insisted on 'the need to understand how and when roles are added or eliminated'. From this perspective, roles can be a useful governance resource and a means for creativity in designing and transforming executive power structures and responding to institutional, market, and organizational complexity (Alvarez and Svejenova, 2005), something we discuss further in Chapter 3. Furthermore, Barley (1990), drawing on Nadel, distinguished nonrelational and relational elements of a role, the latter being particularly relevant when roles are brought together in interaction, as in the TMT. A resource perspective of roles that considers roles 'as tools used in a competitive struggle to control other resources and establish social structure', therefore implies that executive teams and organizations could be viewed as 'the product of role use' (Callero, 1994: 230). We discuss this dynamic further in Chapter 6.

Professional roles identities. The second perspective has grown out of dissatisfaction with the micro-orientation of research on roles and identities and the lack of attention to institutional forces that are particularly relevant for professionalized fields, and accounts for the extra-organizational influences on roles (Chreim, Williams, and Hinings, 2007). This perspective delves into the legitimization of new professional role identities (Goodrick and Reay, 2010).

New senior leadership labels (C-suite titles) and their constitutive vocabularies are used to describe new strategic actors, thereby bringing about new professional role identities, and with them, expectations and capacities for appropriate action (Hacking, 1986; Meyer and Hammerschmid, 2006; Power, 2007). Because they are situated in social space, these roles place their claimants in power-dependent relations with other categories of actors (Meyer and Hammerschmid, 2006) based on 'institutional templates that define the hierarchy of professional groups' (Chreim et al., 2007: 1534). As typologies in an institutional space, new roles and their occupational mandates need to be defined in terms of their value for and fit with prevailing systems (Reay, Golden-Biddle, and Germann, 2006; Fayard, Stigliani, and Bechky, 2017). Hence, role innovation, depicted as the discretion of role incumbents, emanates from existing institutional templates (Chreim et al., 2007).

2.2 Labelling and politics of meaning

The organizing potential of roles is realized through role labelling in the following ways. First, role labels in organizations matter because they formalize new areas of executive attention and action (Alvarez and Svejenova, 2005; Ocasio, 1997, 2011; Power, 2007). They function as devices that help communicate organizational priorities, define problems, and allocate organizational responsibility, with 'accountability for perceived failure and potential blame' (Power, 2007: 83). As Meyer and Rowan (1977: 350) posited, 'affixing the right labels to activities can change them into valuable services and mobilize the commitments of internal participation and external constituents'.

Second, labelling brings new actors to life through the act of naming them (Hacking, 1986). In the context of organizations, job titles constitute such acts of naming. They are also 'recognized shorthand for describing a set of responsibilities held by one employee', and signal 'the knowledge, skills, abilities, and other characteristics that employees who hold the job are likely to possess' (Grant, Berg, and Cable, 2014: 1201). Organizationally, they have significance and implications for the management of talent in organizations (Grant et al., 2014). For employees, they are means for expressing identity and constructing a professional image, and constitute 'prominent identity badges' (Ashforth and Kreiner, 1999: 417).

Third, labelling enables category creation (Granqvist, Grodal, and Woolley, 2013) and helps to 'distinguish novel ideas from each other, [and] contribute to perceived homogeneity within a category' (Meyer et al., 2018: 404). Delmestri et al., (2020: 917) affirm that 'labels, including those associated to categories, not only reflect the reality that surrounds us but also represent our way of ordering it' and that 'the relationship between labels, their meanings, and the actual physical and institutional reality is rather complex, coevolutionary, and performative'.

Finally, a label facilitates engagement in 'politics of meaning', that is, negotiations around meaning that contributes to the formation and legitimation of new categories (Slavich et al., 2020). As research has shown, in and across organizational contexts, the same label can cover a range of different meanings; likewise, a number of different concepts can have the same meaning (Sahlin and Wedlin, 2008; Meyer and Höllerer, 2010). The politics of meaning encompasses the 'political circuitry' of labelling (Logue and Clegg, 2015) consisting of diverse, and sometimes conflicting interests and preferences that drive the introduction, spread, and often rapid legitimation and elaboration of novel ideas in general and new roles in particular.

CXOs' distinctiveness as a category of strategic actors in organizations stems, at least partially, from their labelling as both 'chiefs' and 'officers', which connects them in a system of explicit and implicit meanings (Granqvist et al., 2013). The term 'officer' suggests 'seriousness and officialdom' (Power, 2004: 51) that can convert roles into resources for achieving political ends (Baker and Faulkner, 1991; Logue and Clegg, 2015). This term likens the CXO role to a public 'office' and the impersonal conduct of office-holding (du Gay, 2017), although this could be misleading, as accounts of these roles emphasize the importance of infusing them with personal style, which is contrary to the ethics-of-office idea. (For an elaboration on the style of executive power, see Chapter 5.)

The term 'chief', in turn, conveys leadership, the highest rank, and importance, and could be considered symptomatic of 'hierarchy fetishism' (Gordon, 1972, as cited in Baron and Bielby, 1986), the 'professionalization of everyone' (Wilensky, 1964), and the 'triumph of emptiness', whereby grandiose names are desired and desirable (Alvesson, 2013). Some of these roles—especially CXOs who do not serve on the executive committee and are nominated in accordance with the latest fashion—may be categorized as 'bullshit jobs' (Graeber, 2019). However, in senior CXO roles, the word 'chief' combined with that of 'officer' signals an affinity in tasks and competencies between the new roles and the superordinate chief—the CEO—stirring hopes among new CXO incumbents for a fast track to the top job.

In this book, we employ a political perspective on the labelling and categorization of CXOs as a new category of management elite in and across organizations, thereby addressing calls for the 're-flowering of a more politically-inflected, and societally-relevant, organizational theory' (Zald and Lounsbury, 2010: 965). Next, we explore how extant research has theorized what both classical and contemporary CXO roles mean and how they come to matter.

2.3 Research on CXO roles

In this section, we delve deeper into what we already know from organizational scholarship about the 'classic' roles comprising the traditional core of the C-suite—that is, the CEO and the CFO (with some references to the Chief Operations Officer (COO))—as well as other more recent CXO roles studied in fragmented contributions.

2.3.1 Classic CXO roles

The CEO role. Peter Lorange (2008: 363) described the CEO role as that of a chief orchestrator who sustains an organizational focus on growth, costs, internal issues, and external issues, and as such serves as 'the point of intersection for the divergent and often contradictory concerns emanating from multiple constituencies'. The role is demanding, and involves 'constant juggling between time frames and levels of focus or abstraction', 'rapid switches of attention', and not least, 'the ability to make connections between issues across units and to draw the organization-wide conclusions' (Lorange, 2008: 363). Although accounts of the origins and spread of the CEO role differ, there is overall agreement regarding the importance of the C-suite to the life and well-being of organizations and their members (Selznick, 1969).

The CEO role has become much 'more complex and more publicly scrutinized over time' (Lorange, 2008: 348). In the late nineteenth century, the first modern corporations had 'no corporate headquarters and no salaried managers with the title of 'chief executive'' (Chandler, 1976: 38).[1] The title of CEO was introduced as a way to address the needs of early top management teams to reach agreement and closure on decisions, and to represent corporations to their various constituencies. In 1923, the President of General Motors, Pierre du Pont, appointed Alfred P. Sloan as its first CEO; by the mid-twentieth century, most large American corporations had a chief executive serving as the actual and symbolic head (Chandler, 1976). In a contrasting account, Allison and Potts (1999) asserted that the CEO role dates back to 1955, when the top leader of one of the 200 largest US industrial corporations was given the title, and suggested that it took 20 years for it to spread to all but one of these 200 firms.

Today, the CEO role is ubiquitous across all types of organizations, and continues to evolve. In the wake of recent corporate governance reforms in a growing number of countries, CEOs are found to have less discretion, less

---

[1] In searching the Harvard Business School Baker Library's archives of corporate reports, we came across a much earlier use of the label 'Chief Executive Officer' in the Third Annual Report of the Directors of the Pennsylvania Rail-Road Company to Stockholders (1849: 22), which reveals the existence of a salaried position, also referred to as President. Although what this role had entailed at the time is impossible to grasp in any detail from that brief mention, the report affirms 'that the services of a Chief Executive Officer, not possessing the qualifications of an Engineer, should not command the amount of remuneration now paid'.

autonomy, and more of a short-term focus (Mizruchi and Marshall, 2016). Nevertheless, the CEO remains the most powerful executive in the C-suite.

The CFO role. The emergence and consolidation of the CFO role became one of the key battlegrounds in the still-raging competition between economics and sociology scholars (including organization theorists), and more generally, between functionalist and non-functionalist interpretations of organizational dynamics. Studying the rise of financial executives, Fligstein (1985) attempted to prove the essential tenets of institutional theory, daringly contradicting Chandler's (1977) 'visible hand' hypothesis. Specifically, Fligstein asserted that CFOs became indispensable members of TMTs not because the role represented a necessary functionalist or rational response to economic or market demands, but because of the influence of two forces, neither of which was purely economic. Fligstein (1985: 389) thereby captured the crux of the academic dispute, noting that 'there is a sociology underlying economic processes'.

One of these forces was exogenous to organizations: legal changes implemented to address economic crises, regulate free market competition (e.g. to prevent oligopolies), or address social pathologies (e.g. to prevent corruption). These highly-technical new legal contingencies required in-house specialists to deal with the complexities of new regulations, tax legislation prominent among them. The role of the State was of paramount relevance to neo-institutional scholars, who argued that even free markets cannot be explained without considering non-economic independent variables such as political dynamics or public institutions.

The second force was clearly organizational: occupational groups vying for corporate power. According to Fligstein, CFOs were given seats at executive committee tables and later gained second-in-command status. The CFO role became the best platform for an ascent to a CEO appointment, because incumbents were able to deploy the most convincing set of claims to power and the most sophisticated self-legitimating arguments—that is, they were able to articulate a more developed *intellectual position* (Fligstein, 1987: 56). In Gramscian political vocabulary, this dominant intellectual position would be called 'hegemony'. The arguments sustaining this position do not necessarily need to be 'objective', although they certainly could be. As they are ideological, they should be useful for roles' jurisdictional competitions. Such was the case for CFOs.

Aspirations and claims to institutionalized power by an organizational group cannot be sustained without legitimation, which requires a moral high ground (Anteby, 2010). In a business context, legitimation begs some credible pretence of control over some aspect of strategic uncertainty, that is, the ability to exercise control over a critical issue (Seabrooke and Henriksen 2017). In today's parlance, an individual, role, unit, or project must be 'strategic'. Another expression used to claim legitimacy is that a role 'adds value' by bolstering the bottom line on financial statements and/or controlling some aspect of strategic uncertainty. Given their functional activities and mastery of the numerical language of business, quantitative evaluations, connections to sources of capital, etc., CFOs can argue that they add value and are more strategic than any other functional executive.

Being 'strategic' has become the most popular and forceful justification for new CXOs' participation in executive committees, as we illustrate with numerous examples in this book; some even enjoy direct access to increasingly powerful boards of directors. Indeed, Alvesson (2013) warned that the word 'strategic' has come to suggest 'importance', or some pretention of it, without further specification. Nothing favours the success and spread of an expression like ambiguity or polysemy, which enable words to operate as signifiers without significance.

Financial specialists' upward re-labelling from functional titles such as Directors of Finance to CFOs who not only occupy undisputed central C-suite positions, but even sit on company boards as internal directors, was driven first by the spread of the multidivisional firm, and later by the conceptualization of the firm as a portfolio of investments requiring differentiated financial expertise. Once CFOs achieved second-in-command positions in C-suites at some leading organizations, isomorphic mechanisms kicked in, and mimetic, normative, or coercive diffusion followed. This ascent in the hierarchy by CFOs closely followed the two-step institutionalization sequence proposed by Tolbert and Zucker (1983), whereby a role emerges to address a real or perceived need, and when successful, is adopted by other organizations, either mindfully or uncritically. This is the isomorphic mechanism that neo-institutionalists cite. By 2000, almost all big firms had a CFO, yet prior to the mid-1960s, financial tasks were performed by accountants and treasurers, contemptuously referred to as 'bean counters' positioned well below the executive committee in the corporate hierarchy. This rapid ascent to the top of the organizational structure was highly attractive as a subject of study to institutional scholars, because a full explanation required using variables alien to economics, such as modifications to legal regulations, the role of the state, the transformation from industrial to financial forms of capitalism, and phenomena such as changes in organizational strategies and structures, the evolution of occupations, ideological lines of discourse, etc.

However, the contest between functional and non-functional explanations in the domains of economics and sociology, the former based on the assumption of rational individuals who operate on the market, and the latter on the assumption of more unpredictable and imperfect individuals engaged in a political dynamic, was not fully settled by the story of the rise and triumph of the most important non-CEO chief officers: CFOs. In the conclusion to his piece on the spread of the multidivisional corporation, Fligstein (1985: 389) recognized that the central question remained unanswered: 'Does strategy [related to market/economic factors] cause a certain type of structural power base [i.e., power dynamics] to dominate the firm, or vice versa?' Quite similarly, in the conclusion of a subsequent article, he was still asking about the cause–effect sequence: 'Do subunits come to power as a result of shifts in strategies by competitors or as a result of their already having seized power and shaped strategy according to their perception of the key organizational problems?' (Fligstein, 1987: 57).

As a consequence of the lack of definitive empirical and theoretical answers to these questions, the story of the rise of CFOs did not mark the final, unambiguous victory over economics and Chandlerian functional business history that non-functionalist sociologists and institutionalists had hoped for. For instance, although showing that in later phases of diffusion most firms adopted the multidivisional firm structure 'net of strategy', not 'solely' due to market-driven strategies (Fligstein, 1985: 388), they also had to recognize that the M-form was adopted when managers 'perceived' that the innovations implemented by pioneering firms (e.g. the new CFO role) were successful and rational (Fligstein, 1985: 381). Therefore, calculus and rationality influenced the diffusion process, particularly the first step of diffusion, which begins with an assessment of what works and what does not. Even in the second phase, a perception of usefulness is a prerequisite for the adoption of an innovation. Unless a firm possesses substantial slack, managers will not make decisions that cannot be defended as being functional with regard to the company's bottom line and survival. The assumption is that managers initially adopt an implicit contingency theory when reacting to new challenges from environmental sets, and intuitively adopt institutional theory in the second phase, when fads and fashions have a legitimating role, but only, we argue, insofar as they are not perceived to be contrary to the economic logic of for-profit businesses. The fact that a significant percentage of neo-institutional research has focused on state-owned or not-for-profit organizations explains some of its emphasis on non-rational behaviour.

In his nuanced account of the CFO's rise, Zorn (2004) confirmed the two-step general theory formulated earlier by Tolbert and Zucker (1983). The emergence of the CFO role and its ascent to a seat on the executive committee was first made feasible by organizations' objective need for expertise in capital management due to regulatory changes. Because of entrenchment, legitimacy, and other mechanisms studied extensively by institutionalists, CFOs retained their places in corporate C-suites, even when there were no longer objective needs for the specific expertise that elevated them there in the first place.

Building on Edelman (1990, 1992), Zorn (2004) argued that businesses may respond to environmental demands, both economic and non-economic, through formal adaptation, which may range from new roles and structures to new formal systems, such as due process. Forms—in this case, roles in the C-suite and the structures of executive committees—are important, because they constitute a resource that organizations may use to adapt to their environments, not only functionally, but also symbolically. As a result, structures and roles, while retaining similar names or forms, may feature highly varied dynamics (Edelman, 1990):

> Governance is, after all, peripheral to organizations' core technical or service activities and therefore likely to be considered more malleable than core activities. Furthermore, governance is ripe for symbolic manipulation; formal rules that comply with laws may be coupled only loosely with actual organizational practices.
>
> (Edelman, 1990: 1436)

Thus, 'the construction of compliance becomes a function of internal organizational politics tempered by industry norms and the standards of professional personnel and affirmative action administrators', even in the context of compliance with laws (Edelman, 1992: 1567). Moreover, 'organizations' collective response to law becomes the de facto construction of compliance; it is shaped only at the margins by formal legal institutions' (Edelman, 1992: 1568). When operating in situations of legal ambiguity and weak enforcement mechanisms, decision makers have degrees of freedom to implement novelties. The same leeway applies to decisions on business policies and strategies, as well as on the structures, compositions, and processes of executive committees and TMTs where most CXOs serve, which are not regulated, universal, or institutionalized. There is, then, ample latitude for role crafting and labelling. One of the purposes of this book is to explore whether the dynamics uncovered by Edelman (1990, 1992) and Zorn (2004) apply to the new emerging and proliferating C-level roles, as the roles and committees comprising the executive government of organizations are inherently symbolic.

2.3.2 Contemporary CXO roles

As new roles began to appear on top teams, scholars began paying attention to their particularities, drawing on different perspectives to enhance understanding. For example, whereas the role of the Chief Information Officer (CIO) was originally theorized by Rockart, Ball, and Bullen (1982), in later attempts to review studies of the CIO role, scholars sought to establish a link between the role, necessary capabilities, and performance implications for organizations, and have argued for the need to compare the CIO with other CXO roles (Peppard, 2010). In an exploratory study of another information related role—the Chief Digital Officer (CDO)—Kunisch, Menz, and Langan (2020) noted that among S&P 1500 companies, the CDO role appeared in 2003 but did not gain traction until 2010. They also captured internal variation in role performance, distinguishing two types: generalists and domain specialists. Exploring the role of the Chief Marketing Officer (CMO), Engelen, Lackhoff, and Schmidt (2013) recognized that scholarly work on the role has been scarce, and endeavoured to examine informal sources of CMOs' influence in TMTs (e.g. social capital), seeking to unravel role differences across different cultural contexts. Menz and Scheef (2014) provided a contingency analysis of the presence of Chief Strategy Officers at the top, suggesting that their presence is associated with strategic and structural complexity. Similarly, Strand (2014) sought to understand the reasons behind the establishment of the Chief Sustainability Officer (CSO) role and its effects on respective organizations. Yet, unlike Menz and Scheef, who focused on contingency theory, he drew arguments from strategic leadership and neo-institutional theory. Strand (2014) identified legitimacy crisis and potential external opportunities as driving forces for establishing such a role. Rather than examining the effects of the role on performance, he focused on the possible influences of the CSO role on the structure of the organization. He found that the role was dissolved or removed when the sustainability agenda was bureaucratized: 'the successful implementation of bureaucratic machinery can help considerations to sustainability extend beyond the tenure of a corporate sustainability position within the TMT' (Strand, 2014: 687).

Strand's (2014) study expands the understanding of CXOs by going beyond the reasons for their emergence and their impacts on performance to examining what a role's elimination could mean for the organization:

> TMT position titles are useful indicators of the issues that the corporation deems strategically and/or symbolically significant. . . . we find that it is equally important to bear in mind that the removal of the corporate sustainability position from the TMT does not, in and of itself, indicate that sustainability is any less important at an organization.
>
> (Strand, 2014: 704)

Strand's (2014) findings and arguments connect with our opening reflections in this chapter, namely, the organizing power of roles and their ability to transform not only the top team, but also the broader structure of the organization.

In recent reviews, scholars have attempt to integrate academic research on contemporary CXO roles (Menz, 2012; Radek and Menz, 2020). Menz (2012) noted that the fields in which functional executives have been studied range from accounting and finance to information systems and technology to marketing and strategic management. Nevertheless, interest among organization studies scholars in advancing the understanding of new roles on TMTs has been limited. According to the review, the range of theories applied is vast, and although organization studies scholars have not exhibited a focused interest in the trajectories of these roles, some of the theories employed—such as contingency or stakeholder theories—have organizational origins. The common denominator across theories and roles, Menz noted, is their connection to the upper echelons perspective, particularly Hambrick and Mason's (1984) conception of the organization as a reflection of its TMT, as well as interest in the studied roles' relationship to performance, hence, a rather functional focus. Yet, most studies of CXO roles are inconclusive with regard to specific roles' influence on performance; for example, Menz and Scheef (2014) concluded that having a Chief Strategy Officer did not have a significant influence on firm's performance. Similarly, Nath and Mahajan (2008) found that having a Chief Marketing Officer has no impact on firm performance.

Overall, as shown above, research on current CXO roles is piecemeal, lacking a strong institutional and organizational foundation. This calls for a deeper exploration of the essence of CXO roles in terms of the CXO industry involved in the 'production' of their expertise, identity, and style. We now turn to this CXO industry.

2.4 The CXO industry

We distinguish three main external 'role creators' (Hacking, 1986) that engage in the politics of CXO labelling and framing, with different implications for the legitimation, language, and trajectory of roles: experts, media, and professional networks. *Experts* are consulting and executive search firms that have developed practice areas centred on the C-suite. They regularly produce reports and papers on the state of the art of different roles; by articulating challenges and suggesting courses of action for the future, they contribute to the status and evolution of these roles. *CXO professional networks* are facilitated by role-based associations and clubs that seek to bring together professionals at events and other forms of interaction, and further influence the roles' legitimation by providing direction with regard to burning issues and priorities (setting the agenda), and exemplars to follow and aspire to, thereby celebrating excellence and achievement. The *media*, both traditional and new, sustains interest in and amplifies best practices in management by providing memorable stories and exemplars, or at least titles that draw readers in. These external role creators and legitimators have been defined as carriers and creators of management innovations and fashions (Abrahamson, 1991, 1996; Alvarez, 1997; Kieser, 1997; Sahlin-Andersson and Engwall, 2002), as well as intermediaries in managers' relations with different stakeholders (Engwall and Kippling, 2006). Considered in interaction, they constitute an 'arena for the trading of rhetoric', in which 'different groups of participants bustle about' (Kieser, 1997: 56–7). Next, we discuss in some detail these groups of actors' contributions to CXO expansion and legitimation.

2.4.1 Experts

In an extensive management literature, scholars have examined the role played by consulting firms as significant carriers of management ideas, 'supporting, transporting, and transforming' them (Sahlin-Andersen and Engwall, 2002: 9; Kipping and Engwall, 2002). Researchers have emphasized both their 'insatiable appetite for new clients' and their ability to define new problem areas that demand new expertise (Ernst and Kieser, 2002). What has been less explored is how these experts create and propagate not only management concepts and practices, but also new strategic actors (CXOs) who become continuously dependent on their services to develop their expertise, thereby generating a steady source of revenue for professional service firms (Hill, 2016).

'Over several decades, through proprietary assessment tools, Korn Ferry research has profiled leadership styles of CEOs, COOs, and functional areas (CHRO, CFO [chief financial officer], CMO [chief marketing officer], CIO [chief information officer])' (Ulrich and Filler, 2015: 35). Similarly, 'Spencer Stuart and Weber Shandwick have been monitoring the evolving role of the CCO since 2007 by partnering on a comprehensive quantitative survey of global CCOs. The Rising CCO, now in its fourth instalment, examines the roles, responsibilities and opinions of CCOs in the world's largest companies' (Spencer Stuart and Weber Shandwick, 2012: 1). The last page of an Accenture (2013) report explains that in 2009 'Accenture founded the CSO Circle to provide a unique forum for select strategy executives in which small groups of members convene to share, debate and interact', and provides an overview of the practice of working through circles with other CXO roles, such as:

COO Circle for chief operating officers and equivalent operating executives. CFO Circle for chief finance officers and equivalent finance executives. CHRO Circle for chief human resources officers and equivalent HR executives. CIO Council for chief information officers and equivalent IT executives. CPO Circle for chief procurement officers and equivalent procurement executives. CSCO Circle for chief supply chain officers and equivalent supply chain executives.

(Accenture, 2013, final page)

These examples suggest that roles are an important focus domain of consulting services for companies as well as specific business areas from an identity creation perspective.

Many consulting companies have dedicated arms engaged in producing surveys, reports, and papers on the C-suite as a whole or on specific roles. For example, through its Institute for Business Value (IBV), IBM has conducted regular C-suite surveys since 2003. IBV's 20th (and 4th global) survey titled 'Build your trust advantage: Leadership in the era of data and AI everywhere' was published in 2019 and based on data from 13,484 respondents across six C-suite roles (CEOs, CFOs, CHROs, CIOs, CMOs, and COOs), 20 industries, and 98 countries. In addition to broad overviews, it offers timely advice on key concerns for specific C-suite roles. In relation to COVID-19, IBV published 'The CHRO's guide to workforce re-entry' (June 2020) and 'The CMO's guide for turning mayhem into momentum' (May 2020) with recommendations for these specific CXOs in relation to reopening businesses. Insights are organized by specific business areas led by CXOs. At the time of the writing of this book, these business areas included 'Strategy and General Management, CEO', 'Finance and Risk, CFO', 'Marketing and Sales, CMO', 'Operations and Supply Chain, COO', 'Talent and Skills, CHRO', and 'Technology and Security, CIO'. In particular, 'the urgency of defining the [Chief Strategy Officer] role and identifying best practices and the optimal skill set seems to have increased in recent years as industries in many regions have been called upon to address levels of volatility that were previously unknown' (Accenture, 2013: 3).

Although services related to specific roles could be scattered across practice areas and functional domains, some consulting and search firms bundle C-suite services. For example, Deloitte South Africa has formulated a C-suite offering focused on specific CXOs, such as CEO, CFO, and COO, as well as other chiefs covering IT, HR, marketing, procurement, risk, tax, and audit under the umbrella of the Deloitte Executive Institute and its CXO or transition labs (Deloitte Johannesburg, 2016). In a Deloitte pamphlet, a 'CXO lab' is described as a structured process that 'is all about YOU as a CxO. There will be no one else there from your team' (Deloitte Johannesburg, 2016: 14; capitalization as per original text). These labs support executive transitions and are 'based on Deloitte's extensive research' (Deloitte Johannesburg, 2016: 2). In subsequent chapters, we closely examine the content of 575 reports and papers focused on different CXO roles published by twenty consulting and executive search firms over a twenty-year period. These reports and papers based on surveys or interviews with role holders provide insights into role expertise and identity (Chapter 4), styles of executive power (Chapter 5), the nature of competition and collaboration with other CXOs on TMTs, and the CXO's relationship to the CEO (Chapter 6). They also provide insights into field-level verbal vocabularies and visual discourses (Höllerer et al., 2013) employed in defining and legitimating different CXOs which deserve further in-depth study beyond the scope of this book.

2.4.2 Media

General and specialized traditional media (e.g. publications targeting general and professional management audiences, respectively) and new media (e.g. social media posts, blogs) are platforms for ideas on current and future challenges and opportunities in the trajectories of different CXO roles. They make fashionable ideas of the moment visible to the broader audience. Media stories and publicly available reports produced by consulting and executive search firms can be considered sources of prêt-à-porter ideas for the C-suite (Mazza and Alvarez, 2000). Sophisticated and expensive offerings are reserved for a much more limited market of firms that are able to afford expert support and training to define and realize new CXO roles.

As part of our research for this book, we used Factiva, an international news database produced by Dow Jones, to trace media references to forty CXO roles in addition to the terms 'CEO' and 'C-suite' from their first mentions until September 2018, when the search was conducted. Factiva enables the trajectory of a given CXO label to be visualized over time, highlighting its first mention as well as interest in the topic over time. For example, if one compares the trajectories of the Chief Operating Officer (COO), Chief Diversity Officer (CDO), Chief Human Resources Officer (CHRO), and Chief Strategy Officer (CSO) labels, the following differences come to the fore. First, their dates of first mention differ; for example, the first mention of COO was in 1972, whereas the first mention of CDO was in 1997. Second, the magnitude of interest is highly divergent: CDO and COO are each mentioned less than 10,000 times across the entire period, whereas CHRO is mentioned 30,900 times, and CSO is mentioned over 82,900 times. (Appendix 1 provides another 'window' into the media attention to roles, drawing on Factiva data in the period 2000–2020, and focusing on the clusters of CXO which we introduce and discuss in Chapter 3).

Forbes, a global media company focused on business, technology, entrepreneurship, and leadership, has published a number of articles referring to CXO titles under the heading of 'Leadership' and its subheadings, 'CMO Network', 'CFO Network', and 'CIO Network'. Illustrative titles include 'What is a chief experience officer and why does a company need one?' by Dan Gingiss (December 2019); 'The case against a chief customer officer' by Blake Morgan (January 2020); and 'It is CMO wake-up time', referring to the Chief Marketing Officer, by Larry Light (February 2020). Forbes (2018) has also published guides, such as 'AI: A CXO strategy guide'.

In addition, new media platforms enable authors to contribute opinions on the labelling and trajectories of CXO roles. For example, a LinkedIn post from 29 September 2016 by Michael Show, CEO and founder of the American Council of IT Sourcing and Procurement Executives (ACSPE), titled 'The CPO is dead', suggests that the title of Chief Procurement Officer does not adequately reflect its responsibilities and should be substituted with Chief Value Officer, which is a more strategic title (Show, 2016).

2.4.3 CXO professional networks

Professional associations have been recognized as 'important entities' that engage in discourse that can legitimate adjustments in what professionals do and what it means to be such professionals (Greenwood, Suddaby, and Hinings, 2002). Our exploration of the CXO field revealed a wealth of managerial occupational associations and networks that seek to further professionalize and legitimate specific chief officer roles. Similar to experts, they can define the vocabulary of the roles they cover through white papers, newsletters, or reports on their websites that promote stories, discourses, and best practices, as well as exemplary practitioners. For example, over the course of several years, the Chief Digital Officer (CDO) Club has developed and established a discourse that frames the CDO role as essential, thereby contradicting a discourse suggesting the role has a limited shelf-life. The club also gives awards, maintains a Hall of Fame of CDOs who have become CEOs or board members, and organizes networking events and other role-promoting activities which create ongoing role-relevant content and buzz. Those who run such networks are at times referred to as 'curators', a term usually reserved for those 'whose job is to be in charge of the objects or works of art in a museum or art gallery, etc.' (Oxford Learners' Dictionary). In the context of CXOs, this involves curating role-enhancing experiences, with participants of the highest calibre lined up as speakers.

On its website, the CDO Club describes itself as 'the world's first, largest, and most powerful community of C-Suite digital leaders'. An article about the CDO Club suggests it was started on LinkedIn in 2011 and describes founder David Mathison as a serial entrepreneur who was retirement-ready after selling his businesses 'when he said he noticed the "hockey stick" growth in companies hiring CDOs to assist with their digital transformation efforts' (Schick, 2019). In that article, Mathison is quoted explaining that the CDO Club is also a business: 'We've been doing a lot of work keeping this all community together, but the natural evolution of that are services to help those CDOs get their jobs done. . . . This has become a real business, and now it's time for me to scale.'

Some of these managerial occupational associations and forums are sector- and country-specific (e.g. the National Association of Diversity Officers in Higher Education), whereas others cross boundaries, seeking global legitimation of specific CXO roles (e.g. the Chief Marketing Officer [CMO] Council). The CMO Council, established in 2001:

> serves as the premiere [sic] peer-powered network for senior marketing decision makers. It is the only global network of executives specifically dedicated to high-level knowledge exchange, thought leadership and personal relationship building among senior corporate marketing leaders and brand decision-makers across a wide range of global industries.
> (https://www.cmocouncil.org/about, accessed on
> 23 September 2020)

The CMO Council is distinct relative to other networks and associations in its pursuit of global coverage and its emphasis on knowledge creation and exchange, suggesting professional awareness based on distinctive knowledge. Some of these networks have open membership policies, whereas others are more selective, bringing together CXOs working for organizations of a particular calibre. An example of such exclusivity is the HR Roundtable Group (HRRG), which defines itself on its website as giving 'its members a place to connect, learn from, and share with an exclusive group: Chief Human Resources Officers . . . only from the world's largest, most complex corporations'. Unlike other networks that tend to project confidence-boosting messages about the significance of their respective CXO role occupants, the HRRG features a message that is symptomatic of the overall lack of confidence among CHROs, which we discuss at some length in Chapter 4:

> There may be no lonelier person than the CHRO at a large enterprise. Sure, it's been said the loneliest person is the CEO, but the CEO gets the press, the accolades when things are going well, the recognition for better or for worse. But the CHRO? Who can you lean on? Your CEO? Not likely. Your team? Nope. You can't be completely transparent with them about your challenges. So, yes. The CHRO at a Global 1000 company may be the loneliest person in business. It doesn't have to be that way. The EN [Executive Networks] HR Roundtable Group (HRRG) is a haven for CHROs from the largest, most complex businesses in the world.
>
> (https://www.executivenetworks.com/human-resources-roundtable-group/, accessed on 23 September 2020)

With the ongoing challenge of including more female executives in the C-suite, some networks, such as the New York-based 'Chief', a private network co-founded by Carolyn Childers and Lindsay Kaplanare, seek to enhance diversity and inclusion at the top by focusing exclusively on the needs of women leaders. The co-founders use symbolism and storytelling, for example the metaphor of time travel (Long Lingo and McGinn, 2020), when affirming the need for their work as a network: 'at the current rate of change, it will take over 200 years for women to reach parity in business. We're not waiting eight generations' (https://www.chief.com/, 2020). In the words of co-founder Carolyn Childers, quoted in Aziz (2020):

> Chief launched in January 2019 with 200 Founding Members and has since grown to over 2,000 women across New York, Los Angeles and Chicago, with more than 7,000 on the waitlist. We also just announced our new San Francisco and Boston locations, which are currently accepting applications for digital membership. Members have access to an incredible community of executive women. Chief's signature service,

Core groups, are monthly leadership development meetings with fellow members at similar experience levels, led by best-in-class career coaches. Core groups become a personal board of directors to share perspectives and work through challenges.

In the article, Childers further explained the purpose of Chief as a network, not only in helping more female leaders attain C-suite positions, but also in ensuring they remain there: 'women are brought into leadership roles during periods of crisis or downturn when the chance of failure is highest' (Aziz, 2020).

In addition, similar to organizations operating in a context of uncertainty, associations and clubs for individuals in newly established CXO roles engage in mimetic behaviours, reproducing practices and organizational forms observed in extant clubs and associations recognized as well-functioning and/or legitimate, and sometimes even acquiring them. When announcing the CDO Club's acquisition of the CMO Club, founder Dave Mathison (2020) acknowledged:

> When I started the CDO Club in 2011, I modeled it—and the name—after the CMO Club. My goal was to replicate Pete's CMO community, but with a laser focus on addressing the needs of the Chief Digital Officer, Chief Data Officer, Chief Analytics Officer, and Chief Information Security Officer.

2.4.4 Connections between role theorizers

Professional networks engage in influencing the trajectories of specific CXO roles at 'summits' which bring the roles' elites together to connect and discuss topics of importance for their areas of responsibility. Summits also provide a platform for visibility and celebration through rankings, awards, and halls of fame for the most prominent representatives of the role as exemplars of success and excellence. For example, the Chief Information Officer Network produces annual rankings of the 100 best CIOs. By convening and connecting professionals, setting and controlling agendas, and displaying exemplars of excellence, these summits constitute field-level events that contribute to both field-changing and field maintenance (Schüßler and Sydow, 2015; Gross and Zilber, 2020).

For example, media companies, consulting companies, and renowned business schools are collaborating to establish information exchanges and networking venues to facilitate interactions and support the maintenance of the Chief Information Officer's role (e.g. IDG has established CIO Inside, Deloitte sponsors a CIO Event Series, and MIT's Sloan School of Management runs the MIT Sloan CIO Symposium).

Another example of a role-centred network led by a media company is the WSJ CIO Network, which promises membership benefits, such as connections among 'heads of technology from the world's most influential companies', premier events, and business insights (https://cionetwork.wsj.com/, accessed 23 September 2020). During the current COVID-19 pandemic, it has provided a platform for 'curated conversations and networking, live online'. WSJ also offers the journal print edition as a platform for selected members' voices on timely topics. The WSJ CIO Network annual meetings are denoted as 'flagship events' that convene management and technology leaders 'to explore the CIO's role as a business leader and prepare for the next wave'. A 2013 edition of the Journal Report of the CIO Network (WSJ, 22 January, pp. B11–B17) provides a glimpse of how this network influences the visibility, voice, legitimacy, and not least, the confidence of those in CIO positions. The cover page carries a heading that affirms it is 'A Transformative Time for Companies and Their CIOs' and suggests CIOs have moved from 'denizens of the "back office"' to reporting directly to the CEO (p. B11). Furthermore, among the topics for debate is something we discuss in Chapter 4—namely, how CIOs can become corporate strategists. WSJ also features a CMO network with the mandate to bring together marketing and related top executives.

Overall, actors such as experts, media, and professional networks who serve as carriers, trendsetters, and intermediaries of new management ideas (Abrahamson, 1991, 1996; Kieser, 1997; Sahlin-Andersson and Engwall, 2002; Engwall and Kipping, 2006) contribute to sustaining the increasing variety of CXOs. In performing their work, we suggest that these actors contribute to creating and legitimating not only new management ideas, but also new strategic actors and occupational identities within a 'fast fashion industry' of executive roles. Given their spread, CXOs can be considered a fashionable management idea. What makes it 'fast fashion' is the ongoing introduction and diffusion of new labels and roles, following a fast-paced 'template' of launching a label, initiating events, bringing together different role creators, and establishing awards and halls of fame for remarkable achievements. It is an 'industry', as experts, media, and networks are in the business of producing these new 'strategic actors' and selling services to them. They influence CXO roles' legitimacy, status, and significance, as well as their rise, fall, or transformation and the extent to which they spread across geographies, industries, and organizational contexts. They not only enhance the visibility of CXO labels, but also contribute to 'stirring up managers' fear' (Kieser, 2002: 181) and anxiety, stemming from continuous competition with other CXO roles with which they are constantly being compared and ranked in terms of popularity and status.

In addition, one could argue that their not-so-hidden agenda involves the creation of new strategic actors (Hacking, 1986) who in turn constitute customers of services provided by experts and networks, dynamics that facilitate the evolution of both CXO roles and the respective businesses that serve them. Similar to 'issue professionals' defined in the context of transnational organizing, CXOs operate in two-level professional(-like) and organizational networks as a context of action, and 'claim particular expertise that is not bound by professional associations, formal training, or one-dimensional organizational values' (Henriksen and Seabrooke, 2016: 723).

2.5 Conclusion

In this chapter, we have focused on different aspects of the theorizing of CXO roles. We have outlined the organizing power of executive roles for transforming organizations in general and executive power structures in particular, singling out two main perspectives on the nature and significance of roles as resources and as professional role identities that account for both power-related and institutional dynamics in the shaping of new CXO roles. We also have emphasized the multiple interests and contributions involved in the 'politics of labelling' and categorizing CXO roles as a management category by an active 'fast fashion industry' of skilful, interested, and authoritative theorists who project CXOs as 'panaceas' (Mazza and Strandgaard Pedersen, 2015) for diverse problems and pressures faced by organizations.

Bringing together insights across fragmented classic and contemporary studies of CXO roles, we suggest that although the dominance of the CFO role remains unmatched, other CXO roles are becoming increasingly relevant for the organizational adaptation these problems and pressures require. This could be indicative of a possible shift in the model of organizational control. In this potentially updated model, organizations need to respond not only to investors, but increasingly to a wider and more diverse constellation of extra-organizational actors, including consulting and executive search firms, diverse professional networks, and not least, the media. This extra-organizational constellation of actors is able to swiftly bring new CXO roles to 'life', signalling their belonging to a recognizable and distinct management category of 'chiefs' and 'officers'—or alternatively, send them into oblivion—by shaping the expertise, identities, and styles of those who fill these executive roles, which we explore further in subsequent chapters.

3
CXO Expansion

In February 2019, Levi Strauss & Co. (LS&Co)—the iconic denim company founded in 1853 in San Francisco, California, and at the time, one of the world's largest apparel firms—announced the introduction of a brand new executive role: Chief Strategy and Artificial Intelligence Officer (CSAIO). According to the press release, the CSAIO role was 'designed to help the company translate data analytics into meaningful decisions that drive business value and competitive advantage' (Levi Strauss, 2019). The company's website further clarified that the CSAIO would focus 'on setting the company's holistic digital and corporate strategy and infusing it with data, analytic, and artificial intelligence capabilities to drive business value across LS&Co. globally'. Katia Walsh, the first person to hold this position, previously the first Chief Global Data and Analytics Officer at Vodafone Group, also received a Senior Vice President title and joined the company's global leadership team. Her LinkedIn profile affirmed the role was not only transformative for LS&Co, but also pioneering across industries (LinkedIn, 26 February 2020).

The creation of the CSIAO role at LS&Co. raises some pertinent questions related to the Chief 'X' Officer (CXO) phenomenon, whereby 'X' denotes a growing nomenclature of domains. Would the CSIAO role spread beyond LS&Co. to other organizations? Why name both strategy and artificial intelligence in the same role? Why combine the titles of CSIAO and Senior Vice President in the same position? What does it signal and to whom? And, given Katia Walsh's move from one CXO position to another across organizations, is there a distinctive CXO career path that differs from other career paths at the top of the organizational hierarchy? In this chapter, we investigate some of these and other questions related to the expansion of chief officer roles.

The Changing C-Suite. José Luis Alvarez and Silviya Svejenova, Oxford University Press.
© José Luis Alvarez and Silviya Svejenova (2022). DOI: 10.1093/oso/9780198728429.003.0003

3.1 Directions for understanding expansion

We suggest the following pertinent theoretical directions for thinking about and investigating further the CXO expansion: (a) as a category extension; (b) as an aspect of hyper-organization; and (c) as strategic responses to different types of complexity. The three directions concern both the phenomenon of CXOs as a whole, as well as its sources of internal differentiation across roles in terms of domain and status variation, as well as adoption across types of organizations, industries, and geographies, and not least in terms of response to the complexity these organizations are exposed to in their respective fields.

First, we examine the proliferation of CXOs as a category extension (Delmestri and Greenwood, 2016) of an existing category consisting originally of a limited number of classical roles (e.g. CEO, CFO, COO) with a plethora of contemporary CXOs, in which—as discussed in the previous chapter—the 'chief' and the 'officer' terms are shared signifiers which maintain certain category coherence, while enabling extension to a range of 'X' domains. Second, we connect the rampant inflation of chiefs to the professionalization and myths of management, and argue that the establishment of CXO roles is part of the elaboration of an organization into a hyper-organization and of management into hyper-management (Bromley and Meyer, 2015, 2021). Third, we interpret CXO expansion in the context of an organizational-level institutional pluralism (Kraatz and Block, 2008; Heinze and Weber, 2016; Jancsary et al., 2017), considering the creation and transformation of CXO roles as organizations' strategic (substantial and/or symbolic) responses to four domains of complexity (i.e. institutional, information, primary task, and administrative) and outline respective clusters of chief officer roles. Below we provide insights from the CXO expansion in each of these three theoretical directions and illustrate them accordingly.

3.2 CXOs as a category extension

Our analysis of CXO expansion reveals the emergence of a pattern which goes beyond individual instances of roles with unique attributes, and enables the formulation of a hypothesis on the existence of a new species, to borrow insights from biology on the art of naming (Ohl, 2018), or management category. This category has an important horizontal categorical dimension and a vertical status dimension (Delmestri and Greenwood, 2016), which we detail on continuation. As Delmestri and Greenwood (2016: 510), building on Hofstadter and Sander (2013), explained, category extension is about 'an ongoing display of increasing abstraction', such as the use of the CXO or the C-Suite terms as a collective term covering a range of roles (Appendix 1 shows the growing use of these terms as well as of individual CXO roles in the media, drawing on data from Factiva.)

In that category extension, Delmestri and Greenwood (2016) distinguish 'a category grows horizontally to encompass new sets of situations and acquires different meanings reflected and reproduced through socio-cultural practices' (2016: 510) and vertically 'through status orders' (2016: 511). In the case of CXOs, the horizontal growth takes place by increasing the variation of terms depicted by the middle part of the label, the 'X', whereas the vertical growth is manifested in the status ordering of these roles in terms of their reporting distance from the CEO as the top role, N-1 being the CEO direct reports.

Horizontal categorical dimension. First, there is a horizontal extension, with myriad CXO titles sharing the terms 'chief' and 'officer' with different 'X' terms in the middle denoting their distinctive areas of responsibility. A Wikipedia entry from March 2021 lists sixty-five such titles, whereas our own analysis of the S&P100's top teams based on 2015 data from The Official Board, a global data boutique, providing real-time data on corporate organizational charts and executive moves; (www.theofficialboard.com) reveals seventy-eight unique titles, including CEO. New titles are continually being added to the CXO nomenclature, such as Chief Social Impact Officer, Chief Resilience Officer, and even Chief COVID Officer, among others, including LS&Co's Chief Strategy and Artificial Intelligence Officer described in our opening example. Studying the evolution of this nomenclature could reveal shifts in organizational attention and emerging priorities. For example, Erin Reilly, was recently appointed as the first Chief Social Impact Officer of Twilio, a technology company headquartered in San Francisco with offices in sixteen countries. In a Forbes interview (Farley, 2020), Erin hinted at both substantial and symbolic reasons behind the title:

> Ever since I began leading social impact at Twilio in 2016, I've had a company-wide lens where I look at how we can weave social impact into the entire DNA of our company. My new title is a company-wide acknowledgement of the importance of social impact for all of Twilio.

As some roles lose relevance and, at times, come back from oblivion (e.g. Chief Learning Officer, cf. BCG report – Dyer, Dyrchs, Bailey, Bürkner, and Puckett, 2020 – which argues for reinventing of corporate learning and with that of the role of the CLO), many new titles continue to emerge, acknowledging shifting areas of executive interest and attention. A number of new titles expand and/or morph existing roles into role 'families'. For example, the Chief Marketing Officer role, which was fairly uncommon in the mid-1980s (Gilliatt and Cuming, 1986), is now ubiquitous and being differentiated into a variety of sub-specialties (e.g. Chief Customer, Product, Sales, Experience, Brand, and Digital Officers), and expanding into adjacent areas of executive attention (e.g. Chief Marketing and Technology Officer). An analogous differentiation of the Chief Human Resource Officer role has taken place, involving a proliferation of personnel roles (e.g. Chief People, Talent, Culture, and Leadership Officers). In addition, longstanding roles inspire the creation of new ones. For example, the role of Chief Information Officer has inspired some recent 'relatives' in what can be considered a 'family' of information-related roles, such as Chief Digital, Data, and Artificial Intelligence Officers. Originally defined by Rockart et al. (1982), the Chief Information Officer role has inspired the creation of the Chief Risk Officer (Power, 2005). Moreover, the development of executive expertise and identity, and how these are acted upon, which we discuss further in Chapter 4, influences whether a role fades away, morphs into a variety of related roles, and/or inspires the introduction of new roles. A role's evolution, in turn, could lead to new overlaps in areas of responsibility as well as to competition and collaboration with other CXO roles, on which we elaborate in Chapter 6.

Some CXO titles also appear in less conventional domains, as suggested by labels such as Chief Happiness Officer (CHO), a title held by the fictional character Ronald McDonald, a mascot with his own LinkedIn profile, which claims a seventeen-year tenure as McDonald's CHO and fifty-seven years of service. Mattel's marketing effort at the launch of 'Entrepreneur Barbie', a doll promoting start-up careers to girls, consisted of partnerships with female entrepreneurs. Girls Who Code founder Reshma Saujani, among others, were listed as the doll's 'Chief Inspirational Officers' (Hudson, 2014), providing advice to young entrepreneurial aspirants. Several companies in California- and Denmark-based global company Thornico have Chief Karma Officers. And, if one may wonder what a Chief Listening Officer could possibly do, below is an excerpt of a career description posted on Study.com (2020), a personalized learning platform:

Chief listening officers specialize in monitoring both external and internal communications about organizations. Their primary focus is on gathering information from customers and employees in order to develop ways for an organization to enhance their relationships with both.

This title inflation has led some authors to use the terms 'chief everything officers' (Tobak, 2009) and '"chief" whatnots', (Too many chiefs, *The Economist*, 24 June 2010), resonating with Boltanski's (1987) concern over not only 'symbolic inflation', but also the 'vulgarization' of such titles.

A final feature of this horizontal expansion is that CXO roles are constantly changing, and the turnover of executives occupying such roles is high. According to the website of The Official Board (www.theofficialboard.com, 2020), an organization dedicated to providing real-time data on moves in the ranks of over 77,000 publicly traded or private companies worldwide, 'organizational charts are ever-moving jigsaws': 'out of 100 executives, statistics reveal, 35 will assume another business title within only 12 months'. In addition, executive roles are continuously morphing, not only in terms of new variations of chief officer titles, which we touched upon above, but also in terms of transformed mandates and remits, as well as expanded competences. The need for coordination across disparate domains of complexity leads to boundary-spanning roles (see Chapter 5 for further discussion on boundary work as an aspect of CXO roles and the style of executive power), some of which can be characterized as 'double-hatting' and hybridization (i.e. connecting two areas of executive attention in the same position). Examples of these are LS&Co's Chief Strategy and Artificial Intelligence Officer, which we discussed at the beginning of the chapter, Telefonica's Chief Strategy and Corporate Development Officer, DuPont's Chief Technology and Sustainability Officer, and GE's Chief Marketing and Communications Officer.

Furthermore, although evidence is still limited and inconclusive, the horizontal expansion of CXO roles may create opportunities to address (at least partially) deeply entrenched gender and race inequalities at the top. A recent study of over 100 large US financial institutions by Deloitte (Rogish, Sandler, and Shemluck, 2020: 3) suggests:

Chief diversity and chief learning officers are more likely to be women, representing 86.7 percent and 61.5 percent of these roles, respectively. Women serving as chief brand (46.4 percent) and chief sustainability

(50 percent) officers are nearly or already on par with men. And perhaps more interestingly, over the last decade the share of women as
chief innovation (32.4 percent), chief data analytics or chief digital (28.5
percent), and chief strategy (25.2 percent) officers also exceed their average share in traditional C-suite roles, where their representation has
historically lagged.

The authors explained that this increase is partly attributable to the possibility 'that emerging roles are unencumbered by the obstacles that have
historically impeded women's journey to leadership. . . . [such roles] tend
not to have a set career path, which could result in more avenues [for
women]' (Rogish et al., 2020: 5). Cappelli, Hamori, and Bonet (2014)
compared the appointment of female executives in Fortune 100 executive
positions at three points in time, noting an increase from 0 per cent (1980)
to 11 per cent (2001) to 17.7 per cent (2011). They also observed that

women are slightly more likely to work in the financial services, health
care, and retail industries than elsewhere. They're prominent in the executive ranks of consumer products and, surprisingly, aerospace companies. At the corporations that have the most female executives—Target,
Lockheed Martin, and PepsiCo— women hold half the senior management jobs.

(Cappelli et al., 2014: 78)

Overall, further research is needed on whether, how, and to what extent
the expansion of CXO roles responds to increased institutional pressures
for more women at the top and whether that leads to accelerating women's
C-suite advancement (Bonet, Cappelli, and Hamori, 2020).

Vertical status dimension. Although chief officer titles can be found at
different levels of the organizational hierarchy, they are particularly visible
in Top Management Teams (TMTs), that is, the C-suite, as the following
quote suggests: 'When it comes to job titles, we live in an age of rampant inflation. . . . The rot starts at the top. Not that long ago companies
had just two or three "chief" whatnots. Now they have dozens, collectively
called the "c-suite"' (*The Economist*, 'Too Many Chiefs', 24 June 2010). TMTs
swelled between the mid-1980s and the mid-2000s, doubling the number
of a CEO's direct reports 'from 5 to 10 with approximately three-quarters

of the increase attributed to functional managers rather than general managers', reflecting 'functional centralization' (Guadalupe et al., 2014: 825). Analysing panel data on executive positions, Guadalupe and her colleagues concluded that the executive team expanded in response to changes in firms' diversification and information technology, mostly to include roles with product (e.g. marketing, R&D) and administrative (e.g. finance, law, human resources) functions.

Our exploration into the composition of a number of top teams is in line with Guadalupe and colleagues' (2014) findings that most CXO titles relate to product or administrative functions. For example, Chief Creative Officers, Chief Design Officers, or Chief Experience Officers extend the range of product-oriented roles, whereas Chief Process Officers, Chief Project Officers, or Chief Value Officers in the area of procurement expand the range of administrative roles. However, we also observe CXO roles in other responsibility areas, particularly those related to public accountability and the management of information. Public accountability seems to drive the establishment of roles that address demands by diverse stakeholders. Examples of these are executives with areas of responsibility in sustainability, diversity, risk, and climate change, among others. For example, the Chief Risk Officer role, first introduced in 1993 by GE Capital and subsequently adopted by other (typically, large) companies, serves not only as an internal regulatory agent, but also as a signal to stakeholders of organizational commitment to the internal management of risk (Power, 2005). Another responsibility area of growing importance, particularly in relation to engaging with customers and accomplishing work, is the management of increasingly vast, complex, and dynamic information. The growing importance of information as an area of responsibility is visible in the adoption of titles such as Chief Information Officer, Chief Digital Officer, Chief Data Officer, and/or Chief Artificial Intelligence Officer. The section on strategic responses to complexity in this chapter reveals and explains the main areas in which CXO roles tend to cluster.

Another source of status 'inequality' refers to the roles' spread, as some roles are widely adopted by organizations across sectors whereas others are rather industry-specific (see Appendix 2 on the adoption of 40 CXO roles among 77,426 companies in 89 industries and 244 countries based on March 2020 data from The Official Board (www.theofficialboard.com)). For example, of the 77,426 listed in The Official Board database companies, approximately 80 per cent have a CEO, 40 per cent a CFO, 21 per cent a Chief Operating Officer, 15 per cent a Chief Information Officer, and 5 per cent a Chief Human Resources Officer and a Chief Marketing Officer, showing a significant variation in the adoption (Table 3.2 later in this chapter—in the discussion of CXO expansion as an aspect of hyper-organization—provides a breakdown of adoption by geographic area of the top six CXO roles). This is perhaps not very surprising, as these earlier or more classical C-level roles are less specific to particular industries and they have had a longer and/or stronger institutionalization, as we explained in Chapter 2, in the discussion of the CEO and CFO roles. Other executive roles are rather industry-specific (e.g. Chief Medical and Nursing Officers in hospitals, Chief Scientific Officers in pharmaceutical companies, and Chief Gaming Officers in entertainment companies) and exhibit a more narrow adoption pattern.

Finally, from a status perspective, there is an internal stratification and pecking order amongst CXOs, in terms of reporting structure within the organizational hierarchy and control over financial and other resources. Some CXOs report directly to the CEO and, as such, are situated at reporting level N-1, whereas other positions are situated at the N-2 level and report to the CEO's direct reports, which in some cases are other CXOs (see Table 3.1 for examples and Appendix 2 for a broader overview). If one looks more closely at the forty roles we have overviewed in Appendix 2, only three roles are either predominantly found at the N-2 (the Chief Accounting Officer and the Chief Tax Officer) or almost equally spread between N-1 and N-2 (the Chief Diversity Officer). Such a status distinction reflects a company's priorities as well as its primary and supporting areas of responsibility. For example, with regard to the Chief Data Officer role:

> organizations are almost evenly divided among the top-three options: 34 percent report to the Chief Executive Officer; 31 percent report to the Chief Information Officer; and 34 percent report to a C-suite executive, namely the Chief Operating Officer (17 percent), the Chief Marketing Officer (10 percent) or a technology-related vice president (7 percent).
>
> (IBM Institute for Business Value, 2015)

Some CXOs may also have seats on boards of directors. In a Harvard Business Review posting titled 'Why CIOs make great board directors', Stephenson and Olson (2017) suggested that 'CIOs are the fastest-growing addition to the boardroom', quoting unpublished data from Korn Ferry

Table 3.1 Examples of CXO status (N-1 and N-2 from CEO) from 10 S&P50 companies, 2015[*]

Company[**]	N-1 (direct reports to CEO)	N-2 (reporting to CEO's direct reports)
3M Industrial conglomerates www.3M.com (23 April 2015)	CFO Chief Design Officer Chief Technology Officer	Chief Accounting Officer Chief Compliance Officer
AIG Insurance www.aig.com (14 May 2015)	CFO CEO, Commercial Insurance Chief Information Officer Chief Risk Officer Chief Strategy Officer CEO, Consumer Insurance CEO, Americas CEO, Asia Pacific CEO, Europe, Middle East and Africa Chief Science Officer	Chief Procurement Officer CEO, Aerospace Division CEO, United Guaranty Corporation Chief Operating Officer of Commercial Insurance CEO, Life, Health, and Disability Insurance CEO, Personal Insurance CEO, AIG Financial Distributors CEO of AIG Canada CEO, Latin America and the Caribbean
AT&T Telecommunications www.att.com (10 April 2015)	CFO Chief Compliance Officer CEO, Mobile & Business Solutions Chief Strategy Officer	CEO, Mobility Chief Technology Officer, President and CEO, AT&T Labs Chief Diversity Officer
Cisco Computer networking www.cisco.com (4 June 2015)	CFO Chief Information Officer[***] Chief Operating Officer Chief Human Resources Officer Chief Marketing Officer Chief Security Officer Chief Technology and Strategy Officer	Chief Information Officer CEO, Greater China, Cisco Chief Globalisation Officer Chief Development Officer Chief Technology Officer

Continued

Table 3.1 *Continued*

Company**	N-1 (direct reports to CEO)	N-2 (reporting to CEO's direct reports)
Coca-Cola Company Beverages www.thecoca-colacompany.com (5 May 2015)	CFO Chief Customer and Commercial Leadership Officer Chief Administrative Officer Chief Marketing Officer Chief People Officer Chief Technical Officer	Chief Accounting Officer Chief Strategy Officer Chief Procurement Officer Chief Executive Officer, Coca-Cola China Designate Chief Executive Officer, Coca-Cola Beverages Africa Chief Information Officer Chief Sustainability Officer Chief Science and Health Officer Chief Quality, Safety and Sustainable Operations Officer
Chevron Oil and gas www.chevron.com (29 May 2015)	CFO Chief Governance Officer	Chief Information Officer
Colgate-Palmolive Consumer goods www.colagte.com (1 June 2015)	CFO Chief Information & Business Services Officer Chief Legal Officer Chief Marketing Officer Chief Operating Officer, Emergent Markets and Business Development Chief Operating Officer, Global Innovation and Growth, Europe, South Pacific and Hill's Pet Nutrition Chief Technology Officer	Chief Procurement Officer Chief Ethics and Compliance Officer
eBay Internet www.ebayinc.com (4 June 2015)	CFO Chief Communications Officer CEO Designee, PayPal	Chief Marketing Officer for North America Chief Product Officer Chief Technology Officer

Continued

Table 3.1 *Continued*

Company**	N-1 (direct reports to CEO)	N-2 (reporting to CEO's direct reports)
EMC Computer hardware www.emc.com (11 May 2015)	CFO CEO of VCE CEO, EMC Information Infrastructure Business Chief Marketing Officer Chief Technology Officer Chief Information Officer Chief Operating Officer	Chief Risk Officer CFO, EMC Information Infrastructure Chief Talent Officer Chief Operating Officer, Global Services
General Electric (GE) Industrial conglomerates www.ge.com (19 March 2015)	CFO CEO, GE ASEAN CEO, GE Oil & Gas CEO, GE Africa CEO, GE Business Innovations and Chief Marketing Officer CEO, GE Healthcare Chief Information Officer CEO of Power and Water CEO, GE Aviation CEO, GE Global Growth & Operations	Chief Accounting Officer Chief Communications Officer CEO, GE Lighting CEO, GE Intelligent Platform CEO, GE Appliances and Lighting

Source: Data from The Official Board (www.theofficialboard.com), 2015

*Only CXO roles are listed; if titles include both a CXO component and a President, Vice President or other component, these components are not noted; the number of CXO roles in a company does not capture the size of the executive committee (N-1), or the number of N-2 roles.

**Date information accessed in parentheses.

***Cisco has two Chief Information Officers listed. The N-1 CIO is also Senior Vice President, IT and Cloud & Systems Management Technology Group.

showing 'a 74% increase in the number of CIOs serving on Fortune 100 boards in the past two years'. They further affirmed that 'having an accomplished CIO director is the most effective way to make sure the board identifies the most-pressing technology priorities, establishes greater importance for the technology functions, and plays an active role in attracting top technology leaders'. Whereas the readiness and ability of a CIO to participate in board-level work may be subject to debate, such statements do hint at the increasing involvement of CXOs on boards of directors. Another role considered potentially important at the board level is the Chief Human Resources Officer (CHRO). As suggested by KPMG (Barrett, 2019), a CHRO as an internal director could offer expertise to CEO succession issues, contribute to a stronger focus on culture and diversity, and also satisfy calls from institutional investors for more transparency on human capital management practices, among others. Overall, though, the CFO remains the N-1 role that most often sits on boards of directors as an internal executive director (Mobb, 2018).

Moreover, although our discussion of the horizontal categorical dimension of CXOs emphasized that it brings possibilities for more women and wider diversity in the top team, considering the vertical status dimension of CXOs allows capturing further sources of gender and other inequalities. For example, Mishra's (2018) analysis of data from ISS analytics reveals that only a low percentage of top executive positions in the Russell 3000 are occupied by women (9%). Further, there is a higher concentration of women 'in positions that rarely see a promotion to the top job, such as Human Resources Officer, General Counsel, and Chief Administrative Officer', while 'female executives appear scarcer at roles with profit-and-loss responsibilities that often serve as stepping stones to the CEO role, such as COO, Head of Sales, or CEOs of business units and subsidiary groups'. (According to the Russell 3000 Index (2021: 1) factsheet, it 'measures the performance of the largest 3,000 US companies representing approximately 98% of the investable US equity market'.)

Overall, the horizontal and vertical dimensions of the expansion of CXOs as a management category reveal a complex phenomenon that has achieved both abstraction and internal differentiation, both of which contribute to its persistence. Below we turn to another—complementary—direction for understanding this expansion.

3.3 CXOs as an aspect of hyper-organization

The institutional perspective on the elaboration of organizations into hyper-organizations that cover a wide variety of activities and address a wide range of stakeholders (Bromley and Meyer, 2015), along with recent developments in relation to hyper-management (Bromley and Meyer, 2021) offer useful insights into the proliferation of CXO roles. Seen through this lens, CXO roles covering diverse areas of responsibility and oriented toward different stakeholder groups could be considered an aspect of organizational elaboration 'facilitated by the rise of a conception of society as transcending national boundaries' and of 'expanded ideologies of organization and management' (Meyer, 2002: 34–5). According to Bromley and Meyer (2015), these roles are filled by professionalized managers who have coordination and decision-making expertise, yet lack substantive knowledge (we elaborate on these knowledge gaps in Chapter 4 when we discuss some theoretical ideas on executive expertise and identity). More importantly (for the argument that we put forward in the current chapter), and much in line with globalization trends depicted by Bromley and Meyer (2015), CXO roles have diffused across various types of organizations— for example old and young, big and small, for-profit and non-profit, public and private—as well as across industries and in different geographies (see Appendix 2 for information about the geographic and industry spread of the forty most frequently used titles). Table 3.2 provides an overview of the top six CXO roles (according to the data presented in Appendix 2) across the six main geographical areas. The table shows that in 2020, these CXO

Table 3.2 Percentage of firms with top six CXO titles across geographic areas, 2020

Title geographical area	CEO	CFO	COO	CIO	CHRO	CMO
Africa	92	34	18	9	3	2
Asia	83	31	15	8	3	3
Europe	86	31	15	10	3	3
Oceania	91	47	21	13	4	3
North America	83	52	29	23	9	8
South America	75	23	7	5	2	1
Overall % (across areas)	80	40	21	15	5	5

Source: Data from The Official Board (www.theofficialboard.com), March 2020; see Appendix 2 for detail.

*Abbreviations: CEO (Chief Executive Officer), CFO (Chief Financial Officer), COO (Chief Operating Officer), CIO (Chief Information Officer), CHRO (Chief Human Resources Officer), CMO (Chief Marketing Officer).

**Percentages rounded to nearest whole number.

titles were most prevalent in North American companies and least so in South American companies.

Senior leadership and executive management teams of emblematic US companies such as Coca-Cola, Corning, DuPont, General Electric, and Walmart have various CXOs, as do European multinational corporations such as Erste Group Bank in Austria, The Lego Group in Denmark, Telefonica in Spain, BASF in Germany, and the insurance firm AXA in France. Most British companies have a managing director rather than a CEO. However, firms competing in global markets are among the adopters of CXO titles. For example, GSK's executive team includes a CEO and a CFO, as well as Chief Scientific, Strategy, Commercial, and Digital & Technology officers. Similarly, Chinese companies of global renown, such as Alibaba Group, have a number of CXOs on their senior leadership teams. In addition to a CEO, CFO, and Chief Marketing Officer, Alibaba has Chief Customer, Technology, and People Officers, as well as a combined Chief Risk and Platform Governance Officer's position. The latter spans platform responsibilities, from data and information security, to governance of the group's retail and wholesale marketplaces.

CXOs are also found on the management teams of start-ups, thereby signalling new firms' importance and legitimacy, and/or recognizing core employees beyond stock options and other benefits. In addition, CXO roles could reflect start-ups' current priorities, attention domains, and/or expectations for the future. Such roles could also be established to support and mentor an inexperienced founder-CEO (Bennett and Miles, 2006b). Cole (2017) suggested that if entrepreneurs 'plan to increase revenue by 400% in the next three years', it is important to 'have a superstar Chief Revenue Officer, whereas those who are 'planning to disrupt an entire market with proprietary technology . . . need a business-savvy CTO'. In addition, advice proliferates on how start-ups can use CXO titles vis-à-vis other senior labels and what that implies for the career trajectories of senior leaders in the context of an early-stage organization: 'If you make someone a VP, you can promote them to CxO, but you can't promote a CxO to anything other than CEO' (Byrnes, 2014).

Non-profit and public organizations, as well as organizations affiliated with social movements also adopt CXO titles and adapt them to their specific needs. This can be understood in the context of growing managerialization and an increased emphasis on the importance of value (Bryson, Crosby, and Bloomberg, 2015; Moore, 1995, 2013). The reliance on CXOs in such contexts goes beyond the more customary CEO and CFO roles to include a range of other titles. For example, the executive leadership team of the Bill & Melinda Gates Foundation includes a number of CXOs, similar to the TMT of a business organization (e.g. Chief Business Operations Officer, Chief Strategy Officer, Chief HR Officer; Gates Foundation, 2019). Similarly, The Clinton Foundation's leadership team includes a Chief Communications and Marketing Officer (Clinton Foundation, 2019). However, it also has roles such as Chief Development Officer and Chief Impact and Foreign Policy Officer that are customized to the specificities of the organization's non-profit work, which is focused on developing and influencing foreign policy, and is measured in terms of impact. This customization can also be observed with regard to more conventional titles. For example, in 2019 the me too. movement had a Chief Strategy Officer responsible for field innovation and political strategy, and a Chief Operations Officer responsible for building the movement's infrastructure and foundation, as well as a more traditional Chief Communications Officer responsible for communications strategy, branding, engagement, and media relations (me too. Impact Report, 2019).

Libraries, business schools, and universities also show signs of partial adoption of CXO titles. For example, The New York Public Library's leadership includes a Chief Digital Officer, Chief Branch Library Officer, Chief Operating Officer, Chief External Relations Officer, and Chief Investment Officer (New York Public Library, 2019). Universities have been a bit more conservative in adopting these new titles, but are not completely exempt from it. For example, while we were finishing this book, Harvard University hired a new Chief Diversity and Inclusion Officer, having had a Chief Diversity Officer between 2010 and 2017. Referring to 2018 data from the National Bureau of Economic Research, a recent report by Russell Reynolds Associates suggests that 'more than two-thirds of major U.S. universities had appointed a chief diversity officer or executive-level equivalent', with the role considered 'integral to the strategic direction and success of the institution' (Pihakis et al., 2019: 3). Freie Universität Berlin has a Chief Gender Equality Officer role, which is served by a team. The global business school INSEAD, where one of us works, features a Chief Operating Officer and a Chief People Officer for non-academic staff, and the Dean of the Kedge Business School in France serves as its Chief Academic Officer.

Cities are also sites of CXO innovation: Helsinki has a Chief Design Officer, Palo Alto has a Chief Information Officer, and New York City has recently introduced a Chief Analytics Officer. Cities are also increasingly hiring Chief Resilience Officers. The website of 100 Resilient Cities, an organization created by the Rockefeller Foundation to mark its centennial in 2013, suggests that a Chief Resilience Officer is 'a top-level advisor that reports directly to the city mayor' whose 'task is to establish a compelling resilience vision for his or her city, working across departments and with the local community to maximize innovation and minimize the impact of unforeseen events' (http://www.100resilientcities.org/what-is-a-chief-resilience-officer/). The role can be found in cities around the world, from Medellín, Colombia to Athens, Greece to Wellington, New Zealand.

Chief officer titles also are applied at the country level, either as formal titles or self-monikers. For example, the United States has had a Chief Technology Officer since 2009, when the role was introduced by the then President Barack Obama. In 2015, Obama also introduced the White House's first Chief Digital Officer. According to CNN (2020) reports, in February 2020 former US President Trump used a CXO title in reference to his own role, allegedly saying that he is 'the chief law enforcement officer of the country', a claim contradicting the United States Department of Justice (https://www.justice.gov/ag/about-office) accounts which suggest it is 'the Office of the Attorney General which evolved over the years into the head of the Department of Justice and chief law enforcement officer of the Federal Government'. During the current COVID-19 pandemic, Chief Public Health Officers in cities (e.g. Detroit) and countries (e.g. Canada) have taken centre stage. From start-ups to countries, from formally assigned to self-claimed, CXO titles reflect the overall growing importance of a type of top executive with a distinctive role denoted with the shared label of 'chief' and 'officer'. This new type, as suggested at the outset of this section, could be understood partly through the global expansion of organization and hyper-management (Bromley and Meyer, 2015, 2021), particularly in terms of its universal applicability. In the following section, we move to the middle part of the label—the 'X' in CXO—and seek to conceptualize patterns, or clusters of roles that can be considered to constitute strategic (substantial and/or symbolic) responses to complexity.

3.4 CXOs as strategic responses to complexity

Complexity—'the state of being formed of many parts; the state of being difficult to understand' (Oxford Learner's Dictionaries, 2020)—is the third direction through which to interpret the expansion of CXO titles. Complex systems in an organizational sense are those

> made up of a large number of parts that interact in a nonsimple way. In such systems, the whole is more than the sum of the parts, not in an ultimate, metaphysical sense, but in the important pragmatic sense that, given the properties of the parts and the laws of their interaction, it is not a trivial matter to infer the properties of the whole.
>
> (Simon, 1962: 468)

Both the popular and the academic definition of complexity and complex systems resonate with scholarly depictions of contemporary organizations as pluralistic settings (Kraatz and Block, 2008; Heinze & Weber, 2016; Jancsary et al., 2017). Such settings have diverse objectives (Lawrence and Lorsch, 1967a; Denis, Lamothe and Langley, 2001) and contested power distribution (Pfeffer and Salancik, 1978; Dörrenbächer and Geppert, 2011) that respond to fieldwide and specific critical events by making decisions to adopt and implement specific organizational positions (Chandler, 2014). Leadership teams shape the organizational structures, rules, and frameworks that 'lure, mobilize, and inspire others to make decisions' (Finkelstein, Hambrick, and Canella Jr., 2009: 3). These teams have been likened to 'private governments' (Selznick, 1969) and their members as 'governors' due to the important impacts they have on the wellbeing of organizational stakeholders and members, and 'much else that goes on in the life of a large enterprise' (Selznick, 2005: 37). In this process of governing, members of the senior leadership team 'determine when, why, and how to respond to or anticipate changes in their environment or internal processes'; in turn, these decisions determine 'whether they successfully change their strategies and capabilities, or whether they fail to respond adequately to competition' (Ocasio, 1997: 187). From this perspective, a firm's behaviour is a function of how decision-makers' attention is distributed (Ocasio, 1997) and, particularly, what areas of responsibility and priority are singled out.

We propose that, in current organizational environments, four types of complexity—institutional, information, primary task, and administrative—require ongoing executive attention. We explore whether, to what extent, and how new and changing CXO roles (i.e. the structure and composition of the TMT) can be understood as strategic responses to these complexities. We consider two types of complexity discussed in the literature—institutional and informational complexity—which refer to the growing significance of organizations' public accountability and the transformative influence of ever-evolving information and communication technologies (ICTs). We also consider primary task and administrative complexity, which relate to an organization's operations and administration, as well as to its product or service offerings and the competitive landscape (Guadalupe et al., 2014). We provide a more detailed account on institutional complexity than the other three kinds of complexity discussed, as it is where the organization faces and needs to address the central challenge of engaging with the multiplicity of conflicting demands of logics (Raynard, 2016).

Institutional complexity is brought about by the operation of competing and, at times, even overlapping or incompatible and/or difficult to settle or prioritize prescriptive demands of institutional logics at the field level, which pose important expectations to organizations and can be consequential for their legitimacy and access to resources (Greenwood et al., 2011; Raynard, 2016). It involves 'multifarious and fragmented institutional environments' (Seo and Creed, 2002: 223), characterized by constant flux as well as diverging pressures and prescriptions for organizational behaviour (Greenwood et al., 2011; Martin et al., 2017). In the context of multinational enterprises (MNEs), for example, Kostova and Zaheer (1999: 67) distinguished complexity 'reflected in the multiple domains of the institutional environment and in the multiplicity of institutional environments faced by MNEs'.

Moreover, institutional complexity stems not only from the multiplicity of and competition among institutional expectations, arrangements, and prescriptions, but also from their entanglement (Seo and Creed, 2002) and dynamic influence, which comes in 'institutional waves', 'characterized by peaks and troughs of varying intensity', depending on evolving societal attention directed to critical events (Chandler, 2014: 1724). As Seo and Creed (2002: 228) explained, 'the process by which shifts in the wider institutional contest alter the interpretation of organizational structures and systems represents a 'sedimentation' where one institutional logic ... is layered on another ..., rather than a distinctive transformation where one logic sweeps away the residue of the other'. Hence, new or transformed C-suite roles can be considered strategic responses to fragmented and entangled institutional environments, which not only reflect this sedimentation but also, as Zucker (1987) noted, shape a firm's reputation, resources, and survival.

CXOs operate at the boundaries between organizations and increasingly complex external contexts (Thompson, 1967; Lorsch and Morse, 1974) marked by a growing 'strain toward public accountability' (Selznick, 1969: 45) and demands from the 'audit society' (Power, 1997) to increase the transparency of organizational actions as well as accountability for those actions. These external contexts require members of TMTs to perform complex unstructured tasks with tremendous variability and volatility (Edmondson, Roberto, and Watkins, 2003) and to continuously revise their arenas of attention (Ocasio, 1997; Alvarez and Svejenova, 2005; Shepherd et al., 2017). These tasks and the executive roles that deliver on them are thus largely directed towards navigating institutional complexity. The number and variety of CXO roles being introduced signals the plurality and differentiated nature of the environments in which contemporary organizations operate and whose demands they need to balance.

New CXO roles could be seen as a reaction to substantially increasing demands for accountability and transparency in organizations (Power, 1997). These demands involve ethical and environmentally sustainable organizational behaviour, as captured in the proliferation of Chief Ethics, Sustainability, and Diversity Officers, and more recently, the establishment of the Chief Climate Change Officer role. For example, firms in the fashion industry recently have felt an acute need to address diversity issues, as reflected in the number of recent appointments of Chief Diversity Officers; in some cases, these appointments have been responses to missteps, but in general these positions are important 'to different stakeholders. It matters to employees, to suppliers, to customers, [and] it matters to the different channels you sell into' (Oliver Chen, senior equity analyst at Cowen, as quoted by Malik Chua, 2019). Recent appointments of Chief Compliance Officers reflect coercive measures in specific contexts, for example banking or oil extraction. Relatedly, the appointment of Chief Data Protection Officers is a response to mandatory requirements to specified organizations articulated in recent EU legislation on data protection. Yet, even in such prescribed positions there is some leeway for strategic responses by organizations, not only in terms of whether to appoint an internal candidate or an external one (i.e. a consultant), but also in terms of the relevant background for the role. For example, some have suggested that it is important to find 'someone with a very strong understanding of security and data privacy, instead of appointing someone with only risk management skills and a legal background' (Fragkos, 2016).

Overall, roles that address institutional complexity are established to support organizational legitimacy in the face of continually evolving, conflicting, and intertwined societal demands and institutional pressures. However, creating such roles could result in 'organizational licensing' of more risky behaviours, which occurred after Chief Risk Officers were established by banks in response to regulatory policies (Pernell et al., 2017). Roles aimed at external legitimacy also carry symbolic value, creating opportunities for public scapegoating in cases of corporate misconduct or scandals (Power, 2007).

Institutional complexity is exacerbated by 'how corporations are monitored, covered and represented by media' (Pallas and Fredriksson, 2013: 422) and the growing mediatization of their activities (Pallas, Fredriksson, and Wedlin, 2016). The need to proactively and urgently address the media's framing role of what constitutes legitimate and reputable organizational behaviour has given rise to roles such as Chief Communication, Reputation, Public Relations, and Public Affairs Officers. For example, a 2012 Spencer Stuart and Weber Shandwick report on Chief Communication Officers (CCO) reveals that role occupants consider both positive media coverage and corporate social responsibility (CSR) expertise to be important in supporting organizational reputation:

> Six in 10 CCOs report that their senior management expects them to increase positive media coverage for the company this year. In fact, it is ranked only behind reputation management (65%), signifying management's high regard for the media's role in defining reputation.
>
> (Spencer Stuart and Weber Shandwick, 2012: 3)

> Nearly eight in 10 CCOs (76%) believe that corporate social responsibility (CSR) is critical to safeguarding reputation, and approximately half (52%) say the need for a dedicated CSR communications professional is growing at their companies.
>
> (Spencer Stuart and Weber Shandwick, 2012: 4)

Individuals in these roles are expected to provide rapid and coordinated responses to conflicts, crises, and acts of organizational or management misconduct. Thus, they function as guardians of corporate image and legitimacy, and translate the 'goodness' of the organization to the media and important stakeholders.

Information complexity is associated with a currently relevant transformational force—information and communication technologies (ICTs)—and associated advances and threats. Technology's role has long been recognized as an influential factor in the structuring of organizations (Woodward, 1965). However, recent changes have been defined as transformational not only for organizations, but also for economic and social orders. Some refer to these recent developments as the second machine age, a 'time of astonishing progress with digital technologies—those that have computer hardware, software, and networks at their core', on par with the steam engine (Brynjolfsson and McAfee, 2016: 9). This is viewed as 'an inflection point in the right direction . . . but one that will bring with it some difficult challenges and choices' (Brynjolfsson and McAfee, 2016: 11). Others are rather concerned about and critical of the dehumanizing side of 'surveillance capitalism' and the economy it brings to bear (Zuboff, 2019). Overall, corporate needs to address information complexity fuelled the creation of roles such as the Chief Technology Officer and Chief Information Officer in previous eras, and a wealth of recent additions such as Chief Digital, Data, Analytics, and Artificial Intelligence Officers.

Primary task complexity relates to the main task an organization must perform and/or evolve to ensure its survival (du Gay and Vikkelsø, 2017). It can consist of design, production, and/or delivery of specific products or services, and may involve competing on the market and addressing evolving customer demands, as well as the related need to continually improve product or service offerings. In recent years, notions such as innovation, design, and creativity have become ongoing concerns in product development and commercialization. Lovric and Schneider (2019) affirmed that 'one of the hottest jobs in the C-suite these days is the chief innovation officer, or CINO'. Numerous organizations have Chief Innovation, Creativity, or Design Officers, in addition to more traditional roles, such as Chief Marketing Officer. The latter is supported by a variety of more specific roles, such as Chief Customer, Experience, or Sales Officers. The expansion of such roles may also be related to the rise of the intangible economy and the growing importance of intangible assets (Haskel and Westlake, 2018).

Administrative complexity concerns an organization's internal fragmentation (Fligstein, 1990), as it is composed of multiple units with different degrees of interdependence (Kostova and Zaheer, 1999) and the related need for integration. In our depiction, administrative complexity mostly involves the different demands associated with managing processes and people. For instance, the traditional personnel function at Accenture is deconstructed into various roles to address specific internal audiences: the Chief Leadership Officer is responsible for spotting executives with the potential to rise to the top of the organization, the Chief Talent Officer is responsible for developing people with great potential, and the Chief Human Resources Officer (CHRO) is commonly responsible for traditional, administrative personnel activities. Additional CXO roles aimed at administrative complexity may involve Chief Process or Project Officers, as well as change management roles, such as Chief Transformation or Chief Change Officers. They may also include roles that seek to ensure continuity in organizational intellectual property and learning, such as Chief Knowledge or Learning Officers.

In addition to domain-specific roles that respond to different domains of complexity and localize executive attention, core roles in the C-suite address key constituents with external control of the organization, and pursue attentional integration across the TMT. As shown in Table 3.3, in the current predominant C-suite model, this core consists of the CEO and the CFO, with significant expansion of the CFO's mandate and status in recent years. Previously, the COO had been the 'sidekick' of the CEO and an essential part of the C-suite's core. However, as organizations have restructured their top teams to address demands of emergent extra-organizational networks of institutional investors, financial analysts, and firms seeking to engage in hostile takeovers, the COO role has fallen into obsolescence and has been displaced by the CFO (Zorn et al., 2004).

Recently, some have promoted the idea of people before business and proposed a 'G3' core consisting of the CEO, CFO, and CHRO, arguing that the latter is uniquely positioned to cut across complexities and balance priorities by focusing on talent (Charan, Barton, and Carey, 2015). The main role of the core is to steer the fragmentation of the C-suite in a shared direction and perform two main balancing acts. The first balancing act is between accountability and alignment, predominantly between roles that address external institutional and internal administrative complexity. The second balancing act is between agility and collaboration, pursued through the ongoing refocusing of attention on new domains and integration across domains through collective judgement.

In Table 3.3, we distinguish between the core C-suite roles and other CXO roles, clustered by the types of complexity they address. Using data

Table 3.3 Complexity clusters and CXO roles[*] of S&P100 companies[**], 2015

C-suite core
CEO, CFO, COO

Institutional complexity cluster
Chief Communications Officer
Chief Compliance and Risk Officer
Chief Compliance Officer
Chief Corporate Social Responsibility Officer
Chief Diversity Officer
Chief Ethics and Compliance Officer
Chief Global Diversity and Engagement Officer
Chief Governance Officer
Chief Legal Officer
Chief Progress Officer
Chief Risk Officer
Chief Sustainability Officer
Chief Transaction Compliance Officer

Information complexity cluster
Chief Data and Analytics Officer
Chief Data Officer
Chief Digital Officer
Chief Information Officer
Chief Information Security Officer
Chief Information and Business Services Officer
Chief Information and Global Services Officer
Chief Security Officer
Chief Technology Officer

Primary task complexity cluster
Chief Brand Officer
Chief Business Officer
Chief Commercial Officer
Chief Communications and Marketing Officer
Chief Creative Officer
Chief Customer and Commercial Leadership Officer
Chief Customer Officer
Chief Design Officer
Chief Development Officer
Chief Experience Officer
Chief Growth Officer
Chief Health Strategy Officer
Chief Innovation Officer
Chief Integration and Innovation Officer
Chief Marketing and External Affairs Officer
Chief Marketing Officer
Chief Medical Officer
Chief Merchandising and Supply Chain Officer
Chief Merchandising Officer
Chief Nuclear Officer

Administrative complexity cluster
Chief Accounting Officer
Chief Administrative Officer
Chief Credit Officer
Chief Globalization Officer
Chief HR Officer
Chief Integration Officer
Chief Investment Officer
Chief Leadership Officer
Chief Learning Officer
Chief Legal and Administrative Officer
Chief People Officer
Chief Procurement Officer
Chief Quality, Safety and Sustainable Operations Officer
Chief Talent Officer
Chief Tax Officer

Continued

**Primary task complexity
cluster (continued)**
Chief Technical Officer
Chief Omni-Channel Officer
Chief Partner Resource Officer
Chief Product Officer
Chief Product Supply Officer
Chief Restaurant Officer
Chief Science and Health Officer
Chief Science and Technology Officer
Chief Science Officer
Chief Scientific Officer
Chief Scientific, Clinical and Regulatory
Officer
Chief Store Operations Officer
Chief Stores Officer
Chief Strategy Officer
Chief Strategy and Innovation Officer
Chief Strategy and Marketing Officer
Chief Technology and Strategy Officer
Chief Transmission Officer

Source: CXO roles in S&P100 companies, based on data from The Official Board
(www.theofficialboard.com), May–June 2015.

* Roles spanning domains of two clusters, e.g. Chief Communications and Marketing
Officer, Chief Legal Officer, and Administrative Officer, have been assigned to one of the
clusters.

** The top 10 most frequently found CXOs are CEO (all 100 companies), CFO (96), Chief
Information Officer (48), COO (32), Chief Technology Officer (25), CHRO (23), Chief
Marketing Officer (20), Chief Accounting Officer (19), Chief Risk Officer (15), and Chief
Compliance Officer (13).

from The Official Board (www.theofficialboard.com), we analysed the
compositions of executive teams of companies in the 2015 S&P100 Index,
which measures the performance of large market capitalization companies in the United States. We performed additional searches of corporate
websites to clarify the meaning of specific roles in cases where titles did not
suggest a clear clustering.

Based on the clustering presented in Table 3.3, we selected two to four
roles per cluster as well as the three roles in the core, and performed Factiva
searches on them for the period 2000–2020 (see Appendix 1, Figures A1.1–
A1.6) to get an insight into how these roles are covered by the media (Pallas
and Fredriksson, 2013). Below we briefly summarize the main insights from
this additional analysis.

First, the reference to the C-suite and CXOs as collective labels for these roles, as well as to the specific roles in the core and the selected roles from all four clusters exhibit considerable growth in the media coverage of this period. This could be symptomatic of both an expanding interest in the management category as well as heightened scrutiny of firms and their CXOs in the media. In addition, arguably, such increase in media attention could contribute to the visibility and institutionalization of CXOs as a management category and to the fast legitimation of new roles, as discussed in Chapter 2.

Second, not all roles are attracting similar levels of media scrutiny. For example, until 2005, the C-suite is a less referenced term than CXOs but then it overtakes the latter and is over three times more referenced than it was in 2020 (12,727 mentions of the C-suite vis-à-vis 4,023 of CXO and CXOs). Further, the CEO and the CFO attract a significantly higher following compared to the third role in the C-suite core, the Chief Operating Officer (COO) and, particularly, to other CXO roles across the four clusters. To give an impression of the difference in magnitude, for 2020, for example, the CEO and the CFO have 536,442 and 277,830 mentions, respectively, whereas the COO has 136,955 mentions. Further, the trajectories of the CEO and the CFO closely follow each other (with references to the CEO almost twice as prevalent as that of the CFO), resembling an M form punctuated in 2009 and 2011, arguably by much higher scrutiny in relation to defining stages in the financial crisis. Such a heightened and rather similar interest to the CEO and the CFO is consistent with our discussion in Chapter 2 of their significance as the two most important executive roles.

Third, there are some interesting dynamics in each of the four clusters. With the exception of the Chief Human Resources Officer and the Chief Accounting Officer whose media references grow substantially, the rest of the administrative complexity cluster's roles enjoy much more limited media attention, most likely because they constitute internal, back-office roles of less audience resonance or appeal. As to the information complexity cluster, one could observe fast growth for new roles, such as Chief Digital Officer or Chief Data Officer, yet they are still far from challenging the much more referenced Chief Information Officer. Further, the Chief Digital Officer's popularity is showing some signs of declining interest in the most recent years, most likely relatable to the possible fulfilment of the mandate of this role. From the primary task complexity cluster, it is worth noting that the Chief Marketing Officer role attracts a high number of references, comparable to those of the CFO since 2013, while starting from a significantly lower position in 2000—4521 references—than the CFO who had 77,310 mentions in Factiva that year. In the institutional complexity cluster a number of roles are having a growing following, yet the level of this following is similar to the likes of the Chief Human Resources Officer and the Chief Accounting Officer from the administrative complexity cluster, although way below the references to leading roles in the primary task complexity and information complexity clusters. A potential explanation for that could be the fragmented nature of the different demands stemming from the institutional environment which the roles in that cluster address. It is worth noting that within the institutional complexity cluster, CXOs with domains of sustainability and diversity are mentioned much less often than those with compliance and risk domains, possibly hinting on the resonance these domains have with the audiences served by the media or the importance they have for the scrutiny of firms.

Undoubtedly, the reasons for all these differences in growth of and/or change in media interest across roles and across clusters require a much deeper exploration and discussion of potential causes and related arguments that is beyond the scope of this book's inquiry. Here we wanted to highlight only the main developments which enrich the understanding of the CXO expansion, accounting for the media attention to the core and the four clusters of roles we had outlined. The final point in this discussion is about the symbolic and substantial moves of the CEO as a chief designer of the TMT.

As discussed in Chapter 2, CXO roles are ultimately established by those with the most responsibility for the design of executive power structures in an active 'fast fashion industry' of role makers and breakers (i.e. CEOs or equivalent). As the highest-ranking chief officer, the CEO can tailor the composition of the TMT to substantially and/or symbolically address pertinent problems and demands, thereby directing organizational attention as well as signalling shifts in attention to relevant stakeholders. Scholars have suggested different reasons for creating new roles on the TMT. For example, Hambrick, Finkelstein, and Mooney (2005) noted that excessive executive job demands may lead the CEO to name a COO or add new top management positions. Bennet and Miles (2006b) suggested that a COO role might be designed to complement the style and knowledge of the top-ranking chief officer, to develop or test a potential successor, or to install a second-in-command to drive strategic transformation, etc. In addition, organizations can introduce new CXO positions as a currency of appreciation when other incentives are lacking or insufficient.

CEOs tend to account for such design interventions in their TMTs in press releases and media interviews, as well as during investor relations meetings where they publicly justify the introduction, transformation, or elimination of C-level roles, mostly based on the current strategic direction or a forthcoming transformation. For example, Johan Lundgren, easyJet Group's CEO, explained the creation of a new position on his TMT in a 2018 *Financial Times* interview:

> I'm changing the structure in that I am creating the new position of chief data officer, who will report directly to myself and will further build on work we have already done with data science to exploit the opportunity of the billions of data points [we have] within the organisation.
>
> (Rovnick, 2018)

In a 2014 investor relations meeting, the then Chairman and CEO of the multinational telecommunications company Telefonica presented a new organizational structure 'that is completely focused on clients and incorporates this digital offering as the main focus for commercial policies' (company website), motivating the creation of two new roles on the revenue and cost sides, respectively: the Chief Digital Commercial Officer and the Chief Global Resources Officer.

Overall, the theoretical lens of strategic responses to complexity is particularly useful in connecting the diverse kinds of complexity encountered by organizations and revealing how specific CXO roles on the top team are expected to constitute substantial and/or symbolic responses to such complexities. We propose that attention-defining organizational responses to different types of complexity influence the clustering of CXO roles. Whereas previous sources have recognized the importance of the product and administrative clusters for expanding the C-suite (Guadalupe et al., 2014), here we suggest that the information complexity cluster, and particularly the institutional complexity cluster are the arenas for the most recent transformation of the C-suite and the changing dynamics of power in it.

3.5 Conclusion

In our exploration of CXO expansion, we have sought to provide a the-oretical perspective on why such roles, which share 'chief' and 'officer' in their titles, can be found across different types of organizations and geographies by pursuing three theoretical directions: category extension, hyper-organization, and strategic responses to complexity. We have also sought to explain why and how the 'X' differs in CXO titles by distin-guishing main types of complexity driving the elaboration of CXO roles and the strategic responses these CXO roles constitute. Distinguishing the four types of complexity— institutional, information, primary task, and administrative—enabled us to discern different arenas of top management attention and respective clusters of CXO roles addressing these arenas. The institutional arena is served by roles that help address a variety of external stakeholders as well as issues of interest for them, such as diver-sity, risk, or sustainability. The information arena is increasingly populated by technology-driven roles that have been added to the rather 'classic' Chief Information Officer role (e.g. Chief Data, Digital, Cloud, or Artificial Intelligence Officers).

Roles in both institutional and information arenas are largely conver-gent across organizations, and so are those related to administration of internal processes and people. The primary variation of roles is observed in the primary task arena, as that is where organizational distinctiveness in terms of business operations and customers is observed and played out. The four arenas or clusters can be mapped along two main complexity dimensions that are in constant tension and in need of integration: the technology–customer axis, which captures the market complexity of orga-nizations, and the internal–external stakeholder axis, which accounts for the range of different audiences and their interests, particularly the need to connect institutional and organizational complexity. We also acknowl-edged the theoretical difference between the substantial and the symbolic aspects of these strategic responses. Adding different CXOs to the top team enables organizations to focus on different types of complexity and orga-nizational needs and to develop substantial and/or symbolic responses to them. Yet, in addition to their introduction, these diverse roles need to have their expertise domain and professional role identity defined, as well as the style of their executive power. In the following chapters, we delve further into the executive expertise and identity, and the style of executive power.

4

Executive Expertise and Identity

In Chapter 3, we explored CXO roles as an expanding management category and proposed two ways of thinking about the increasing number of these roles and their nomenclature. First, viewing this phenomenon as an aspect of hyper-organization helps to explain the growing number of 'chief officer' roles as well as the versatility of their adoption across different contexts (e.g., geographies, industries, types of organizations, etc.). Second, viewing this phenomenon as a set of strategic responses to different types of complexities enables a better understanding of the expanding nomenclature of these roles (i.e. increasing variation in the attention domain of top management, i.e. the 'X' in CXO). This enabled us to organize the different roles into clusters or 'families' aimed at addressing particular types of complexities, thereby also revealing potential internal competition over areas of responsibility, status, and resources. In this chapter, we shift our focus from explanations of expanding numbers and nomenclature to theoretical examination and illustration of the essence of these roles, exploring common themes in the vocabulary of their executive expertise and role identity.

Our use of the term 'executive' as a qualifier of CXO expertise and role identity aligns with Peter Drucker's (in Harris, 1993: 122) preference for the term over that of 'manager':

> While we're on the subject of words, I'm not comfortable with the word manager anymore, because it implies subordinates. I find myself using executive more, because it implies responsibility for an area, not necessarily dominion over people. . . . In the traditional organization—the organization of the last 100 years—the skeleton, or internal structure, was a combination of rank and power. In the emerging organization, it has to be mutual understanding and responsibility.

Drucker's definition of executive resonates with what we observe in depictions of CXOs in consulting and executive search reports. In these, CXOs'

The Changing C-Suite. José Luis Alvarez and Silviya Svejenova, Oxford University Press.
© José Luis Alvarez and Silviya Svejenova (2022). DOI: 10.1093/oso/9780198728429.003.0004

roles are discussed in terms of their responsibilities for work in specific domains as well as their orientation toward fostering mutual understanding and shared responsibility aimed at collaboration and synergies with other roles (the latter we discuss in further detail in Chapter 6).

We regard expertise as 'the ability to accomplish complicated tasks' through a combination of knowledge and action (Abbott, 1991: 19) and the related gaining of influence (Mikes, Hall, and Millo, 2013), yet acknowledge that this ability unfolds in 'a network linking together agents, devices, concepts, and institutional and spatial arrangements' (Eyal, 2013: 864). In addition to expertise, a role is also defined by a professional role identity, as we advanced in Chapter 2 in our discussion regarding the organizing power of roles. Here, we draw on a notion of identities as socially constructed and negotiated 'locations in social space', which place organizational actors in relations of power-dependency vis- à-vis other social categories of actors, and involve expectations (and associated capacities) for appropriate actions; 'identity work, thus, is the micro-level enactment of social structure' (Meyer and Hammerschmid, 2006: 1001). Having a particular role identity involves fulfilling these expectations, 'coordinating and negotiating inter-action with role partners, and manipulating the environment to control the resources for which the role has responsibility' (Stets and Burke, 2000: 226). Yet, if these expectations are constantly shifting, this may contribute to identity volatility, as we will explore later in this chapter.

The following quote aptly illustrates the main points of our argument, namely the action orientation of executive expertise related to value, strategy, and transformation (e.g. CDOs are expected to drive value and change, and grow data as a strategic asset), and the volatility of the CXO identity, as the role and associated expectations are evolving rapidly:

> The role of the chief data officer (CDO), a very recent addition to the C-suite, is evolving rapidly as data becomes increasingly pivotal to an organization's business strategy and success. CDOs are now responsible for much more than regulatory compliance-driven data governance and stewardship. They're being asked to champion data, and protect and grow its value as a strategic asset. They're being asked to drive change, enable and support analytics and innovation, and lay the foundation for exploiting the possibility of artificial intelligence. They're under pressure to drive value from analytics, achieve operational efficiencies, and keep costs under control.
>
> (Deloitte, 2018: 3)

Below, we first provide some definitions of executive expertise and role identity, and vocabularies associated with an overarching analytical perspective of these concepts. Then, we delve into the action orientation of executive expertise and the dimensions of volatility associated with executive role identity as it relates to different types of roles. We then dive deeper into CXOs' endless search for identity. We conclude the chapter by suggesting how the shared action orientation of executive expertise is countered by the volatility of executive role identities, thereby creating a tension that contributes to weak professionalization of executive roles.

4.1 Vocabularies of expertise and identity

In 1981, the Society for Management Information Systems (SMIS), which in 1982 became the Society for Information Management (SIM)[1], commissioned a positioning paper to define the future of the information system executive, known as the Chief Information Officer (CIO). According to public accounts, a team of academics from the Center for Information System Research at MIT's Sloan School of Management were given a mandate to develop a model of this rather new role that could inspire professional development, related events, and future research—in other words, to define aspects of the executive role's expertise and identity. The paper, which subsequently appeared in *MIS Quarterly*, noted that 'the title of "CIO," or any other combination of letters or words, seems awkward' and demands a 'clearer definition, therefore, of the role and requisite personal and managerial attributes of the person with corporate responsibility for this function' (Rockart et al., 1982: 1). It also suggested that a change from a line to a staff orientation and moving towards a corporate-level responsibility for strategy would be essential for the future of the information executive role.

In light of the ever-increasing importance of information and fast-paced innovation in ICTs, many aspects of the CIO role have changed since the publication of that paper, which drew on consultations with academics and professionals. Nevertheless, it remains an important milestone in understanding the theorizing of this role. It contributed to the construction of the vocabulary of this role (which was new at the time), and highlighted the main aspects of its expertise and role identity. Since then, a variety of

---

[1] SIM defines itself as 'the premier network for IT leadership' (https://www.simnet.org/about-sim/new-item6) and currently boasts a membership of over 5,000 CIOs, other IT senior leaders, academics, and consultants.

interests have continued to shape the role's executive expertise and identity, including those of experts (e.g. Deloitte's CIO Insider, IBM's CIO Office), professional networks (e.g. the above mentioned SIM, the European CIO Association), media and communications organizations (e.g. the *Wall Street Journal*'s WSJ CIO Network or IDG Communications' CIO), academic institutions (e.g. the MIT Sloan CIO Symposium, which is a joint initiative of the institution's alumni and researchers) and scholars (e.g. Banker et al., 2011).

Alongside these developments in support of the CIO role, its expertise and identity have been continually challenged by competing claims in its domain of expertise made by newly created CXO roles, such as Chief Digital Officer, Chief Data Officer, or Chief Artificial Intelligence Officer. Yet, the importance of the CIO has been continually asserted and the role's expertise and identity have constantly evolved, thereby maintaining its presence in the C-suite for several decades.

In order to investigate the central and distinctive aspects of the essence of CXOs, in this chapter we focus on the vocabularies of their expertise and identity, as revealed in the texts of consulting and executive search firm reports on CXO roles. Vocabularies of organizing (Ocasio and Joseph, 2005) are semiotic systems of words, and motives are recurrently used by members of social collectives to form conventions and generate categories 'representing specialized knowledge, identities, and valuations' that are consequential for thinking, communicating, and acting in organizations (Loewenstein, 2014: 79). Their elements and structures—word frequencies, clusters of key words coalescing in frames, and relations to specific practices—bring together cognition and experience in meaning making (Loewenstein, Ocasio, and Jones, 2012). Shared professional vocabularies, for example, facilitate coordination by providing common ground for organizing (Loewenstein, 2014). Studies of vocabularies enable insights across levels. For example, they signal identity and competency within the logic of a profession (Jones and Livne-Tarandach, 2008), reveal how institutional logics shape a new role category, support jurisdictional competition, either vertical or horizontal (Dunn and Jones, 2010; Jones et al., 2012), or depict how new role identities achieve consistency and become institutionalized (Rao et al., 2003).

Importantly, broader discourses influence and provide building blocks for these vocabularies of executive expertise and identity. Such discourses are collections of both texts and practices that constitute systems of power used by actors as they engage in contests (Hardy and Phillips, 2004). Texts, such as consulting and executive search firm reports on CXO roles, can have influential power and textual agency (Vaara et al., 2010). Seeking to uncover, reveal, or disclose what is implicit, hidden, or otherwise not immediately obvious in such texts requires deep reading and critical analysis (Fairclough, 1989; van Dijk, 1995). It also requires alertness to certain discursive attributional tendencies, as well as cognitive and politically motivated biases that are embedded in the management literature and in articles on managers and their work (Laamanen, Lamberg, and Vaara, 2015).

We discuss two main directions in the vocabularies of CXOs' executive expertise and role identity. First, we delve into executive expertise, revealing a shared action orientation across roles. As elaborated in reports produced by consultancies and executive search firms, at the heart of this action orientation is the theorized ability of managers not only to respond to rules and pressures, but also to 'define and provide solutions for newly constructed problems not fully specifiable by legal and accounting rules' (Bromley and Meyer, 2015: 94). We illustrate this action orientation with three main aspects of the 'vocabulary' used in reports on CXO roles: value, strategy, and transformation. Second, we discuss the volatility of the CXO's role identity, emphasizing a shared ongoing demand for its evolution, while surfacing differential role assertiveness and role endurance across roles.

4.2 Action orientation of executive expertise

Our exploration of CXO reports produced by consultancies and executive search firms suggests a shared vocabulary of executive expertise centred on each role's action orientation and various terms used to describe the domain of this action (e.g. creativity, sustainability, risk, etc.). Abbott (1991: 19) noted that a 'focus on action . . . emphasizes an executive agent, who may in fact merely organize others' knowledge'. In the case of CXOs, this action orientation involves much more than integrating the knowledge of others. It unfolds in relation to three connected areas that CXOs share: value, strategy, and transformation.

4.2.1 Value

Value is among the conceptual darlings of strategy theorists and practitioners, and an essential part of its rhetoric, as captured in the manifold value-related terms in use, such as value creation, value propositions, value chains, and shareholder value (Kornberger, 2017). While undoubtedly within the family of core strategy concepts, we single out the notion of value in role-centred reports as a distinct aspect of CXOs' executive expertise, as it signals action orientation directed toward impacting organizational performance. John Berisford, now President of Standard & Poor's, explained that 'an effective C-suite leader must operate like a CEO—thinking broadly about the levers to pull to create value' (Korn Ferry Institute, 2016: 1).

Reports summarizing the CFO role have described the role's evolution towards value creation. For example, the authors of Accenture's (2014: 9) 'High Performance Finance Study' affirmed that 'for CFOs to leverage the opportune challenges of complexity and the digital revolution, they must serve as the value architect for the enterprise and drive business value'. The report 'confirms the role's growing strategic influence, and reveals the CFO in a new light, as the architect of business value' (2014: 5) and suggests that the CFO needs to be 'playing a broader role as the business value architect of wider transformation efforts that are focused on agility and profitable growth' (2014: 34). The report articulated the action orientation of the CFO's executive expertise, which involves connecting strategic influence, business value, and transformation efforts.

The evolving expertise of other roles has also been defined in terms of contributions to value. For example, according to the Deloitte CIO Program's '2015 Global CIO Survey', CIOs create value for their organizations in three fundamental ways:

> as trusted operators who bolster the bottom line by optimizing cost structures, increasing operational efficiency, and driving performance reliability; as change instigators who lead technology-enabled business transformation; and as business co-creators who influence and execute business strategy.
>
> (Deloitte, 2016)

Similar to the depiction of CFOs in the Accenture (2014) report, this definition of the CIO suggests a connection between value, business transformation, and business strategy. In an Accenture Business Process Management (BPM) White Paper, Franz and Kirchmer (2012: 3) affirmed that:

> The CPO [Chief Process Officer] is the organization's main propagator and advocate for value-driven BPM, whose controlling practice is the process of process management. A process approach enables a systematic definition and rollout of a BPM capability, as well as its ongoing management, with one goal in mind: value creation.

From a skills perspective, performance and value orientation require the ability to accurately predict and develop strategic responses, as noted in an IBM report: 'Both the CMO and CIO are under considerable pressure to accurately predict the future, develop strategic responses, and execute and deliver value' (Baird and Ban, 2012: 3).

It is suggested that delivering performance and value increases the value of certain roles, while devaluing others. For example, a Pricewaterhouse Coopers report (2008: 21) explained that the COO role is being devalued by that of the Chief Information Officer (CIO) due to software-driven internal processes:

> Now consider the other force—strategic value. More and more internal processes are delivered or enhanced with the help of software. This devalues the COO relative to the CIO. Social networking automates customer interaction, devaluing the Chief Sales Officer versus the CIO. And IT drives innovation and facilitates and creates new business models, devaluing the head of R&D relative to the CIO.

Some go even further, suggesting value needs to be included in the role's title, as in the following example (Show, 2016):

> Our job is no longer just sourcing, buying, and managing the supply chain—it is much more. Our leaders are involved in every facet of the business and their job is clear. It is to create value. By definition the title of Chief Procurement Officer is no longer accurate or reflective of the

job's responsibilities. The title doesn't even sound strategic. So I say kill
it and demand the correct and more strategic title: **Chief Value Officer**.

(Show, 2016, bold in original)

Finally, the value potential of some CXO roles may require collaboration
and recognition from other parts of the organization. For example, a report
produced by Bain & Company (Heinrich, Heric, Goldman, and Cichocki,
2014: 1) suggests that even Chief Legal Officers (CLOs) play a strategic role,
especially in connecting legal and business strategy, however:

> The catch is that legal can't become a more strategic resource entirely
> on its own. For a legal department to strategically add value, other de-
> partments must recognize it as a high-value but also expensive resource.
> In our experience working with companies around the world, though,
> there's a wide perception gap between CLOs and CEOs on what legal
> teams add to business results.

The value focus is then a universal, essential, and defining requirement for
all CXOs, even the most operational ones, as the title of this report illustrates: *The Chief Process Officer: A Role to Drive Value* (Franz and Kirchmer,
2012). When corporate functions do not deliver value, they 'stumble', to use
the expressive word in the title of Kunisch, Müller-Stewens, and Campbell
(2014).

4.2.2 Strategy

As discussed earlier, when envisioning the trajectory of the CIO role in its
early days, Rockart et al. (1982) anticipated its evolution towards a strategy responsibility. A quarter of a century later, a PricewaterhouseCoopers
(2008: 3) report affirmed that 'the best CIOs not only keep the electronic
plumbing in good repair, but also help define and execute forward-looking
business strategies', which 'clears the path for more strategic value and
promises more clout and responsibility than CIOs have ever had before'.
Later in the report (2008: 16, 21), the authors acknowledged that 'the CIO
is becoming increasingly thought of as a chief innovator, chief strategist,
chief process officer, or all three . . . s/he is everywhere, setting the agenda
and driving strategy while running operations'. Minus the responsibilities

for 'electronic plumbing', this could be a description of a CEO's job. Such a strategy orientation is not only characteristic of the CIO, but also, as we illustrate below, other CXO roles. For example, to mention two less typical contenders for a strategic role, Chief Tax Officers are considered to 'drive strategic value' (KPMG International, 2018: 2) and Chief Procurement Officers, such as ASML's (the Dutch high-tech company) CPO, have a 'significant input in shaping the company's strategy' (Accenture Strategy report by Nowosel, Terrill, and Timmermans, 2015: 17). Nowosel et al. (2015: 18) go further to affirm that 'business strategy parameters will be owned by the chief procurement officer'. Across CXO-centred papers and reports, these roles typically are portrayed as highly important and increasingly relevant for strategy making and implementation.

This emphasis on 'strategy' resonates with Mantere's (2013: 1414) depiction of '"organizational strategy" as a language game that governs the use of the strategy vocabulary at the level of the organization', allowing for a certain degree of role crafting within the discourses prescribed by experts, such as consulting and executive search firms. It also echoes a cautionary note articulated by Knights and Morgan (1991: 260) that strategy, as a technology of power:

> creates as much as it responds to the problems it professes to resolve. Furthermore, strategists do not usually reflect upon the 'truth' and disciplinary effects of their own discourse. Nevertheless, strategic discourse engages individuals in practices through which they discover the very 'truth' of what they are—viz. a 'strategic actor'. In short, the truth effect of the mechanisms of power of the discourse is to define for the individual what it is to be human—to constitute or re-constitute their subjectivity.

The emphasis on strategy in the CXO descriptions is also in sync with an overall tendency for occupational roles to be conceived as strategic (Alvesson, 2013). Nevertheless, 'if we want to understand strategy, we must understand strategists' (Finkelstein et al., 2009: 5); thus, exploring the strategy orientation of CXO roles is important. As argued in a Deloitte report (Kelly, 2014b: 116), there is an important connection between the labelling of new strategy actors and the evolution of organizational strategy:

> The growing importance of specialist and focused functions has not only reshaped the C-suite over the last 20 years or so—it has also reshaped

the role and locus of strategy-making. Over the last decade, strategy has largely devolved from the corporate level to more specific areas of enterprise endeavour. Most firms today have a broad array of distinct strategies—for example, talent strategy, customer strategy, technology strategy, finance strategy, innovation strategy, and government relations strategy—each typically 'owned' by a C-suite executive. There have been substantial benefits from this more granular approach to strategy— but it has often resulted in a trade-off between strategic and operational excellence at multiple functional levels, and strategic coherence at the enterprise level.

The term 'strategic' is employed in the reports in at least two different ways: in reference to (a) the growing strategic importance of some roles vis-à-vis others, and (b) the CXO's direct involvement in or supervision of strategy development and implementation activities. First, many reports suggest the growing strategic importance of certain roles and identify underlying drivers, which differ across roles. For example, it is suggested that the strategic importance of the CFO role has increased to the point where it is equivalent to that of the CEO in some organizations. According to a Deloitte report (Kelly, 2014a: xiv), CFOs are the real strategists behind internationalization, not CEOs: 'While the chief executive officer (CEO) is ultimately accountable for the successful growth of the company, the CFO is often the person to assume the helm of strategic decision making abroad, particularly in emerging economies where little organizational infrastructure is in place.'

Similarly, an IBM Institute for Business Value (2016: 5–6) report likened Chief Marketing Officers (CMOs) to 'torchbearers', suggesting that the CMO's role is to seek new opportunities and business models, including those in adjacent markets: 'First movers have always enjoyed certain advantages, such as the "buzz" they generate and the ability to charge premium prices. And the challenge to reach the market first is now greater than ever, as the locus of innovation shifts from firms to ecosystems.'

Likewise, an Egon Zehnder (2016) report on the CMO role justified and explained its strategic contribution, suggesting that 'together, increased accountability and complexity have expanded the CMO's span of control. Today's CMOs are more often asked to help the CEO shape overall business strategy, and have a larger voice in determining how resources should be allocated across the business' (2016: 6), and that CEOs 'need CMOs who can be full business partners in crafting and executing a whole new breed of growth strategies' (2016: 10).

Likewise, CHROs are depicted as key business partners in driving strategy, performance, accountability, culture, and change (National Association of Corporate Directors [NACD], 2013: 20). A report from executive search firm Korn Ferry Institute (2012: 11) explained why the strategic focus of CXO roles is increasing: 'As industries and brands redefine themselves within their new operating landscape, the traditional roles of public affairs, communications, investor relations, and marketing are taking on greater strategic importance and, in some cases, morphing into larger roles as companies listen, communicate, and engage with their numerous stakeholders.'

For some roles, involvement in strategy stems from the complexity of the primary task in the context of internationalization or heightened competition, whereas for others, it stems from institutional complexity and needs for accountability and stakeholder engagement.

Second, these reports depict engagement with strategy in different ways. It could be an advisory capacity, as exemplified in Korn Ferry's report on the Chief Communications Officer (CCO) (Marshall, Fowler, and Olson, 2015):

> strategy marks the No. 1 difference between what is defined as a best-in-class corporate affairs officer today versus 10 or even five years ago. The biggest change is the demand to give strategic advice to the CEO; moreover, the CCO, as with other C-suite roles, is expected to contribute in shaping enterprise strategy ... not only to advise leadership during challenges and crises, but also to take part in defining the company's strategic direction and articulating an updated corporate narrative.
>
> (Marshall et al., 2015: 2)

References to the involvement of certain roles in strategy also suggest the need for a specific skillset and an executive constellation of CXOs. For example, as CEOs quoted in the reports acknowledge, there is a need for CCOs who are more than just functional experts, that is, 'multidimensional strategists' who have a good understanding of the business, and are able to solve problems (Korn Ferry Institute, 2012: 11). Drawing on interviews with CEOs, a 2015 KPMG report suggests that the CFO is someone CEOs rely on for strategic guidance. The report goes on to affirm that strategy work requires exceptional qualities which are characteristic of 'renaissance' professionals:

> To manage all of these dynamics requires a truly exceptional individual that we call the Renaissance CFO, an individual who builds on the wisdom of the past, embraces the technology of the present and imagines the innovation of the future. Any senior finance executive must assume many roles—from comptroller to technology evangelist—but the Renaissance CFO is an individual who embraces and transcends all of these roles to be a leader within the organization and beyond the finance function.
>
> (KPMG International, 2015: 5)

This 'hyper' language around the Renaissance CFO points to the continuity the role is expected to provide across past–present–future, as well as the abilities of the role occupant to assume and combine many roles, yet simultaneously transcend these by acting as a leader. Based on CEO interviews, the report suggests that nearly a third of CFOs fail to live up to such expectations. McKinsey & Company highlighted the active strategy-shaping role of the Chief Digital Officer (CDO), yet also emphasized the importance of collaborating with others in a strategic constellation: 'Getting the strategy right requires the CDO to work closely with the CEO, the chief information officer (CIO), business-unit leaders, and the chief financial officer; the CDO also needs to be an active participant in and shaper of the strategy' (Rickards, Smaje, and Sohoni, 2015: 2). Overal, the strategic relevance of the CDO is 'evolving rapidly as data becomes increasingly pivotal to an organization's business strategy and success' Deloitte (2018).

An interesting paradox in relation to CXOs and strategy, and one on which we elaborate in the last part of this chapter, is that both new and traditional executive roles are framed as predominantly 'strategic', and Chief Strategy Officers (CSOs) have practically vanished from TMTs, despite their high prevalence and importance until the early 2010s (IBM Institute for Business Value, 2021). CSOs' theatre of operation is strategy. Yet the role could have a different focus along the strategy process, from formulation to execution, and take different forms (e.g. internal consultant, specialist, coach, or change agent) (Powell and Angwin, 2012). It is referred to as a 'a portmanteau job' (Whittington, 2019: 71) and considered the least defined role in the C-suite, marked by ambiguity, a changing scope, and relationships with various stakeholders, as described in a Boston Consulting Group report (Kachaner and Stewart, 2013). As we discuss later in this chapter, the ill-defined nature of the CSO role contributes to an undifferentiated executive identity and anxiety over the role's endurance.

Overall, reports suggest that the failure of a CXO to engage in strategy and have strategic significance for the CEO and the organization has consequences for the likelihood of role incumbents to rise to the very top of organizations. For instance, the dwindling sway of COOs is attributed to 'focusing for too long on the operational basics, while ignoring the chance to grab a more strategic role within the organization' (Ernst & Young, 2014: 2). Strategic focus is second only to transformational efforts as the most important characteristic for COO executives to become CEOs (Ernst & Young, 2013).

4.2.3 Transformation

CXO roles are also depicted as transformative, not only because they involve responsibilities for organizational change and innovation, but also because they are constantly evolving, which we also discuss as an aspect of role identities. Illustrations of claimed expertise in organizational change include, for example, Deloitte's (2018) 'Chief Data Officers 2.0' report, which affirms that 'CDOs [are] ... being asked to drive change' and 'enable and support analytics and innovation'. According to McKinsey Digital (Rickards et al., 2015: 1), the CDO 'is now a 'transformer in chief', charged with coordinating and managing comprehensive changes that address everything from updating how a company works to building out entirely new businesses'.

A report produced by Accenture Interactive (Shah, Hartman, and Whipple, 2014: 3) suggests the CMO role is characterized by the ability 'to envision a transformation that bridges the entire customer experience, including sales, service and product', yet they can only become 'more visible change agents for digital transformation' by 'collaborating with other C-suite executives and drawing on external partners to boost internal expertise' (see Chapter 6 for further analysis on collaboration and competition in the C-suite). In a publication by Deloitte University Press on Tech trends and the fusion of business and IT, Kark and Vanderslice (2015: 5) argued that CIOs can be considered Chief Integration Officers who are able to 'potentially transform the business without losing sight of feasibility, complexity, and risk'.

The transformational capacity demanded by CXOs is associated with their capacity to envision new organizational paths and collaborate with other CXO roles in the C-suite (see Chapter 6) and develop connections to relevant external parties, thereby playing integrating and boundary-spanning roles (see Chapter 5). Shah et al., (2014) described this transformational capacity in an Accenture Interactive Report on CMOs:

> Digital is changing the world and chief marketing officers (CMOs) know it. They are embracing digital channels with fervor, but it's time to do more. ... Given CMOs' understanding of the brand and the customer, they are the natural leaders, able to envision a transformation that bridges the entire customer experience, including sales, service and product. ... By collaborating with other C-suite executives and drawing on external partners to boost internal expertise, CMOs can become more visible change agents for digital transformation.
>
> (Shah et al., 2014: 3)

Another manifestation of change and transformation is a CXO's ability to break down organizational silos. For example, the mandate for the Chief Experience Officer is to break down silos between the different parts of a business that impact the customer experience, starting with IT and marketing (Accenture, 2014: 4). Role-centred reports also acknowledge that successfully enacting change requires situational knowledge of the organization's strategy history and those who have created it, which is something that can be delivered by experienced CSOs (Breene, Nunes, and Shill, 2007: 89): 'Indeed, a CSO's long experience within a single company—specifically, his or her deep knowledge of the chief architects of the existing strategy and its history—can be crucial for building the federation necessary to enact change.' As the title of another report—*The Agility-Creating Strategy Officer: Bringing Speed to Change* (Accenture, 2013)—suggests, along with numerous similar others, change is a *sine qua non* of CXOs.

In addition to the transformational expertise suggested for CXO roles, some organizations have a dedicated Chief Transformation Officer. Similar to CSOs, Chief Transformation Officers struggle to differentiate themselves from other strategy-involved CXOs. In the case of the Chief

Transformation Officer, the contested expertise relates to change management. In a McKinsey & Company Recovery & Transformation Services article, Gorter, Hudson, and Scott (2016) revealed the inherent challenges associated with a role dedicated to transformation, likening the activities of the Chief Transformation Officer (abbreviated in the quote below as CTO, not to be confused with Chief Technology Officer) to those of 'a military drill sergeant':

> The CTO is a high-level orchestrator of a complex process that involves large numbers of discrete initiatives. Responsibility for making the day-to-day decisions and implementing those initiatives lies with line managers, but the CTO's job is to make sure the job is done. This is not always easy.
>
> Gorter, Hudson, and Scott (2016: 1–2)

> He or she acts as the face of the transformation, sets the tone, spurs enthusiasm, and challenges current wisdom. Like a military drill sergeant who demands daily push-ups and ten-mile runs, the CTO has the objective to make the organization fitter so as to sustain the effort over the longer term.
>
> Gorter, Hudson, and Scott (2016: 1–2)

Similarly, in a *McKinsey Digital* article, Rickards et al., (2015: 1) called the CDO a 'transformer in chief', 'charged with coordinating and managing comprehensive changes that address everything from updating how a company works to building out entirely new businesses'.

These two examples invite a couple of reflections. First, both the CDO and CTO are described in terms of their responsibility for organizational transformation, which suggests potential conflicts in organizations that may have both. Second, the quotes reveal the multiplicity and fragmented nature of discourse on roles part of which is due to professional service firms' operating with network structures: the CDO role is discussed in a report by McKinsey's Digital division, whereas the CTO role is discussed in a report by McKinsey's Recovery & Transformation Services division. This may suggest not only an overlap in expertise, but also, as shown in the next section, volatility in expectations regarding CXOs' role identities.

Overall, the emphasis on strategy, value, and transformation across CXOs suggests a shared, action-oriented base of executive expertise, thereby indicating that such roles could be considered to be part of a higher-order category of top executives.

4.3 Volatility of executive role identity

In addition to action-oriented executive expertise, CXOs have expectations regarding the ongoing evolution of their executive role identity (Figure 4.1). Despite these shared expectations, this theorization captures differences implied by the 'X' in CXO labels (e.g., operations, information, HR, strategy, among others) associated with different levels of role assertiveness and role endurance. We first discuss the expectations of ongoing role evolution as the shared aspect of identity theorization across CXOs. We then move on to accounting for some of the differences in terms of role assertiveness and role endurance.

4.3.1 Ongoing evolution

When reading CXO reports and articles, one cannot help but notice a frequent emphasis on one aspect, regardless of which role is being theorized: its ongoing evolution. Below, we provide a brief illustration of this aspect, arguing that it reflects the volatility of both role descriptions and the role

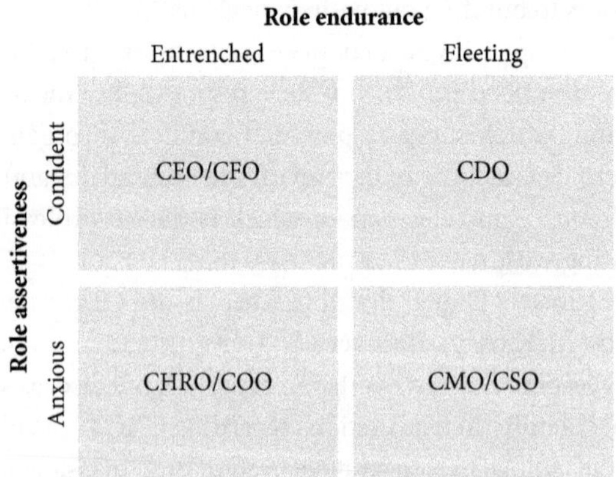

Fig. 4.1 Volatility of CXOs' role identities

identities of incumbents who enact these descriptions (or prescriptions) in different organizational settings and fields.

The reports refer to the importance of the ongoing evolution of CXO roles in different ways. For example, the version of the role being theorized is constantly updated (e.g. 1.0, 2.0, 3.0), as the following illustration reveals. A Deloitte Canada (2015) article titled 'CMO 2.0 takes charge' suggests that the CMO is a 'big role' with 'even bigger expectations', further clarifying that the aim of the report is to explore 'the drastically changing and ever evolving role and expectations of the new Chief Marketing Officer', who 'must be adept at building and managing complex teams, influencing the executive table, and running marketing as a business within a business' (Deloitte Canada, 2015: 5). Part and parcel of this new CMO is strategic agility: 'Organizations will increasingly demand that their CMOs bring to their role analytics and technology skills and a keen understanding of business and finance. Those who can quickly bring these qualities to bear will be well positioned to thrive in this ever more crucial role' (2015: 7).

A Bain & Company blog entry titled 'CHRO 3.0: The New Chief Human Resources Officer', acknowledged that the title 'may sound a bit like a Star Wars character, but it's actually the latest evolution of the chief human resources officer' (Allen, 2013). The text also reviews previous 1.0 and 2.0 versions of the CHRO, clarifying main differences. References to evolution are directed not only to specific roles, but also to the entire C-suite, as in the Deloitte Insight article titled 'The C-suite: Time for Version 3.0?', for example, which offers a vision for the 'next-generation C-suite' that 'secure[s] alignment and coherence across multiple dimensions of essential change, without defaulting back to the command-and-control arrangements of a bygone era' (Kelly, 2014b: 122).

The reports explicitly highlight the importance of continuous role evolution and change, referring to 'the new' CXO as an alternative to 'the old' or 'conventional' one, suggesting new domains of responsibility and new capabilities to address these domains, and even proclaiming certain roles as 'super-heroes', for example the Chief Data Officer, as 'the new hero of big data and analytics' (IBM Institute for Business Value, 2015). This ongoing reference to the need to evolve and become something else, something different, fuels anxieties regarding the responsibilities and performance expectations associated with a given role, its strategic relevance, as well as its endurance in the C-suite. Another aspect contributing to this role anxiety is the need to rapidly adjust to bigger and increasingly demanding roles. For example, a 2015 report by Deloitte Canada announced the arrival of CMO 2.0 as a 'leader for a new era', positing that 'as competition increases and new and non-traditional players emerge, chief marketing officers (CMOs) find themselves with far bigger roles—and far greater expectation—than ever before' (Deloitte Canada, 2015: 1). The report portrayed the 'traditional CMO' as an executive who was trained in a business school and focused on brand, advertising, marketing, mass marketing, and targeted strategies. By contrast, executives in the CMO 2.0 role will come from a variety of backgrounds, for example engineering, data science, mathematics, and 'will need to demonstrate an ability to drive growth, be strategically agile and navigate complex operational issues' (Deloitte Canada, 2015: 6).

4.3.1 Role identity assertiveness and endurance

Based on our overview of reports produced by consultancies and executive search firms, we suggest that executive role identities can be understood along two dimensions related to the respective role expectations expressed in experts' reports and by role occupants: role assertiveness and role endurance. Along these two dimensions, four distinctive groups of role identities emerge. The first group includes entrenched roles characterized by confidence in the role's ongoing C-suite and organizational significance and status, such as the CFO, a traditional core C-suite role, which has been examined extensively in the organizational literature (e.g., Fligstein, 1987; Zorn, 2004). The second group includes fleeting roles characterized by confidence in the role's current and near future strategic importance, as well as an understanding of its imminent obsolescence once its mandate is fulfilled. This group is exemplified by the Chief Digital Officer, a recently created role reflecting technological advances. Such confidence stems from the recognized importance of tech chiefs at the top. The 2021 IBM CEO Study revealed that 'tech chiefs are rated at the very top of the C-suite, alongside Chief Financial Officers (CFOs) and Chief Operating Officers (COOs)' (IBM Institute for Business Value, 2021: 10), given that technology is playing an increasingly important role, particularly during the COVID-19 pandemic and the transition to the post-pandemic world. The anticipated obsolescence is illustrated in an excerpt from a Spencer Stuart report (Alexander et al., 2015: 3), which provides further examples of roles with a limited duration:

> The strategic reason for creating the CXO role should drive decisions about when to evolve or phase out the position. A chief integration officer by definition is required only as long as needed to oversee the successful integration of a newly acquired or merged business. Likewise, CXO positions established to provide specific development experience to individual executives may no longer be needed once the individuals move into their next role. When the goal is to build a new organizational muscle—in digital or innovation, for example—the CEO may dissolve the role once the capabilities and responsibility for the area are sufficiently integrated into the business. It is not unusual for individuals in these roles to work themselves out of a job.

The third group includes entrenched roles characterized by anxiety about the role's standing and status in the C-suite. An example is the CHRO, a traditional organizational role that has continually struggled to achieve higher status, and was only recently given a chief officer title.

The fourth group includes fleeting roles characterized by anxiety about their ownership of their responsibility domain. The Chief Strategy Officer (CSO) role, which has strategy as a core area of responsibility, could be considered part of this group, as the core area of responsibility is contested by expectations that all CXO roles should be involved in shaping and delivering strategy, as illustrated in the previous section. As concluded in the most recent CEO study by the IBM Institute for Business Value (2021: 11), the 'strategy role fell off the map', from 67 per cent of CEOs naming the CSO as an essential role (second to CFOs) in 2013, to 6 per cent of them doing so in 2021. Our identity-driven role distinctions are based on a comparison of vocabularies and the discourses in which these are embedded.

Confident and entrenched role identities (e.g CFO, CFO). These roles are depicted as high status and relevant in top teams over time, hence our reference to their role identities as both confident and entrenched. Whereas the leading role of the CEO remains unchallenged for the most part, the CFO has risen in importance from 'bean counter', back-office status (Fligstein, 1987; Zorn, 2004), to a position that has been particularly strengthened in the wake of corporate scandals. As suggested by Tulimieri and Banai (2010: 242):

The passage of the Sarbanes-Oxley Law threw the CFO into the forefront of the boardroom, and together with the audit committee of the board of directors created a new balance of power between the CEO and the CFO. With that law, the role of the CFO has undergone a metamorphosis unlike any role in business history.

CFOs are currently recognized as co-leaders of organizations, often on par with CEOs, having 'evolved from being 'policemen' to serving as valued strategic business partners' and becoming 'the Chief Focus Officer' (IBM Business Consulting Services, 2003: 4). The role also has been labelled 'chief frontier officer' (Deloitte CFO Insights, 2014) and 'chief "future" officer' (Barnes, 2019) by Deloitte, and 'chief focus officer' by IBM (Bramante, Pillen, and Simpson, 2003). The rise of the CFO has also paved the way for and coincided with the displacement of the COO, which has become a more anxious and less entrenched position. In fact, the CEO–COO–CFO triad has been phased out, with the CEO–CFO emerging as the 'dynamic duo' in the 1990s (Zorn et al., 2004). CFOs are so impactful that the right personality pairing with CEOs can predict the success of merger operations, with the CFO playing the more prudent role and the CEO assuming the more risk-oriented position (Chen and Shi, 2019). Yet, even in the case of such a confident and entrenched role identity as the CFO's role identity, consulting and executive search advisors call for caution. They urge the role incumbents to 'take pre-emptive steps to future-proof their role', as 'digitization, data, stakeholder scrutiny and risk volatility are changing the rules of the game', resulting 'in the increasingly diverse DNA of finance leaders worldwide, with an accepted definition of the CFO role increasingly difficult to pin down' (Klimas and Corson, 2016: 29). Remaining influential in the organization's 'inner circle', these reports suggest, 'proactively shape their role in response to the major forces transforming the business environment' (ibid.).

Confident, yet fleeting role identities (e.g., Chief Digital Officer). Role reports, articles, and summit presentations acknowledge the fleeting value of some executive roles and envision their obsolescence. New roles rarely have a strong knowledge base as a potential source of professional jurisdiction (Abbott, 1988); instead, they are based on specific skills, which erodes their potential for persistence and makes them fleeting structures in a continuously updated taxonomy of executive roles. For example, the title of a PricewaterhouseCoopers report on the new CDO role (Friedrich, Péladeau, and Mueller, 2015), 'Adapt, disrupt, transform, disappear', suggested the role's inherent obsolescence. In 2015, Travelex's CDO acknowledged, 'If I'm successful, my role should not exist in three to four years' time because digital will cut across the whole organization and we will be a fully digitally embraced organization' (Boyden, 2015: 3). Another CDO affirmed, 'My job is to make this role redundant' (Hill, 2016).

Anxious and entrenched role identities (e.g. CHRO, COO). Reports characterize CHRO and COO roles as indispensable, yet with an uneasy status, as they continue to struggle for recognition and stability. CHROs fought for status and a place in the C-suite for a long time, and recently gained it. (We discuss CHROs' 'restless role identity' at length later in this chapter.) The COO role also has endured over time while struggling to clarify its identity. As mentioned in the previous chapter, the COO historically had been the 'sidekick' of the CEO, yet fell into obsolescence late in the twentieth century (Zorn et al., 2004). Because it lacks a consensus job description and is characterized by variability, the COO role has been surrounded by confusion: 'Board members aren't sure when the position will add value. Recruiters don't have an obvious pool to tap. CEOs don't know whom to trust. Potential COOs don't know whether the job is right for them' (Bennett and Miles, 2006b: 78). Yet, in recent years the role has been experiencing a comeback, which could be interpreted as a reflection of the role's integrative potential by connecting distinct areas of responsibility such as data analytics, customer experience, business model development and execution, and operational efficiency. According to insights from a Global C-suite Study (IBM Institute for Business Value, 2020) based on input from 2,099 COOs: 'Torchbearer COOs are not only better at using data to make decisions, they have a better grasp of what customers want' (2020: 15); moreover, they 'have established a new path to value by infusing their strategies, operations, and culture with data' (2020: 5).

Anxious and fleeting roles (e.g. Chief Marketing Officer, Chief Strategy Officer) Another theme in discourses related to CXO roles is that they challenge the positions of previously existing roles, creating anxiety about their endurance, and causing those who occupy such roles to attempt to strengthen their jurisdictions, as revealed in a quote from a CMO on the CMO Summit website:

Chief Marketing Officers are being challenged to fortify their positions, expand authority and assert ownership of critical leadership roles in their organizations. They are surrounded by title inflation and new sub-divisions in the C-suite including new 'chiefs' of revenue, digital, data, customer experience, relationships, insights and innovation. Turf-conflicts multiply and responsibilities are being sub-divided and diluted, and in many organizations, marketing still struggles for legitimacy and credibility, leaving the definition of the CMO role in flux ... and in question.

(http://cmosummit.org)

An Accenture report on the CMO role (Zealley, El-Warraky, and McGrath, 2019: 6) lends further insight into this anxiety, noting that 'in the past, we have observed a widespread sense of uncertainty and inertia when it comes to the daunting task of becoming hyper-relevant' and suggesting that CMOs should pursue such hyper-relevance.

The CSO also falls into this category, as the role's task identity is problematic. Breene et al., (2007) explained this in an Accenture report:

Our initial observation was that CSOs are, in many ways, as diverse as the titles they hold. They do not emerge from predictable backgrounds with easy-to-map career paths or aspirations, and their skills, experiences, best practices, and preferences run the gamut. Yet, deeper exploration revealed many common traits in these individuals—characteristics that, taken together, help define a consistent, although often unfamiliar or misunderstood, role. Fundamentally, these are people who wield the authority, and have the complex range of skills, to make strategy happen. To borrow a term from French cinema, they act as *réalisateurs*.

(Breene et al., 2007: 87)

Incumbent Chief Strategy Officers are vulnerable because their responsibilities are not well-defined and their competencies are not sufficiently differentiated. The leading strategy role is framed as a jack-of-all-trades and a multitasker, and thus can be easily replaced by many different types of seasoned senior executives in the job market. Moreover, because strategy is one of the CEO's most important responsibilities, the CEO must have a trusting relationship with the Chief Strategy Officer that is stronger than their relationships with other CXOs, except perhaps the CFO and Chief Legal Officer. As a result, their fate is intricately intertwined with that of the CEO (Whittington, Caillvet, and Yakis-Douglas, 2011).

Just as Chief Human Resources Officers must do more than manage the personnel function to gain a seat at the top management table, Chief Strategy Officers need to be more than mere strategy professionals. Another quote from the Accenture report illustrates this point:

> It's easy to misjudge the role of the chief strategy officer, in part because the title itself is misleading. These executives are not, for example, pure strategists ... they are not specialists who have breathed in only the rarefied air of strategy. ... Rather, they are seasoned executives with a strong strategy orientation who have typically led major initiatives or businesses and worn many operating hats before taking on the role.
>
> (Breene et al., 2007: 87)

Overall, CXOs in this category constantly need to justify their C-suite positions. Reports on these roles suggest, for example, that CMOs must prove that they serve the business ends and strategy better than individuals in any newly created roles with deeper customer insights, such as the CDO or Chief Customer Officer. Likewise, CSOs must add value beyond the strategy activities associated with all other C-suite roles. As noted previously, a *sine qua non* for a 'seat at the C-suite table' is (at least the appearance of) a minimum level of strategic acumen. Overall, despite their endurance in the C-suite, CMO and CSO roles are still often treated with suspicion—sometimes bordering on cynicism—in the middle management political chatter of large corporations (Raskino, 2015: 1). In Section 4.4, we delve into some implications of these role-related anxieties associated with a perpetual quest to establish an enduring identity.

4.4 CXOs endlessly searching for identity

Whereas some executive roles are on the rise, such as those created in the wake of technological advancements, others are in decline (e.g. the COO role). Overall, as we discussed at some length in Chapter 2, CFOs appear to have been the most successful in terms of gaining power and keeping it, thereby becoming the benchmark against which other CXOs measure their progress—the role that all other CXOs envy. In contrast, other roles have never been considered strong enough to be perceived as well-established members of top management. Most notably, 'the history of personnel specialists as a group is the history of the struggle for status to become full members of the management team' (Anthony and Crichton, 1969: 165; quoted in Watson, 1977: 52). Strategists have encountered similar challenges, as they have struggled to differentiate themselves from the 'developing multi-skilled identity of the successful manager' (Whittington et al., 2011: 541).

While such roles have never been considered so weak or unnecessary as to have no chance of obtaining a seat at the C-suite table, they have never been counted as strong enough to have a guaranteed one, either. Or, to use another relevant measure, incumbents in such roles have never seen themselves as being likely to become CEOs. Individuals in these roles are locked in a permanent struggle, and their identities are characterized by insecurity over their status, and uncertainty as to the tasks they need to perform to have direct access to the CEO position. Here, we examine one such instance of an 'anxious role' in anticipation of important C-suite dynamics (to be discussed further in Chapter 6).

In particular, we examine the case of those executives who, at the beginning of the history of large organizations, were called 'personnel managers' or 'directors of industrial relations'. Later, in the 1990s, they became known as 'human resources managers', and a bit over a decade ago, the 'Chief Human Resources Officer' title emerged (Wright et al., 2011). However, in a fascinating recent development involving the deconstruction and fission of an executive role, heads of personnel management have inhabited a variety of somewhat related roles, which we referred to earlier as a 'family of roles'. These roles include, among others, Chief People Officers, Chief Talent Officers, Chief Learning Officers, Chief Leadership Officers, Chief Engagement Officers, and even Chief Wellbeing Officers (see MacGregor and Simpson, 2018, for a description), without much if any clarity on generalized labelling practices.

Modifications to a role's label suggest weakness. For example, CFOs do not need to update their label, as their power is clear, and their status is not at risk. The following quote from an interview with Martin Crapper, Executive Managing Partner of Redline, an executive search firm, sharply clarifies the 'label anxiety' of HR executives, and points to the artificial distinctions between roles. These labels seem to reflect a post-modern executive role naming trend, without any correspondence to objectives or well-defined tasks:

Some see the title of Chief People Officer as a gimmicky rebrand of a traditional Chief Human Resources Officer. However, many companies with a Chief People Officer will argue that the role is more strategic. . . . Chief Human Resource Officers will often focus on policy and process, whereas a Chief People Officer is more about people, culture and workplace strategies. Chief Talent Officers are sometimes a catch-all for the other two, and other times have very defined roles around finding the right talent to fill needed positions.

(Raymond, 2021: online source)

In any case, as we showed in the section on executive expertise, theorizers of new roles tend to emphasize that these roles focus on the entire business, adding value to the whole and contributing to the overall strategic direction and organizational transformation, not just their specialization. For instance, Lundberg and Westerman (2020: 93) justified the need for a Chief Learning Officer, claiming that 'learning is no longer just a Human Resources function . . . it is a core part of your business'. The role is further legitimized with common refrains, such as 'to be successful, learning departments have to be leaner, agile and, of course, above all, strategic'.

The adoption of these labelling fads by personnel managers has elicited sharp criticism. This is nothing new, however. The legitimacy of personnel expertise has been questioned for decades, as evidenced in the following quote:

This claim of personnel specialists . . . [to be in] control of labour . . . both at the individual and collective levels, should continue to pose a problem. . . . Perhaps this contradiction is one reason for the rapidly changing hit parade of psycho-sociological gimmickry deployed by the profession . . . with such a strong tradition of offering whatever service promises to advance or secure its own position.

(Armstrong, 1985: 144)

Although it may be just a coincidence, Drucker (1954), in a reference which we cite in subsequent pages, also criticized this preoccupation with HR gimmickry.

Another interesting example of an anxious chief officer role devoid of any time-honoured tradition is the CSO. CSOs are perhaps even more anxious than CHROs, because they do not have a secure seat at the executive committee table. For HR professionals, self-doubt stems from the need to prove their executive expertise (i.e. to demonstrate that they serve business needs and add strategic value) and to overcome the perception that they exhibit 'insufficient identification with management and overidentification with employees' (Foulknes, 2015: 469). In contrast, CSOs struggle to carve out a distinct expertise and identity vis-à-vis other senior executives, who, in their struggle to access the top team, almost always try to assume or at least claim responsibility for as much of the strategic function as possible, thereby directly contesting the core of the CSO's attention domain. Strategy executives thus run the risk of being dispossessed of strategy as the only source of their specificity. As we showed in the vocabulary analysis in the first part of this chapter, drawing on a wealth of reports from executive search firms and consultancies, all CXOs—regardless of their 'X'— are defined as and expected to contribute to the organization's strategic direction. This begs the question: If all CXOs are (to be) strategic, is the CSO role even necessary?

Both heads of HR and strategy executives, albeit for different reasons, lack confidence in their status as top managers and have ill-defined role identities. We could go so far as to say that they are defined by a lack of identity, or, even more precisely, by an endless search for it. This self-doubt has consequences for their status. As James Burnham (1941: 36) stated in his book on the managerial revolution, the indispensable quality of any person or group that wishes to lead and hold power and privilege in society is 'boundless self-confidence'. Personnel managers and strategy executives have never had it.

The lack of confidence in the value of the HR function is widely recognized. In a collection of pieces written by CHROs for CHROs, Wright et al. (2011: 83) bemoaned their fate:

> Why do HR leaders and their constituents work so hard, accomplish so much, and yet still often encounter questions and doubts about their real impact? Undoubtedly the work that leaders do is valuable, so why is HR still struggling with its identity after over fifty years of progress? How can so much work and accomplishment still be achieving outcomes that are less than optimal?
>
> (Wright et al., 2011: 83)

The issue of status is so salient to HR executives that the very first paragraph of Wright et al.'s (2011: 1) work includes a quote from the book *Winning* by

Jack Welch, former CEO of General Electric and later management guru: 'Without a doubt, the head of HR should be the second most important person in any organization.'

It can be said that the defining trait of CHROs is not so much the role's expansion from administrative tasks to a focus on strategic or added value, but rather the search for status. Although most heads of human resources currently have seats at TMT tables, they still feel far separated from CEOs and CFOs, the latter being their role of reference, the measuring stick of the power of all N-1s. Quite revealingly, many works on human resources or the CHRO role begin with a historical account of the function's rather dissatisfying evolution (see for example, Ulrich, Schiemann, and Sartain, 2015, and Wright et al., 2011).

Members of the Human Resources community—incumbents in personnel roles, as well as affiliated journalists, consultants, and other actors in the field—are engaged in practice building and status enhancement activities that involve 'self-casting' of the occupation and 'alter casting' of other roles. The main yardstick is the power of the CFO, which cannot be surpassed, but perhaps can be equalled. CFOs cannot be replaced by CHROs, as the horizontal differentiation between the roles is too great. Some have proposed that CFOs should oversee financial and physical assets (i.e. 'hard' assets) whereas CHROs should manage human talent (i.e. 'soft' assets). Chief People Officers, to use a newer term, aspire to the same status and hierarchy as CFOs. For instance, Charan et al. (2015) proposed a three-pronged leadership team with the CEO as *primus inter pares* and the *pares*, the CFO and the personnel chief, ruling over each of the two main sectors of the organizational sphere.

The struggle for status and equality with the CFO is not easy. Historically, the reputation of the HR function has been poor, with pioneering management guru Peter Drucker (1954) delivering a well-known, almost 'classic' blow to 'personnel administration':

The constant worry of all personnel administrators is their inability to prove that they are making a contribution to the enterprise. Their preoccupation is with the search for a "gimmick" that will impress their management associates. Their persistent complaint is that they lack status. For personnel administration—using the term in its common usage—is largely a collection of incidental techniques without much internal cohesion. Some wit once said maliciously that it puts together and calls "personnel management" all those things that do not deal with the work of people and that are not management.

(Drucker, 1954: 275)

Although CFOs have had decades to become the power brokers they are today, CHROs suspect that they do not have the same 'runway' (Benko, Gorman, and Rose-Steinberg, 2014: 58). The ultimate reason for 'CFO envy' is a lack of direct access by other roles to the CEO, who is the uncontested, ultimate source of power. The reason lies in the very task of CFOs: 'Why does the CFO have the ability to always see the CEO any time she or he wants? It is because the CFO has the numbers' (Wright et al., 2011: 21).

This acutely painful self-consciousness of personnel managers reminds us of G. W. F. Hegel's (1807/2019) notion of 'unhappy conscience' in *The Phenomenology of the Spirit*: a debilitating state of mind caused by separations or dichotomies that impede a unified self and self-confident identity. Examples of these fault lines were, for the German philosopher, the juxtapositions between what is changeable and what is eternal, between the mortal and the divine, the universal and the individual, the infinite and the finite. This unhappy conscience dwells in self-contradiction and self-negation, as reflected in the title of a chapter in Ulrich et al.'s (2015) book, '*The Future of HR is Beyond HR*', and in the Heidrick and Struggles (2014) report 'Transforming the Future of CHRO as Chief Change Officer'. It is significant that this self-negation is one of the main recurring messages spread by Dave Ulrich, one of the thinkers and consultants with more doctrinal sway over the personnel occupation: 'HR is not about HR' but about creating value for others, and HR professionals need to reinvent themselves to deliver value. In a very Hegelian dialectic evolution, the personnel function has taken on successive names and forms to overcome its consolidation limitations, but none of those has so far fully overcome these.

In what remains the best sociological work on the human resources function to this day, Watson (1977) illustrated the first and foundational tension of personnel professionals during the interwar period as being caught between serving employers (the buyers of labour) and employees (the sellers of labour). Emerging from the social welfare movement, personnel managers initially were part-time volunteers who eventually became full-time employees to help rein in social conflict in factory settings. Their conflicting loyalties became tangible in the tensions between the rationalization of labour and scientific management practices, and the protection of workers' welfare. It will be interesting to observe whether the roles that are currently emerging to deal with grand challenges such as climate change, diversity, sustainability, etc. show similarly divided loyalties, as these roles are often filled by individuals with activist backgrounds. Weber and Waeger (2017) pointed to this issue as a potentially fruitful avenue of research for scholars in the open systems perspective tradition.

Role strain for personnel managers diminished after World War II as Western countries fully embraced capitalism, thereby clarifying where their ultimate allegiances should lie. A period of professional role affirmation followed in what was called the 'personnel' function. Administrative tasks such as recruitment, compensation, and benefits were systematized and codified, and professional accreditations emerged, along with the typical instruments for occupational community building—magazines, professional associations, awards, etc. It soon became clear, however, that professionalization and knowledge formalization in management does not necessarily produce power. For example, Cappelli (2015: 56) called human resources tasks 'administrivia'. In one of the most telling and straightforward proposals regarding the rearrangement of activities to bolster a function's power, Charan (2014) suggested what Armstrong (1985) called a 'vertical fission': a split of the personnel function into two status levels. Below the line would be 'administrivia' tasks with high determinacy, as they are routine, replicable, and based on easily transmittable knowledge. Charan (2014) proposed that those charged with these tasks, which provide little added value, should report to the CFO, as they did when personnel administration was a department under the accounting function. Boudreau (2015) acknowledged the danger of routinization, which he referred to as the 'profession trap', and called on human resources leaders to open up to other functions and topics, and avoid being too defensive and territorial.

Another option for discharging bureaucratic activities is outsourcing them, as many companies already do in practice. Above the line would be strategic activities of low determinacy, reserved for elite human resources professionals who are able to create value. This vertical fission, Armstrong (1985) argued, is a tactic used in some occupations to ensure the exclusivity of the highest-level professionals and erect some closure mechanisms over a particular field (see Kellogg, 2019 for an interesting example of a contest between a profession, i.e. medical doctors, and a semi-profession, i.e. hospital managers).

Long ago, personnel managers recognized that in order to gain power, they must come to terms with the unassailable force of the bottom line. Some have come to suggest that HR can make a case for the impact of its initiatives on the business:

> The precise ROI of an important new idea in HR is impossible to measure. That doesn't mean that HR can't make its case, or that you can't observe the idea's impact. You can map the logical connections between an effective HR initiative and desired business outcomes. Focus on what can be measured along that path, and extrapolate where you can't measure precisely. That's exactly what every other management discipline does.
>
> (Boudreau and Rice, 2015: 78)

The consequences of failing to adopt this perspective for relationships with CEOs are clear, as a personnel specialist confessed to Watson (1977: 146): 'If personnel management does not provide this specialism and equip itself to maintain a constructive dialogue with general management, sharing interests and objectives, then it risks relegating itself permanently to inferior status. There will be other claimants to the new role.'

The need for the people function to become strategic to make it into the C-suite has been acknowledged in practically all articles on the function since the 1990s (see e.g. Wright et al., 2011; Benko et al., 2014; Charan, 2014; Ulrich and Filler, 2014; Charan et al., 2015; Ulrich et al., 2015), and all reports produced by consultancies and executive search firms. (see e.g. Artho et al., 2020; Spencer Stuart, 2017a; Doliva, 2014; Kosminsky and Cannon, n.d.). For example: 'One way to gauge the current and future trajectory of an organization's talent platform is to evaluate HR's project/program portfolio: How well does each directly align with the strategy of the business? The portfolio of investments will yield the organization's future currency' (Benko et al., 2014: 54). Guarino (2016) also provided a straightforward description of the dynamics at play:

> The CHRO needs to be a businessperson with the same goals and understanding of the business as the CEO and CFO. Only then can the CHRO bring forward the human capital portion of the strategy, which would

then align with the CEO's and CFO's vision. When the CHRO stands separate and apart from these two key partners, he or she stands alone and unaligned.

(Guarino, 2016: 9)

Nevertheless, renowned management guru Ram Charan (2014) expressed scepticism that most personnel managers will ever be able to adopt CEOs' viewpoints on business needs, because many do not have professional backgrounds in operations. According to estimates by the executive search firm Korn Ferry Institute (2008), only 40 per cent of HR professionals have such experience. Charan's (2014: 34) indictment of CHROs is harsh:

It's a rare CHRO who can serve in such an active role. Most of them are process-oriented generalists who have expertise in personnel benefits, compensation, and labour relations. They are focused on internal matters, such as engagement, empowerment, and managing cultural issues. What they can't do very well is relate HR to real-world business needs. They don't know how key decisions are made, and they have great difficulty analyzing why people—or whole parts of the organization—aren't meeting the business's performance goals.

(Charan, 2014: 34)

Defenders of the personnel profession are so cognizant of these criticisms that they feel the need to directly respond to them. In a report for Korn Ferry, Ulrich and Filler (2014: 8) argued that CHROs should be able to aspire to the CEO role, because they 'are cut from the same cloth', with similar emotional competencies, leadership, and thinking styles. Enthusiastically endorsing this hypothesis, a consultant from the same executive search firm authored a report titled 'Why CHROs Really Are CEOs' (Guarino, 2016).

Overall, our exploration reveals some of the sources of role weakness in the C-suite. First, when a CXO role is decomposable into easy-to-learn tasks, or when the required competencies are too common, the role becomes too accessible to new entrants. Second, when a role is closely intertwined with that of the CEO, that strength becomes a liability when the CEO is replaced or loses power.

4.5 Conclusion

In this chapter, we analysed the vocabularies used by consulting and executive search firms to theorize the executive expertise and professional role identities of CXO roles. We revealed a shared emphasis on action orientation in defining CXO role expertise and singled out strategy, value, and transformation as its main components. These three notions are rather broad and general; because they can mean almost anything, they are adaptable to different contexts. Their meanings are inherently defined by those who make them operational by performing their work.

CXOs' overlapping jurisdictional domains (Abbott, 1988) could suggest that the roles are variations of a higher order management category—that of top executives. On the one hand, the range of roles for which strategic relevance is claimed may be considered a push towards more distributed involvement in strategy, which is practised through collective leadership (Denis et al., 2001). On the other hand, it may be indicative of even stronger CEO control over an organization's strategic direction, whereby the CEO, as the top chief officer, retains the power to decide which roles are granted CXO status, their jurisdictions—both vertical (who reports to whom) and horizontal (who does what)—and the fates of those who aspire to become chief officers. Paradoxically, competition among C-suite executives to become more strategic could strengthen the CEO position as chief strategist and architect of language games (Eccles and Nohria, 1992) that could influence internal competition.

We also revealed the volatility of CXOs' role identities, which can be understood as an interplay of different forces. One force creates shared expectations across CXOs to continue to evolve their competences. The other force differentiates specific CXO roles from overlapping executive expertise in strategy, value, and transformation, and the aforementioned shared expectations. The interplay of these forces shapes CXO identities in different ways, leading to different degrees of assertiveness and endurance across roles over time. Some roles such as CFOs remain firmly lodged in TMTs, whereas others (e.g., Chief Human Resources Officers, Chief Strategy Officers) constantly strive to establish identities that can strengthen their status. CXO labels and their vocabularies of executive expertise and identity enable incumbents to position themselves as strategic actors with professional identities, expectations, and capacities for action (Hacking, 1986; Meyer and Hammerschmid, 2006; Power, 2007). Overall, taken together and considered as a distinctive group, CXOs share some aspects with transnational professionals in that they are highly mobile across settings and are expected to shape practices across the national contexts in which their organizations operate; however, their main difference from this class of boundary-crossing professionals is in the nature of executive knowledge, which is action-oriented and practice-driven, rather than high-level abstract knowledge characteristic of transnational professionals (Harrington and Seabrooke, 2020). For many disputed distinct CXO role identities, the combination of an action orientation as a shared ground of executive expertise and volatile expectations for ongoing evolution constitutes a challenge for the professionalization of CXO roles, and suggests they may 'just' be occupations, or at most, 'weak professions' (Fligstein and McAdam, 2012b), without unequivocal expertise and distinct identities. In Chapter 5, we focus on the CXO style and explore additional aspects that potentially influence this weak professionalization.

5

The Style of Executive Power

Style is a profile of the comingling of network relationships and discursive processes across switchings that result from and also shift situations.

White, 2008: 113

In Chapter 4, we proposed three main tasks specific to CXO roles: adding value, contributing to strategy, and acting as change agents who facilitate organizational adaptation to the environment. These tasks are the 'what' of CXOs' roles—the scripts that stipulate what their characters should represent. As in dramaturgy, where roles are acted out depending on the unique characteristics of the director and the actors, social roles are enacted in different ways. The source of these differences is what we call 'style', a durable and recognizable pattern of choices and actions (Godart, 2018: 114). White (2008: 112) likened styles to the rhythms that add variation to the disciplined notes that comprise a melody, or to actors' performances of a script. Without a distinct style (the 'how' of CXOs' behaviour), these would not be able to perform their roles. Styles – both precursors and followers of identity (Fontdevila, Opazo, and White, 2011) – provide a good balance between consistency and lability, as Canales and Greenberg (2016) showed for CFOs' relationships with stakeholders.

In a piece on White's (2008) notion of style, Boorman (2011) stated that understanding it requires applying both network and institutional analysis to the observation of concrete examples, a method he called 'bureaucracy watching' (2011: 182). In this book we do not report 'CXO watching' but rather base our arguments on the rhetoric regarding what CXOs do and ought to do. Doctrines generated and amplified by professional services firms, such as consultancies and executive search firms, are essential to

The Changing C-Suite. José Luis Alvarez and Silviya Svejenova, Oxford University Press.
© José Luis Alvarez and Silviya Svejenova (2022). DOI: 10.1093/oso/9780198728429.003.0005

the display of CXO styles in action, and provide useful justifications (i.e. rhetoric) for CXOs jockeying for seats at the TMT table. As Fontdevila et al. (2011) asserted, rhetoric is as important to style as behaviour, as it has normative capacity, feeds the discourse of communities, and allows for reflective practices. As White posited in the quote at the beginning of this chapter, there is a degree of explicitness about styles, as they are levers for action accompanied by discourses about themselves. Emphasizing this point, he described professionalism as a focus on 'the syntax rather than the content' and 'an obsession with appearance and form' (White, 2008: 137). In this chapter, we make the styles of CXOs explicit by analysing texts produced by consultancies and executive search firms regarding what CXOs do, as well as what they should do.

The chapter is organized as follows. First, as institutional approaches are one of our main perspectives, we outline the ongoing debates on the engagement with issues of power by neo-institutional scholars and organizational institutionalists (see Ocasio and Gai, 2020, for an explanation of the difference between the two), highlighting the insufficient attention to the upper echelons of organizations, where many CXOs operate. This is puzzling, as the upper echelons are precisely where decisions are made regarding the diffusion of important practices and structures that constitute a central focus for these scholars. We argue how a return to political perspectives of organization could not only enhance understanding of executive roles in general and the style of executive power in particular; it can also help extend the power and leadership agenda of neo-institutional research. Second, we provide numerous examples of CXO styles and of what they should be according to professional services firms in the consulting and executive search industries in a form of 'CXO rhetoric reading'. We contend that the most distinct features of CXO styles are the incessant building of social capital via networking and of political capital via reputation, and the use of these resources to exert the influence required to successfully perform internal and external interfacing tasks—what White referred to as acting across a variety of social settings. Third, we relate the exploration of networking and influencing activities to the abundant academic research on boundary spanners, and suggest that these roles are the predecessors of CXOs. Finally, we argue that there is a distinct psychological profile for individuals capable of exhibiting the CXO style, but that personality is a scarce resource, which reduces the pool of candidates able to efficiently perform CXO roles.

5.1 Executive power and political perspectives

How neo-institutionalism has dealt with power has been a subject of intense debate. Critical management and other organizational scholars have insistently lamented power's lack of centrality in neo-institutional theory (e.g. Fleming and Spicer, 2005, 2014; Munir, 2015; Mees-Buss and Welch, 2019; Willmott, 2015, 2019). Institutional scholars have responded to this ongoing critique, reminding how power has been on the neo-institutional research agenda since the perspective's early days and until present (Greenwood and Meyer, 2008; Drori, 2020). For example, in a seminal piece on institutional isomorphism, DiMaggio and Powell (1983: 157) acknowledged that the 'examination of the diffusion of similar organizational strategies and structures should be a productive means for assessing the influence of elite interests'. Connecting with Lukes' (1974) work, they pointed out to the importance of investigating two forms of power: to define norms and standards directing behaviour and to engage in critical intervention. Yet, as Greenwood and Meyer (2008: 262) emphasized, 'the attention to the power dimension and political consequences of institutional processes that DiMaggio and Powell highlighted in their 1983 piece was largely lost in subsequent institutional work and has only begun to recapture serious attention'. In an eloquent defence of the critical power of institutional theory, Drori (2020: 3) affirmed that 'social power broadly defined is a solid foundation for institutional theory's approach to social processes, outcomes and action'.

Where there seems to be more agreement is that powerful senior managers, of whom CXOs are growing in number and importance, are an ideal phenomenon for institutional studies of executive power in transformation. This is so because the actors responsible for adapting organizations to their environments are executives at the top of organizational hierarchies. It is at the level where TMTs operate, and where not only the most relevant encounters between the internal and external environments take place, but also where decisions about institutionalization and diffusion are made (Menz, Kunisch, and Collis, 2015). Zald and Lounsbury (2010) asserted that what they called 'command posts' should be the focus of institutional studies. TMTs are those 'command posts'. Therefore, attention to executive committees is not the consequence of an ideological conservative bias, but a logical research strategy when the priority is explaining organizational transformations, as Ocasio and Gai (2020) suggested for organizational institutionalism. In the end, there are very few cases of bottom-up transformations in business organizations.

This refocusing would also entail returning to leadership as the priority of institutionalism's 'founding father', Philip Selznick, and its role in advancing social action while navigating technical and institutional demands which remains poorly understood (Kraatz, 2009; Besharov and Khurana, 2015; Raffaelli and Glynn, 2015). Tracing institutionalism back to its origins reveals that it was intimately linked to views of organizations as polities or open systems. As this perspective is relevant to our phenomenon, a quick review is in order.

Political perspectives on organizations are based on the hypothesis that organizations are open, multi-goal, non-unitary systems whose functioning depends upon the active balancing of the demands of multiple social groups with different interests and claims on resources, and where roles linking organizations to their environments are critical. It has had a chequered history in organizational theory. Political theories have enjoyed periods of strong influence, but have also gone through phases of obscurity. Nevertheless, they consistently resurface in a variety of forms, always retaining their core features. What follows is a summary of the essential features that are relevant to our arguments about executive roles.

First, by approaching organizations as arenas with a competing plurality of interests at play, political theories of organizations contrast with most economic views of firms, which grant shareholders the status of undisputed 'principals'. Both political theories of organizations and classic institutional theories, which were quite convergent in their early days, hold a pessimistic view of organizations (Perrow, 1986), as both schools recognize that grappling with the pressures of constituents may lead to co-optation: concessions to pressure that end up causing an organization's primary, original purpose to drift and the organization to pursue new aims—the so-called 'displacement of goals'. This features a fascinating resemblance to the loss of 'virtue' that Machiavelli perceived in Italian Renaissance city-states, which he called *corruzione*. Because organizations are open systems and, therefore, require external input for survival and performance, they are, from a political point of view, fragile regimes. Years later, resource dependency theory provided a variety of examples of mechanisms for coping with external contingencies. Today, at senior executive levels, CXOs are the main group of managers responsible for managing dependencies.

The earliest conceptions of modern organizations were highly political. Weber (1978), Etzioni (1961), and Bendix (1974) identified the presence of ideologies of power and subordination as a *sine qua non* organizational trait, without which internal cohesion and legitimacy are not possible. Ideologies of power and subordination in organizations need to be aligned with, or at least not openly contradict, hegemonic ideas in society. The general absence of ideology (for some notable exceptions, see Weiss and Miller, 1987; Meyer et al., 2009 and their edited volume on Institutions and Ideology in *Research in the Sociology of Organizations*) from recent organizational theory is impoverishing, as social action is difficult to explain without it (Hafenbradl and Waeger, 2017; Mees-Buss and Welch, 2019). Weber (1978) tasked superordinates with managing the diversity of motivations present in organizations. These have two components: (a) an orientation to the task assigned by those in command, and (b) an orientation towards the legitimacy of those issuing decisions. When these two orientations are positive, there exists 'compliance' (Etzioni, 1961), the minimum requisite for the functioning of an organization.

A second fundamental characteristic of organizations from a political perspective, originally highlighted by Michels (1915), is that most important political dynamics take place at the level of organizational elites, not only because this is where organizational decisions, including those about adaptation tactics, are made, but also because it is the location of critical environmental interfaces, especially those of a political, social, and institutional nature. However, research interest in the top levels of organizations as the areas where relevant external and internal pressures converge was subsequently abandoned by scholars of the human relations school, as they chose to focus on team dynamics at the worker level.

Political views of organizations emerged again in studies on organizational design and structures. The most explicit work in this regard was produced by European scholars, both continental sociologists (Crozier, 1964) and the British Aston group, which developed the 'contingency theory of organizational power'. They recognized that incumbency in organizational positions or roles introduces bias into decision-making, both conscious (e.g. to advance personal, role, departmental, and unit interests) and unconscious. To understand actors' dispositions, decisions, and ultimately, actions, organizational structures, both formal and informal, must be considered. Organizational politics are inevitable, both at the apex level, leading to the displacement of goals under external pressures, and between functions. Organizational design and organizational politics are intimately intertwined.

With the success of the contingency approach, the topics of power and organizational politics attracted influential scholars such as Petti-grew (1973), Pfeffer and Salancik (1978), Bacharach and Lawler (1980), and others. However, as institutionalism evolved into neo-institutionalism (the most successful organizational theory of the 1980s and subsequent decades), and recently into organizational institutionalism, interest in theorizing political dynamics in organizations faded. As we have already argued, this is surprising, because at the core of institutionalism lies recognition of the importance of legitimacy, which needs to be secured symbolically. Because symbols are not unequivocal in their production, dissemination, and reception, and are amenable to a variety of intentions, interpretations, and use, the politics of symbolism should have been a key part of the development of this theory.

From an institutionalist perspective, the actions of organizational leaders (i.e. the CEO and C-suite executives) to ensure survival or performance in response to pressures from the fields in which they are embedded must be legitimate, 'at least in appearance', as Battilana and D'Aunno (2009: 31) so revealingly expressed. Leaders employ different mechanisms to send signals to the constituencies engaged in evaluating the legitimacy of their organizations. Some signals may be veracious, but others may be *trompe l'oeils* to give the appearance of compliance or alignment without actually practising it. The signalling may be performed by replicating the practices of model organizations—what neo-institutionalists call mimetic isomorphism—or by using formal structures as symbolic tools or facades to signal acquiescence to the environment's demands, but decoupling those symbols from the buffered technical core (i.e. using formal structure as a decoy), as explained by structural elaboration theory (Edelman, 1992). Researchers have been studying organizational impression management for decades. Among others, Elsbach and Sutton (1992) studied the impression tactics of the environmental group Earth First, and of the minorities' rights group Act Up. Similarly, Jung (2014, 2016) described the use of dramaturgy to impress the financial community with downsizing decisions. Joseph et al. (2014: 1837) also recognized these games of managing appearances, and even of disguising non-compliance with environmental demands: 'Organizations strategically react to institutional mandates by searching for structural forms that signal compliance, but which, in practice, protect and promote the interests of powerful internal elites.'

Other scholars have identified numerous analogous tactics in boards of directors (e.g. Westphal and Zajac, 2001; Stern and Westphal, 2010; Westphal and Graeber, 2010). Hambrick and Lovelace (2018: 111) articulated similar arguments, suggesting that CEOs may use symbols for the purposes of 'deception or guile'. The quite publicized recent political activism by CEOs, proclaiming, for instance, their allegiance to stakeholders over shareholders (as the influential USA Business Roundtable did in 2019) and taking progressive stands on social issues can often be explained by pure economic or tactical interests (Bebchuk and Tallarita, 2020; Gangopadhyay and HomRoy, 2020). Crilly, Zollo and Hansen (2016) showed how imperceptible communication nuances make 'faking it' to constituencies so feasible.

In an agenda-defining book on institutional work (Lawrence, Suddaby, and Leca, 2009a), Kraatz (2009: 59) opened his splendid chapter on Selznick with a despondent anonymous quote: 'The most important thing is integrity. Once you figure out how to fake that you've got it made.' That this sentence heads a chapter on the work of Philip Selznick, of all institutionalists, reveals the unresolved ethical challenges about executive work and organizational life pointed to by early institutionalism. Kraatz (2009: 82) ended the depiction of organizational leadership as types of institutional work with another quote, again full of moral despair: 'Perhaps what we really see is only powerful people faking integrity in the effort to buy political support and effectively mask their wholly selfish agenda.'

Thus, from a neo-institutional perspective, symbolic displays of value alignment, whether sincere or merely for show, are essential to gaining legitimacy. In any case, it is impossible to 'unagentically' engage in the social construction of reality, especially when the tactic is to deceive and mislead constituencies for the purposes of organizational adaptation and legitimation. There is no institutionalization in the Selznick sense without intention, without calculation of the effect of influence tactics on constituencies, and as argued by Fligstein (1997, 2001), without the political prowess of organizational leaders to make such decisions and efficiently execute them. Institutionalization cannot be explained without political agency and what psychologists call Machiavellian intelligence. It is appropriate to say that neo-institutionalism makes the most political assumptions of all organizational theories, at least in the popular sense of politics as games of deception, most probably unfair to a true understanding of the Florentine's work (Lee, 2020).

Ironically, neo-institutionalism did not build sufficiently on those assumptions, mostly because of its lack of attention to the roles being played in the upper echelons of organizations. Nevertheless, a few insightful pieces recognize the Machiavellian genealogy of 'agency'. Levy and Scully (2007), building explicitly upon Machiavelli, related institutional theory to the work of the Italian revolutionary Antonio Gramsci, who proposed a new Prince, who was not meant to be a single individual, but rather a collective or organic leader. In Gramsci's Italian context, the Prince was to be the Italian Communist Party (PCI). Hargrave and Van de Ven (2009) also came close to recognizing the political roots of institutional theory when they selected Saul Alinsky, the reflective social activist, to epitomize the figure of a political entrepreneur.

Because social skills such as networking form the basis for influence tactics and other political behaviours used by CXOs as they fulfil their external adaptation and internal integration role responsibilities, in Section 5.2 we examine the descriptions and prescriptions by consultancies and executive search firms of those competencies for CXOs.

5.2 How CXOs do what they do

The number of examples in reports on CXOs produced by professional services firms in which networking is revealed as the primary tool used by CXOs to exert influence and get things done is staggering. The language used in some sections of these reports provides a powerful illustration.

For CXOs, building both internal and external relationships is critical. According to a Capgemini post (Sehgal, 2020), it is important for Chief Digital Officers to be naturally good at networking'. Networking for influence needs to span all internal organizational sectors, including corporate governance levels:

> In today's climate, the culture and practices within a business can change as quickly as those in the external market. Chief Digital Officers, therefore, must be able to build relationships across all levels and functions of the organization—from the Board down to the front line—and effectively manage conflict.
>
> (Russell Reynolds Associates, 2012a: 3)

Chief Risk Officers (CROs) also need to cultivate extensive contacts:

CROs do not work in isolation. They deal with multiple internal and external groups and, therefore, must be able to develop and leverage relationships. They have to be able to collaborate across teams, establish and cultivate networks of people in a complex matrix organization, and use relationships strategically to accomplish objectives.

(Business Insurance, 2009: 2)

Networking is also a critical skill for Chief Procurement Officers (CPOs):

The CPO must understand the needs and strategies of the organization to align with the expectations of leadership and to establish trust and strong relationships with business stakeholders. The ability to forge strong stakeholder relationships is a 'make or break' skill for a successful CPO because it allows for the development of a 'pull' model for engaging with the business units and functions.

(Russell Reynolds, 2012b: 2)

These relationships, essential to any CXO, are to be promoted in circles, conferences, and congresses, best practices meetings, and similar professional events where the driving purpose is 'to leverage metrics to demonstrate cost savings and procurement's organizational value' (Accenture, 2011: 124).

The importance of external networking for Chief Human Resource Officers (CHROs) and of building social capital is explicit in a report from Spencer Stuart (2017a):

To stay abreast of new trends and developments, HR leaders aspiring to become CHROs should develop relationships and networks with other HR leaders . . . by attending HR seminars/training programs, reading academic and leadership journals and maintaining strong ties with mentors across industries.

(Spencer Stuart, 2017a: 2–3)

The same logic applies to Chief Sustainability Officers:

> Overwhelmingly, survey respondents and interviewees highlighted the importance of building relationships at all levels within their organisation, across functions.
>
> (Spencer Stuart, 2017b: 9)

According to a McKinsey article, for roles such as the Chief Digital Officer (CDO), the amount of time that should be invested in external networking is substantial:

> Successful CDOs ... build networks of people, technologies, and ideas far outside of their compan[ies] ... Some CDOs spend as much as 50 percent of their time working with external partners to build effective working relationships that take advantage of every organization's capabilities. ... At a more pedestrian level, they regularly invite technologists or entrepreneurs to team lunches.
>
> (Rickards, Smake, and Sohoni, 2015: 4)

As the next fragment from the same source reflects, internal networking is also vital for Chief Digital Officers, and should be practised without delay.

> Building an internal network is just as important because company systems and technologies need to be flexible enough to work with outside parties. ... Some CDOs realize too late that functions such as compliance, finance, human resources, legal, procurement, and risk also need to change to support a more digitally focused company ... brokering compromises and testing new ways of operating that are necessary to make progress will be virtually impossible if a CDO doesn't build internal networks early and engage with leaders across the business.
>
> (Rickards et al., 2015: 4)

The same logic applies to Chief Information Officers:

> [A CIO who exerts] organizational influence involves and gains commitments of stakeholders early [and] convinces critical business constituencies to sponsor significant enterprise system implementations. Projects driven purely by IT have a high failure rate. Working cross-functionally across the entire C-Suite is a very different skill.
>
> (Russell Reynolds, 2009: 4)

A balanced approach to different constituents, maintaining equidistance, was already recognized as *sine qua non* for integrators in the literature of the late 1960s. The same applies to current CXOs in their relationships with different constituencies. Of course, this is especially relevant to human resources roles:

> CHROs are a stabilizing influence on the executive team. These are individuals who have spent their careers dealing with heated, emotional situations, and they understand how to make people feel listened to and engaged with. CHROs have some of the strongest active listening skills among members of the C-suite, making them especially valuable sounding boards and advisors within the senior ranks.
>
> (Russell Reynolds, 2017: 7)

Exerting influence based on social capital requires social sophistication and calculation on the part of CXOs:

> Key success factors for the CHRO are 'primarily in being able to manage stakeholders and build really strong credible relationships with the Chair, other non-executive directors, the CEO, and ExCo [executive committee] colleagues ... gaining their trust and respect for the value and integrity you bring'. Pam Walkden agrees, seeing the importance of 'sensitivity to a different kind of relationships with peers on the ExCo'. ... You also need to know who needs to know about what, and in what order. Not only that, but you need to become skilled at understanding the nuances of communication between those parties. ... One of our CHRO interviewees says, you have to be 'seen as working for the organisation, not just the CEO ... supporting the CEO, but not just a cheerleader for management'. Steven Baert agrees, declaring that 'HRDs [human resources directors] who are too keen to serve and to please will not be right for the role'.
>
> (KPMG, 2017: 10)

Ulrich and Wilson Burns (2018) described human resource professionals as 'pivots' from theory to practice, giving them recommendations on how to exercise influence: building trust, connecting to the goals and values of stakeholders, gathering information, being aware of the teachings of cognitive dissonance theory for networking (where little exchanges serve as bridges to future larger quid pro quos), and adapting to the style of influence targets.

The following quote elaborates on influence aptitudes for another group of CXOs, Chief Strategy Officers, who need to be mindful of political and social capital.

> Comparing the skills Chief Strategy Officers [CSOs] say they were hired for with the skills they seek to improve on now reveals that while communication and consensus building will remain paramount, analytical skills will become relatively less important going forward, replaced by interpersonal sales skills. Conflict management and persuasion take the third- and fourth-place slots, respectively, in the future skill set, replacing problem-solving abilities and an analytical approach in the hiring skill set. This suggests that analytical skills and industry experience may be necessary but insufficient when seeking out a CSO. The power of persuasion will become increasingly important in a CSO as organizations seek to become more agile.
>
> (Accenture, 2013: 4)

The same logic about influence and collaboration applies to other roles, such as the Chief Information Officer.

> C-suite executives are increasingly finding that the most effective way to manage is through influence rather than control. The gentle arts of listening and persuasion are practiced by successful influencers and best applied in an environment of collaboration. Barriers between functions and divisions need to be dismantled—along with many of their systems, processes and norms—to enable groups that have not encountered each other to work together towards a common goal, exploring new solutions and learning from each other. Chief Information Officers are in a unique position when it comes to leading cross-functional collaboration and, while they're at it, increasing their influence in the business.
>
> (Spencer Stuart, 2018b: 3)

For CFOs, who possess clout other functional heads 'do not come close to' (Karaian, 2014: ix), networking and political capacities are also indispensable. In fact, Karaian's text on CFOs has a chapter titled: 'Relationships: Colleagues and Partners, Friends and Foes'. In the first issue of Ernst &

Young's (2010) series 'The DNA of CFOs', the possibility of conflicts of interest between roles at the top is recognized (2010: 2) and CFOs are advised to 'make friends and influence people' (2010: 25).

Efficient networking and influence tactics in organizations, when applied successfully, improve the chances of CXOs advancing in their careers or even becoming CEOs. One of the reports on Chief Marketing Officers states that among the best ways to make a successful transition to a CEO role is 'developing close working relationships with other functions' and 'play[ing] the role of the integrator' (Spencer Stuart, 2015: 4). Likewise, in an Accenture (2013: 7) report, Chief Strategy Officers were advised to 'learn how to influence at both [the] line and matrix level[s]: you may be good at command and control, but as CEO you should also be good at influencing. You need to explore this early on in your career to understand whether you are good at both'. Adopting a political theory perspective, Soderstrom and Weber (2020) illustrated the activist and influence tactics employed by sustainability advocates within organizations. Without the successful application of these collective mobilization tactics, senior roles and domains do not become established.

Without exception, discourses on how CXOs get things done converge on a distinct style: a particular way of doing things that is highly social (networking) and political (influencing). This is essential to them, because their roles are about cutting across hierarchies, boundaries, social circles, and identities to create and capture added value and facilitate strategic adaptation, as discussed in the previous chapter. White (2008), a sociologist who was highly focused on what makes action and disruption feasible in organizations, defined leadership as cutting through the locked-in expectations created by rules and structures. Without discourse about their own relational work, social agents cannot deploy their style (Fontdevila, 2018). A diffusion so extensive and intensive of roles, tasks, and nomenclature as the CXO phenomenon can only be understood as the combined, mutually beneficial efforts of a number of social actors similar to the one described by Godart and Galunic (2019) for high fashion. Managers are not 'marionettes' of consultants; rather, they have a mutually beneficial interdependence. In addition to professional services, managers gain access to narrative materials for identity building and role competition, and consultants reap the rewards of engagements.

Investigating how leaders network across internal and external boundaries to exert their influence to accomplish integration is not novel to scholarly work. In fact, a robust literature on boundary spanning is dedicated to this topic. Section 5.3 is devoted to this literature.

5.3 Boundary spanning and integration

Schotter et al. (2017: 404) defined boundary spanning as the 'set of communication and coordination activities performed by individuals within an organization and between organizations to integrate activities across multiple cultural, institutional and organizational contexts'. Others have examined and theorized boundary spanning through concepts, such as cross-boundary or boundary work (Gieryn, 1983; Kellogg et al., 2006; Stjerne and Svejenova, 2016; Langley et al., 2019; Lawrence and Phillips, 2019). Lawrence and Phillips (2019) emphasised the purposeful and reflexive efforts involved in the shaping of social and organizational boundaries. Langley et al. (2019) distinguished between competitive, collaborative, and configurational boundary work, the latter capturing 'research in which managers, institutional entrepreneurs, or leaders work to reshape the boundary landscape of others to orient emerging patterns of competition and collaboration, often combining elements of both' (720).

There are two main types of boundary spanners. One is external spanners, who serve as inter-organizational interfaces, for instance, by maintaining legitimacy with important outside groups. A second type is internal integrators, who serve as intra-organizational diffusers through information selection, transmission, and interpretation. Below, we briefly summarize the academic research on these roles and the reasons why some theories have been more active and productive than others in studying them.

This research endeavour is challenging. Schotter et al. (2017) and Weber and Waeger (2017) still recently affirmed that our understanding of boundary spanners remains limited. Complex, global organizations are not homogeneous entities with easily comparable units, subject to analogous diffusion of practice processes. Rather, they are asymmetrical networks (Nohria and Ghoshal, 1997) where power distribution is in permanent contestation and flux (Dörrenbächer and Geppert, 2011; Schotter et al., 2017). Boundary spanners thus must be able to adapt to a wide variety of circumstances that are situationally determined. The fact that individuals in certain roles, even senior executives, may serve as boundary spanners who help legitimate new practices and spread them, does not guarantee that all organizational actors will rapidly and easily adopt such practices, even when they are endorsed by the TMT. Resistance to novelty is a common challenge encountered by managers of all ranks.

The two functions—inter-organizational spanning and intra-organizational integration—could be performed by a single manager or by several. Tushman (1977b) and Tushman and Scanlan (1981a, 1981b) argued that it is best when both external spanning and internal integration tasks are performed by the same manager—a dual role. This person must be 'ambidextrous', to use Tushman's well-known term, or 'amphibious', as Powell and Sandholtz (2012) put it. But it is not easy to find individuals who have the competencies to be boundary spanners. Schotter et al. (2017: 404) affirmed that only a small number of managers with unique skill sets are able to successfully engage in boundary spanning. The fact that merely a minor percentage of executives have the psychological profile to display the right style in this very particular and demanding role is central to our arguments about the CXO identity. Later in the chapter, we elaborate on the rare distinct personality traits of CXOs that enable them to apply social and political skills to their tasks.

In organization theory, boundary spanners have been studied by applying the lenses of contingency theory and its more focused offspring, resource dependency theory. Spanning and integrating roles, which were studied by scholars in the 1960s and 1970s, were the predecessors of the new CXO roles. These are designed precisely to fulfil the functions of the former. For example, several new CXO roles, such as Chief Diversity Officers, Chief Corporate Responsibility Officers, Chief Compliance Officers, and Chief Climate Change Officers, as well as other external-facing roles, such as Chief Procurement Officers or Chief Supply Chain Officers, primarily fulfil an inter-organizational external spanning function. These executives are responsible for addressing pressures stemming from political, social, and symbolic environments—the contexts that best fit institutional arguments—as well as operative contexts. Executives in other new CXO roles, such as Chief Innovation Officers, Chief Digital Officers, and Chief Transformational Officers, as well as those in more traditional roles, such as Chief Operating Officers, primarily (but not exclusively) serve as intra-organizational integrators.

Whereas contingency theory emphasized internal integrating roles, resource dependency theory focused more on studying external spanning roles. Chronologically, contingency theory was elaborated first. Lawrence and Lorsch (1967b) studied the then-emerging role of internal integrators. Years later, Aldrich and Herker (1977), Tushman (1977), and Tushman and Scanlan (1981a, 1981b) helped clarify the role of boundary spanners as linchpins who serve as interface managers in the adaptive function of organizations. The work of these scholars reveals the core functions, behaviours, and personality traits of boundary-spanning role incumbents, many of whom decades later were re-labelled CXOs. The difference between the boundary spanners of the late 1960s, then mostly project managers, and the CXOs of the twenty-first century, is not one of nature. The current proliferation and increased power of non-market contexts and of new technologies multiplies the need for boundary spanning. Boundary spanners are no longer just project managers leading temporary units or teams, as they were in the last decades of the twentieth century. Rather, these managers, many of whom have been elevated to the upper hierarchical ranks and been newly baptized as CXOs, often sit on expanded executive committees.

In their pioneering article on integrators, Lawrence and Lorsch (1967b) defined the essence of who new CXOs are and what they do, and why they are called 'chief officers'. They argued that integrators are like general managers who report to the ultimate superordinate general manager, the CEO (1967b: 142–3). Using a very telling term, Tinker and Lowe (1978) dubbed the CEO role the 'superordinate integrator'. CXOs can be conceptualized as 'ceos' (without capital letters), 'mini CEOs', or potential CEOs in the making. While not superordinates, today's chief 'still-less-than-executive' officers (i.e. N-1s, and some N-2s) fulfil similar fundamental functions and exhibit many of the same behaviours and personality traits as CEOs (i.e. Ns). This is currently being argued, for instance, by supporters of the human resources function (Ulrich and Filler, 2014). Lawrence and Lorsch (1967b) summarized the main CEO functions as attaining unity of effort or integration, solving non-routine challenges, managing conflicts, and developing contexts conducive to effective decision-making.

Contingency theory scholars of the late 1960s and 1970s argued that, for the work of integrators and spanners to be efficient, special managerial capabilities are required, which, in turn, require particular psychological profiles. Two decades later, Fligstein (1997) likewise argued that institutionalization requires agents to have specific competencies, particularly social skill. These, in turn, demand specific personality traits. As mentioned previously, Schotter et al. (2017) recently posed a similar argument.

Integrators who effectively discharge their duties exhibit some common stylistic traits on which scholars basically agree. Lawrence and Lorsch
(1967b: 147) found that effective integrators display balanced cognitive and
motivational orientations toward the units being integrated, which may be
functions, divisions, or even corporations: 'hav[ing] balanced orientations
means that they share more ways of thinking and more behaviour patterns
with the functional managers than those managers normally do with each
other'.

Forty years later, O'Mahony and Bechky (2008) similarly found that integrators must strike a delicate balance between parties (whether units or
individuals) in order to be effective:

> a boundary role . . . need not collapse or merge divergent worlds but . . .
> preserve each world's integrity while building a bridge between them . . .
> only by preserving the boundaries that separated the two parties could
> boundary organizations sustain the ability to represent either party.
>
> (O'Mahony and Bechky, 2008: 450)

Bridging different worlds requires integrators to be bilingual (Uyterhoeven,
1972) or bi-cultural (Schotter et al., 2017), with cultural 'in-betweenness'
competencies (Yagi and Klienberg, 2011), and a flexible style to accommo-
date differences. Being 'ambidextrous' is another way to name these dual
capacities, without which the work of a leader, external and/or internal,
becomes insufficient (Galunic, 2020).

Tushman and Scanlan (1981b) affirmed that boundary spanning is, basically, an informal process based on oral communication, and high-quality
upward and downward information flows—hence the criticality of networking. This requires internal communication stars, who tend to be more
educated, boast excellent reputations as experts and professionals, and enjoy high status; in other words, they have the personal power sources that
allow them to deploy the right style. Especially for those operating from
central positions, networking skills are critical (Ibarra, 1992; Beechler et al.
2004). Long Lingo and O'Mahony (2010) also emphasized the relevance
of relational skills and synthesis capabilities for boundary spanners. Johnson and Duxbury (2010) proposed that expatriates, who epitomize the
boundary spanning function in multinational enterprises, must engage
in relationship building, information and intelligence gathering, coordinating and negotiating, representing, intermediating, and other activities.

Birkinshaw, Ambos, and Bouquet (2017) attributed the spearheading, facilitating, reconciling, and lubricating functions to boundary spanners. Using a felicitous expression that both institutionalists and scholars working in the tradition of political theories of organizations would relish, Williams (2002: 109) called them 'entrepreneurs of power', who understand the interdependencies and fissures between strategic players, and are competent at 'reticulism'. As 'catalytic' agents, boundary spanners are good at establishing and maintaining alliances, councils, joint ventures, coalitions, partnerships, community budgets, coupling, etc., all of which are integrative devices (Williams, 2002). Their 'tool kit' for action, to use Swidler's (1986) term, is plenty of social and political gear. Their style is defined by their comfort with the use of these tools.

Individuals whose core responsibilities involve internal and external spanning tasks (e.g. CXOs), and who do not have the appropriate psychological profile, cannot hone the social and political style necessary to successfully fulfil their duties. We describe this profile in Section 5.4.

5.4 Personality profile of CXOs

The literature clearly reveals that efficient integrators have a particular psychological profile. In their ground-breaking work, Lawrence and Lorsch (1967b: 146) quoted an integrator who said: 'My major tool is my personality'. Forty years later O'Mahony and Bechky (2008: 408) used the expression 'governance by personality'. Personality characteristics supporting these relational and political competencies are *sine qua non*. Williams (2002, 2013) affirmed that boundary spanners should be social initiators who are self-confident, status-seeking, flexible, and assertive, and who exhibit social poise. There are so many requirements for proficient boundary spanners that Williams (2013) expressed scepticism that most executives could realistically possess so many rare and demanding traits. Overall, integrators and spanners must have personality profiles that enable them to manage the dynamics of power and influence underlying the essential tasks of spanning work (i.e. negotiating, mediating, bargaining, brokering, and networking). March (1962: 672) referred to these executives as 'political brokers', whereas Schotter et al. (2017) called them 'policy entrepreneurs' (p. 413) who 'conflate position and role' (p. 405)—that is, executives who are able to craft their own roles and adapt them to their own operating styles to improve self-motivation and self-efficacy. Grant et al. (2014) revealed the strong motivation generated by autonomous role definition and role labelling. The lack of institutionalization of many CXO roles facilitates the proliferation of self-anointed titles, especially with regard to new roles (e.g. Chief Content Officer; Russell Reynolds, 2020b). These titles are part of the negotiating back and forth, of the co-evolution of structures and new managerial roles (Sandhu and Kulik, 2019). The weak formalization of processes associated with the adoption of new roles— especially in new domains of action such as sustainability, as well as in senior management teams—strengthens the argument that it is often managers (i.e. their abilities and interests) who create or precede the role, not the other way around. As part of that influence, managers fight for status-giving or popular titles, hence the relevance of their particular personality traits.

The importance of autonomous action orientation for managers who span horizontal and hierarchical boundaries is also recognized in other streams of the management literature. Joseph Bower (1986), one of the most influential scholars in the field of business policy and general management, posed the concept of 'impetus' in his classic text on resource allocation, in which he described the bottom-up dynamics involved in allocating funds to corporate initiatives. This construct may be helpful for a better understanding of the relevance of personal traits for the successful performance of CXO roles. Impetus is the force enacted by managers to secure funding; it is what persuades managers to commit to sponsoring a project, sustains the rate at which this is successfully carried out, and helps secure project commitments from successively higher levels of the organizational hierarchy. Because high-impetus executives such as CXOs put their careers and reputations for good business judgement on the line, they must exercise caution when committing to roles or projects, and compute the personal costs and benefits of those commitments *a priori* (Bower, 1986). For taking risks, incumbents who are successful in these roles are rewarded with a boost in their professional trajectories. Relevant to our argument is Bower's emphasis on the importance of the personal characteristics of managers who are capable of displaying impetus. Importantly, impetus is not a management technique; it is a personality trait.

Another classic managerial view of senior roles also stresses the importance of personal characteristics to explain executive success. Vancil (1978) proposed three dimensions to analyse senior management roles and the power of their incumbents. The first dimension is the 'responsibility structure' or 'the set of corporate activities with which a manager is concerned and for which he is held accountable'; the second dimension is the 'authority structure', which refers to the 'set of corporate resources under the custody of a manager and for which he has the power to decide how the resources are utilized' (Vancil, 1978: 35). Vancil, along with scholars who worked on the topic of executive power, such as Uyterhoeven (1972), Luthans and Stewart (1977) and Kotter (1985), challenged the myth of executives being all-powerful social actors. For these scholars, a power deficit is intrinsic to the function of even senior management, originating in the gap between the results they are held accountable for, given their responsibility, and the resources they control to achieve these results (i.e. their authority), the latter being systematically inferior to the former.

Vancil argued that the only exceptions to this power gap are CEOs, whose responsibility and authority are equivalent. When Vancil published his book in 1978, the superordinates of most large US and European companies served as both CEOs and Chairs of their Board of Directors. For these individuals, there was no gap between responsibility and authority; they did not suffer from a power deficit, wielding so much influence that years later they were critically dubbed as 'imperial' or 'baronial' CEOs. However, after a couple of decades of corporate governance reforms, which have very intensely promoted the breakdown of the CEO–Board Chair duality, CEOs' decision-making rights and autonomy have been curtailed, and the board chair is often the new N *tout court*. Thus, CEOs of the first decades of the twenty-first century are in the same position as the N-1s in the second half of the twentieth century, in that they have more responsibility than authority. Many CEOs today are members, but are not leaders of the highest superordinate committee: the board of directors, which is, in turn, subject to the decisions by the general assembly of owners or shareholders. Therefore, similar to their subordinates of years past, current CEOs must actively fill in the gaps between the goals against which they are evaluated (i.e. their responsibilities), and the structural resources available to them (i.e. their authority).

Whereas Vancil's first two dimensions are formal or structural, the third dimension by which executives' power is evaluated is personal, and therefore highly related to personality. This personal dimension reflects *who* these executives are, as personal resources are required to close the responsibility-authority gap as much as possible. Vancil (1978) called this third dimension 'autonomy', defined as the 'freedom to take action' (p. 4), the 'perception of power to initiate change' and the 'ability to influence events' (p. 51). In other words, autonomy is the self-confidence managers enjoy because of the personal power they derive from possessing the influencing skills necessary to accomplish their tasks. This is particularly important in contexts such as complex enterprises, where executives have to 'make sense, manipulate, negotiate, and partially construct their institutional environments' in the words used by Kostova, Roth, and Dacin (2008: 1001); or need to be 'necessarily adept at building coalitions, cutting deals, and other forms of pragmatic action', in a similar view by Kraatz (2009: 64). Vancil's autonomy, then, is very similar to Bower's impetus, and both stem primarily from executives' personalities.

Yet another term related to both autonomy and impetus is 'energy'. One of the founding fathers of the United States, Alexander Hamilton, proposed energy as the distinctive characteristic of executive power (Mansfield, 1989, and Eastland, 1992). Energy is indispensable to sustain the friction facing change agents. In short, impetus, energy, and autonomy are the character baseline of the CXO's style.

As Fligstein (1997) recognized, some people are better institutional entrepreneurs than others, as not all personalities facilitate agency or action similarly. Agency and action are to sociology what impetus and autonomy are to management studies. According to Fligstein (1997: 398), the main psychological characteristic that enables change agents to enact social skill is the ability to entertain plausible predictive hypotheses of how relevant constituencies or stakeholders may react to the focal actor's initiatives, and then develop or adjust their own action plans and deploy corresponding behaviours: 'strategic actors have to imaginatively identify with the states of others'. Fligstein and McAdam (2012b: 291) expanded on the same point: 'certain individuals possess a highly developed cognitive capacity for reading people and environments, framing lines of action, and mobilizing people in the service of these action "frames"'. Mayo and Nohria (2005) called these capacities 'contextual intelligence'.

Fligstein and McAdam's quote points to the concept of 'Machiavellian intelligence' and the associated social hypothesis for the development of human brain articulated by de Waal (1982) and Byrne and Whitten (1988). For these theories, humans have innate capabilities to entertain conjectures about other actors' true intentions and potential lines of action and, in response, design and display behaviours that may include deception and guile. Yet, once again, these capabilities are not equally distributed; not all people, not all managers, and not even all senior executives are psychologically endowed with similar levels of empathy, strategic imagination, and self-presentation skills.

In the following paragraphs, we attempt to identify the basic personality traits of the ideal CXO. Our arguments are based on the most academically-backed personality theory, the NEO-AC (an anagram for neuroticism, extroversion, openness to experience, agreeableness, and conscientiousness), also known as the Five Factor Model, or Big 5, which provides initial indications of how different basic profiles affect a person's propensity for action. Neuroticism, or a lack of emotional stability, is associated with defensiveness and the tendency to withdraw from uncertain action, and is the best predictor of a subpar ability to read stakeholders, which results in fragile agency. Overwhelmed by changing circumstances, neurotic actors lack the will to act as change or adaptation agents. They have the psychological profile of what some neo-institutionalists call 'doves'. The 'muscularity' or agency that neo-institutionalists demand from institutional entrepreneurs—a willingness to engage others, deploy deliberate action, and seize opportunities for transforming the status quo—derives mostly from 'dominance', one of the sub-facets of extroversion, as well as from openness to experience.

Another psychological trait not included in the Five Factor model, self-monitoring, predicts which managers are better equipped for strategic intelligence, empathy (Snyder, 1974), and network brokering aptitudes (Oh and Kilduff, 2008; King, 2020) and adds to the main traits of the ideal personality of CXOs. This is foundational to the ability to understand others' situations and realistically imagine their probable lines of action. Self-monitoring allows individuals to flexibly adapt their behaviour to different environments.

The self-monitoring construct has three basic components. First, high self-monitors grasp the behaviours necessary to be successful in, or at least to adapt to, a particular environment. This social reading capability closely resembles the already referred to Machiavellian intelligence. Interestingly, CEOs seem to differ from non-CEOs in that they are more 'efficient readers of people' (Russell Reynolds, 2012a); specifically, they actively seek to understand people and adapt to different audiences, and are socially confident. Second, these individuals are able to behave as needed to properly react to people and circumstances. Thus, self-monitoring is not just a cognitive capability, but a behavioural capacity evidenced by the self-regulation of expressive displays, equivalent to the accurate performance of a dramaturgical script. Among other behaviours, these individuals are able to easily influence individual stakeholders, fit into a specific corporate culture, and convince others to change. Third, self-monitoring is the capacity to self-observe and self-assess the validity of one's own adaptive behaviour, and if necessary, self-regulate and self-adjust it. Thus, high self-monitors have an acute awareness of others and themselves in action, characteristics shared by the psychological construct popularly known as emotional intelligence.

CXOs need to count on psychological profiles that enable them to feel comfortable with social dynamics and with exercising influence. Personality is the microfoundation of CXOs' style.

5.5 Conclusion

In their thorough review of political perspectives on organizations, Weber and Waeger (2017) underlined that boundary-spanning processes linking internal activities with external conditions constitute the key element of open polity perspectives, and that a more complete unpacking of those processes is warranted. Half a century ago, contingency theorists had well-articulated the main tasks and profiles of boundary-spanning roles and their incumbents. However, neo-institutionalists have not sufficiently studied these processes and roles, another manifestation of their nonchalance toward issues of power and politics in organizations. Responding to Weber and Waeger's (2017) call for a return to political theories of organizations, we have argued in this chapter that boundary spanners and integrators are the forerunners of CXOs, that efficiently executing the tasks of both roles requires social and political prowess, and that efficient incumbents exhibit similar profiles and personality traits.

CXO roles require interpretation, as they help CEOs adapt their organizations to a wider variety of changing environmental contingencies. CXO roles provide actors with ample latitude to determine how they should be performed. White's (2008) concept of 'style' works especially well to capture how senior executives enact these roles. Styles that strike the right balance between discipline and adaptability provide organizational actors the necessary leeway to move across structures and social boundaries—that is, to engage in the spanning and integrating required to adapt organizations to environmental pressures. Styles are essentially relational (Fontdevila, 2018). They manifest in and are legitimated by the discourses instantiated in the texts of intermediaries and legitimizers of senior executive practices, such as executive search firms and consultancies.

We have used reports by these organizations, which are simultaneously descriptive and normative, as the empirical basis for our arguments. The many texts quoted in this and other chapters of the book provide supporting evidence. The cultivation of social capital for networking and the mustering of political capital for influence capture the essence of the CXO's style. This is their 'how', the way they do their 'what'. The formal knowledge CXOs employ defines their expertise less than their political and social style does. Although social and political competencies certainly are requirements for executives in other management roles, such competencies are not as essential or distinctive as they are for CXOs. In the mid-twentieth century, Selznick (1957: 61), the classic institutionalist, famously affirmed that although 'administrators' (the term often used at that time for top executives of either private or public organizations) 'are called leaders, their profession is politics'. This description applies to CXOs today. The only modification of this quote that we would propose is to replace 'profession' with 'occupation' for reasons that will be spelled out in Chapter 7.

Drawing on a variety of sources, we have also argued that the skilled use of influence tactics depends on a set of psychological capabilities that are unevenly distributed across the managerial population. Only the minority of executives who are dominant, open to experience, and high self-monitors possess personality characteristics that enable them to apply their energy, impetus, and autonomy to their social and political tasks—that is, their style—amidst the uncertainty, ambiguity, and imperfection of life in the upper echelons of organizational hierarchies.

6

Top Team Dynamics

> *The increase in C-suite roles has helped to diversify the expertise and experience in the executive ranks, yet failed to solve a bigger problem: Emerging challenges do not touch just one function or business line at a time. Solving those problems requires the ability to see and work horizontally across the company, not vertically within a single segment.*
>
> **Abbatiello, Bécotte, and Handcock, 2020: 3**

In 2020, Russell Reynolds Associates, a leading executive search firm, published a report titled 'The End of Executive Expertise? Rethinking the C-suite' (Abbatiello, Bécotte, and Handcock, 2020), which—as the epigraph reveals—acknowledges the diverse expertise at the top of organizations due to the increased number of CXO roles. The authors argued that in response to a wealth of external pressures, organizations 'are moving fast to hire new executives into the C-suite that have the necessary expertise to deal with them' (Abbatiello et al., 2020: 2). Individuals hired for these newly created CXO positions have expanded TMTs' expertise in essential areas of responsibility in response to external pressures:

> Chief digital officers, chief data officers, and to a lesser extent chief artificial intelligence officers and chief privacy officers have emerged in response to digitalization. In most organizations, these new roles exist alongside a legacy chief information officer, leading to lack of clarity around responsibilities and decision making. . . .
>
> Elsewhere in the organization, human resources has similarly seen a growth of new roles—chief culture officer, chief people officer, chief talent officer, chief diversity and inclusion officer—and the resurgence of the chief learning officer.
>
> (Abbatiello et al., 2020: 2–3)

The Changing C-Suite. José Luis Alvarez and Silviya Svejenova, Oxford University Press.
© José Luis Alvarez and Silviya Svejenova (2022). DOI: 10.1093/oso/9780198728429.003.0006

Yet, the authors of the Russell Reynolds report also cautioned about how emerging challenges and ongoing external pressures call not only for additional expertise, but also for organizational resilience. This in turn requires leadership to bring diverse expertise and experiences together in a highly functional top team that works horizontally across the organization, allowing the organization to anticipate and adapt to both incremental change and major disruptions:

> To succeed, CEOs need to push the C-suite into an 'age of contextual integration', leading a group of executives who adapt quickly to changing circumstances, are unafraid to wade into new terrain, and who manage horizontally with one another, not vertically alongside each other. This is as much about the CEO defining a new set of norms for how the group will operate as it is selecting a set of leaders with a different profile.
>
> (Abbatiello et al., 2020: 2–3)

In this chapter, we examine some of the dynamics and challenges involved in enabling the growing number of CXOs on TMTs to 'manage horizontally with one another, not vertically alongside each other', as the above quote suggests. To do so, we shift the lens once more, this time from the nature of CXO roles in terms of claims related to their executive expertise, role identity, and style of executive power, to their 'teamness', that is, their relationships and ways of working with one another. We first provide an overview of some core contributions on the nature and dynamics of TMTs, highlighting their evolution, characteristics (e.g. structure, composition, processes), as well as main challenges and benefits. With this, we seek to provide a foundation for readers who may be less familiar with them, and to organize extant insights for their subsequent illustration in the rest of the chapter, which focuses on the dynamics and challenges of TMT relationships.

For this illustration, we return to the vocabulary approach introduced in Chapter 4 and employ it to unravel three main aspects. First, we conceptualize and illustrate aspects of competition among CXOs in TMTs, revealing some tensions and balancing acts. Second, we theorize the nature and dynamics of collaboration among CXOs and with the CEO, articulating characteristics and benefits. Third, we explore the vocabulary of 'teamness', overviewing claims that suggest the obsolescence of and/or challenges with the current TMT model and put forward ideas for transforming it. We conclude by recognizing the unique role of the CEO as the chief designer and sensegiver who shapes individual CXO roles and the C-suite model as a whole. However, we also acknowledge the importance of experimenting with and going beyond CEO-centred models to more distributed executive constellations that can enable organizational resilience and ensure temporal flexibility as organizations seek to address and align multiple future horizons.

6.1 An overview of teams at the top

An executive committee, senior leadership team, or TMT is the group of senior managers reporting directly to the CEO, meeting regularly for the common purpose of shaping the collective work of an enterprise in accordance with its values and strategic objectives. According to Wageman et al., (2008), the primary responsibilities of an executive committee are: defining or modifying the organization's strategy (which the board of directors typically must approve), acquiring and deploying capital (when significant amounts of capital are involved, the board of directors also has the final word), building organizational capabilities (e.g. staff competencies, processes, etc.), managing strategic initiatives (e.g. new product launches), monitoring performance, and integrating significant acquisitions. Wageman et al. (2008) proposed four basic functions to be performed by TMTs: information (to ensure alignment between the different elements of the organizational system); consultation (to debate and provide counsel on crucial decisions); coordination (of the operative requirements of integration); and decision-making (critical and strategic decisions).

6.1.1 Origins and evolution

Executive committees have not been around since the emergence of large organizations. Their history reveals their evolving functions, which are intimately intertwined with the emergence of the M-form (i.e. the multidivisional organization). This basic structure emerged when organizational size, growth, and complexity overwhelmed the capacities of the CEOs of functional organizations, which were dominant until the Second World War. The structural answer to the shortcomings of functional organizations was to delegate down and empower managers to lead a new type of operational unit, divisions, which initially covered specific territories and, later, clients or technologies. Following the logic of Ashby's law of requisite variety (i.e. only variety can absorb variety), organizations became more internally differentiated to mirror an increasingly differentiated external environment. In the 1960s, as companies began to launch even more differentiated and specialized products, and more companies began operating in more territories, these divisions were subdivided and labelled 'strategic business units' (SBUs), following General Electric's lead. As contingency theory states, all differentiation requires integration mechanisms to counterbalance the centrifugal forces it generates and to promote cooperation between highly autonomous units. Examples of centripetal mechanisms include well-aligned incentive systems, a common culture, managerial rotation, product managers, and groups such as councils, temporary teams, permanent cross-unit teams, etc. The most crucial integration team in complex organizations, and the highest in the hierarchy, is the executive committee, with CEOs fulfilling the ultimate integrating role.

Executive committees have a clear origin in the history of organizations, emerging with the spread of multi-divisional firms and the need for a TMT to function as an integration mechanism. As the M-form spread in the United States and executive committees became 'institutionalized', Mylander (1955) published an article in the *Harvard Business Review* addressing the challenges facing the then-pioneering executive committees, many of which remain salient today. Mylander built on the ground-breaking experience of the senior team at DuPont, a large chemical enterprise that initiated a broad product differentiation strategy in the 1920s. DuPont's executive committee, which met on Wednesdays, had nine members, plus the vice-president and president. The guiding principle was that the executive committee manages the company, and the executives manage the different businesses. The committee's only restrictions related to decisions that lay with the board of directors, such as auditing policies, the compensation of top executives, and the most consequential financial commitments— issues constituting core board responsibilities today. The executives in charge of the autonomous business units had broad leeway for decision-making over their businesses' technical, productive, commercial, and other functional areas, and even had the capacity to decide whether to use internal services for legal, advertising, public relations, and research and development activities (among others), or to hire external firms that were fully independent from DuPont, which was a very advanced practice at the time.

6.1.2 Characteristics

Executive committees are not a universal necessity in all organizations. Only highly complex companies need them to integrate differentiation. Moreover, not all executive committees work as real teams. Often, they fall short of the team concept and function merely as 'groups' or 'working groups', exhibiting a low degree of behavioural integration (see, e.g., data related to Spanish executive committees presented by Gallo et al., 1998). A working group is an aggregation of individuals who interact mostly to exchange information, best practices, and different perspectives, and to make decisions that will improve their capacity to fulfil their individual responsibilities. To truly be called a 'team', a group of executives should display several characteristics, which we elaborate below.

> *Common purpose.* The team should have some specific goals beyond the sum of its members' individual objectives. The very existence of an executive committee (as distinct from unilateral reporting between heads of units and the CEO acting as a hub) entails a common purpose: the overall good of the entire enterprise.

> *Interdependence.* This is the need for tasks to be shared in order to accomplish objectives. For instance, developing the strategy of a complex organization requires collaboration between the main units for collecting, sharing, and processing data, evaluating scenarios, etc. However, that is not necessarily the case for every complex organization, as revealed in the following quote by Wagman et al. (2008):

Not every organization needs an integrated senior leadership team. . . . Indeed, if yours is, in essence, a holding company, if you are managing a number of highly independent and unrelated businesses, your senior leaders would gain very little from interacting, given the cost of bringing them together (or the opportunity costs of pulling them away from their individual accountabilities for the time it takes to conduct a proper meeting).

(Wagman et al., 2008: 31)

Clarity of roles and consequences. Team members must have clearly defined roles. Role expectations may come from the formal or the informal organization, but team members need to know what is expected of them. On executive committees, senior managers ideally should think of themselves not as representatives of their units or silos, but as generalists with a common stake and interest in the enterprise as a whole.

Both individual and common responsibility. Because a common purpose exists and accomplishing it requires interdependent collaboration, a firm's performance cannot be attributed to a single individual on the TMT. To use Durkheim's (1893) vocabulary, solidarity should be organic, not just mechanical. However, in most business systems, legal solidarity is mandatory only for boards of directors, not for executive committees.

Presence of synergies. What is achieved by a team should exceed that which could be obtained by its members working individually and in an uncoordinated manner. Moreover, the team's added value minus the so-called 'process costs' stemming from interaction time (i.e. decisions made by teams are slower than those made by an individual), frictions (i.e. personal conflicts), development costs (e.g. building teamwork skills), etc. should be superior to that of the individuals' contributions plus 'group' work (which is not yet teamwork).

Next, we build on Hackman's (1989) list of teams' general characteristics, which explain why and when team decisions are better than individual ones, adjusting his arguments to senior management teams:

- Team decisions better represent the range of interests and perspectives present in any complex or differentiated enterprise. Thus, an executive committee must reflect the heterogeneity or diversity of the organization, which requires a minimum size of three members.
- Innovation and creativity are more likely in a group with a variety of competencies and perspectives than in one with homogenous membership. Senior teams are often diverse in their composition, as their members represent different functions and the main business

units of companies. However, poorly designed teams and poorly led decision-making processes produce homogeneity, groupthink, etc.

- The members of the executive committee will better implement decisions when they have participated in decision-making processes, as they will better understand the advantages and disadvantages of such decisions and what is required to put them successfully into practice, will know their leaders better, etc.
- If executive committee members feel that they have been engaged, listened to, and allowed to participate in decision-making processes, they will probably feel that such processes have been fair, which should increase their motivation.
- Most executive committees meet regularly (weekly, at many companies), which may produce habits of implicit knowledge exchange, the learning of non-verbal communication cues, understanding of cultural nuances, etc. that make communication more efficient.

Membership on an executive committee is a great opportunity for learning and professional development, given the perspective it offers, the heterogeneity of competencies represented on such teams, the exchange of information produced, the influence exercised, etc. Such teams could serve as effective learning platforms for executive leadership.

6.1.3 Benefits

The previous points are the general characteristics that executive committees must possess to merit the 'team' label. Next, we outline the benefits of teams in general, and the specific characteristics and functions of executive teams at the top, building on Ancona and Nadler (1989).

> *The relevance of the external environment.* Organizational apexes are convergence points for the most relevant external contingencies: economic (main clients, main suppliers of material or financial resources, etc.), political (e.g. relationships with governments) and social (lobbies, interest groups, etc.) Executive committees are the teams that interface most with normative institutional forces, operating where the threat of strategic uncertainty is strongest.

The complexity of decisions and tasks. There are two basic types of decisions. Routine decisions are clearly right or wrong, and the most critical criterion is precision. These are Category I or 'problem-solving' tasks. Executive committees, and even boards of directors make routine decisions. However, and more importantly, executive committees must also deal with less structured, non-recurring problems with fewer precedents and imperfect solutions. These are Category II or 'decision-making' tasks performed by boards of directors, CEOs, and senior teams. In the absence of established rules, the values and styles of the executives involved play a crucial role in Category II decisions. As a consequence, differences in values and styles may lead to irreconcilable differences among team members. It is in these predicaments, called 'weak situations', that the role of the team leader—in the case of executive committees, the CEO—is most relevant. Harrison (1999) detailed the characteristics of these critical decisions:

- The goal is to improve the organization over the long term.
- An effort is made to make the best decision among a set of alternatives, each of which could reasonably attain the goal.
- The decision is made under a high degree of uncertainty, due to imperfect information, time and cost restrictions, and cognitive limitations of the decision-maker.
- The decision usually results in at least some degree of change for the organization as a whole, or for some important functions or programmes.
- The decision necessarily requires committing scarce resources, and therefore incurs some opportunity costs. Strategy involves saying no, renouncing possibilities, and limiting the number of possible futures. This is the reason why this type of decision-making is so stressful: it is psychologically challenging for human beings to relinquish possibilities.
- The act of selecting between alternatives is a means to an end (the achievement of an objective), not an end in itself.
- In situations with few precedents and significant uncertainty, decision-makers tend to overestimate their chances of success.
- The success of a decision is verifiable based on the achievement of objectives, or the failure to do so.

- Differences in values may lead to inherent structural conflicts among members of top management teams.

Top management teams are highly visible. The rest of the organization pays a great deal of attention both to the substance of top managers' decisions and to their styles as the symbolic embodiment of organizational culture. The executive committee is responsible for making and implementing major organizational decisions affecting areas ranging from strategy to structures to personnel, including, either directly or through policies, decisions affecting the compensation packages and careers of all employees. Only personnel policies affecting the members of the executive committee itself escape their own purview, as such decisions rest with the CEO and the board of directors.

Executive committees reduce the structural isolation of CEOs at the organizational apex (Krachenberg et al., 1993). CEOs are lonely for several reasons. Executives working at the peak of organizational hierarchies must process an overwhelming amount of information. This overflow of inputs can be dealt with in one of two ways: by increasing the resources available for information processing (e.g. forming an executive committee), or reducing the amount of information from outside sources (e.g. the market) and the internal organization that must be processed. However, opting to reduce the amount of information to be processed may further isolate top management.

Top management teams are instruments of CEOs. According to Vancil (see Vancil and Green, 1984: 66), one of the first management scholars to explore the dynamics of top management teams, the corporate world is more civilized and predictable when the CEO 'reigns' and the top management committee 'reins'. These dynamics largely depend on how CEOs perceive their executive function and the way they govern:

The primary advantage of top management committees is that they are flexible, personal tools for enhancing leadership effectiveness. Committees are easy to form and continue to exist only at the pleasure of the CEO. Their agendas are entirely in the CEO's hands, and they afford an excellent means of sending signals down into the organization.

(Vancil and Green, 1984: 73)

Frisch (2012: 63) also emphasized the role of senior management teams as tools contingent on the personal and strategic view of the CEO, on how the CEO views the job, and on what priorities the CEO establishes for the organization, affirming:

> There is no one best way. . . . 'Ed Brennan (the late chairman and CEO of Sears, Roebuck, and Co.) told me that *an organizational structure should be based on who you are—what your personality is as a leader.* I used to think that was wrong, but now I realize that's the only way an organization can function'. (emphasis in original)

Wageman et al. (2008: xiv) also recognized the lack of institutionalization, or of normative, homogenous practices in the structure, composition, and processes of senior teams, and their dependence on CEOs' skills and preferences:

> There is no single best way for a chief executive to create and sustain the conditions that increase the chances that a group of senior executives will develop into a superb leadership team], nor any fixed set of steps to follow in structuring, launching, and leading senior teams. Instead, we find that great leaders draw on their particular skills and preferences to create these conditions in ways that are tuned to the unique circumstances in which their teams operate.
>
> (Wageman et al., 2008: xiv)

Having provided an overview of the benefits of having and working with teams at the top, in Section 6.1.4 we describe some important challenges.

6.1.4 Challenges

Katzenbach (1998, see also Katzenbach and Smith, 1993), one of the most influential scholars on teams, suggested that real teams at the top are rare, and work well only under particular circumstances, and when they fit the leadership style of the CEO. Katzenbach argued that non-team approaches such as individual reporting (with the CEO as a hub), transitory teams, functional teams, and working groups more often meet the complex and urgent challenges typically faced by senior leaders of large, complex organizations. Others have also questioned the teamness in the C-suite (Pettigrew, 1992; Hambrick, 1994) and distinguished between a stable core group and a dynamic periphery (Roberto, 2003).

Another problem that Katzenbach spotted is an excess of unnecessary teams at the top; notably, this problem is not unique to the highest organizational layers. Common acceptance of the culture of participation and teamwork leads to situations where decisions should have been made individually, by the CEO. The challenges to the proper functioning of an executive committee are so pervasive that 'teaming at the top' is an unnatural act: 'it is abundantly clear that non-teams work at the top. There is a natural order of things; it tends to be hierarchical' (Katzenbach, 1998: 41).

The designing of upper management groups may prompt an interesting debate: should it be a single top team, or several teams? If so, should there be hierarchies between them, and what kinds of integrating mechanisms should be structured? Investigating these questions, Frisch (2012) argued against conceiving of formal, permanent, senior management teams as strategic decision-making bodies, calling this notion a myth. Rather, most critical decisions are made by *ad hoc*, non-institutionalized teams with unofficial status and fluid membership, where the most important requirement is the trust of the CEO, not one's position in the organizational hierarchy. For non-strategic decisions, Frisch endorsed the existence of a portfolio of upper teams with different configurations based on the types of decisions and tasks involved. Frisch (2012) asserted that the typical formal senior management team, composed of between eight and fourteen members, should just aim for what Wageman et al. (2008)) identified as the informational function of senior teams (i.e. the alignment function), whereas larger teams should focus on counselling, generating ideas, etc.

Both practitioners and scholars agree that the work of executive committees is less than perfect. Scholars such as Woolbridge and Floyd (1990), Hambrick (1995), Amason (1996), Eisenhardt, Kahwajy, and Bourgeois (1997, 1998), and Katzenbach (1998), among others, have identified the most recurring problems with top management teams, which we summarize below.

The primary challenge for leaders of senior teams is managing the tensions that divide the focus of their members, who must simultaneously play at least two roles, as part-time members of the senior team, and full-time leaders of business units (e.g. vice-presidents), functions (e.g. Chief Marketing Officers, etc.) or processes (e.g., Chief Sustainability Officers, etc.). While there is no such thing as a top management team comprised solely of full-time members, team members are not just part time consultants or *consiglieri* either. Senior leaders need to understand the company with the depth that only holding a full-time, high-responsibility position in the organization provides. Without full-time responsibility for a business unit, function, or service, members of executive committees cannot fulfil one of their essential functions: to serve as channels of communication and alignment between the CEO and lower levels of the organization. Organizational stretch and discipline are not possible without them.

However, when top managers serve as part-time executive committee members and full-time managers, their activities are most often asymmetrical in favour of their business units, leading to the crucial problem of teams in the upper echelons, which typically are not teams, but working groups that lack behavioural integration. Beyond a lack of attention or dedication, this asymmetry is reinforced, for example, by compensation systems, as most companies still do not reward service on the executive committee. Hambrick (1995: 111) dubbed this problem 'fragmentation': 'This is the case of the team that it is not a team at all, but rather a mere constellation of senior executives pursuing their own agendas, with a minimum of collaboration or exchange among them.' Katzenbach (1998) cited additional reasons for fragmentation, among which that the composition of executive committees is determined by the representative quality of their members. Executives participate on executive committees because they are heads of departments or business units, regardless of their decision-making competencies. Sometimes, fragmentation is inevitable. At some companies, the concerted work of senior executives is non-existent because it is not needed. To express this in the vocabulary of Thompson (1967), at some companies, managers at the top do not need to engage in 'mutual' or 'reciprocal' interaction. In these cases, committees are simply mechanisms for information sharing. Hackman (2002) labelled these groups without real interaction 'co-acting groups' in which members' responsibilities do not require cooperation from others to fulfil.

Second, when the fragmentation of top committees, which manifests as intra-team conflict or unproductive rivalries, is very intense, the CEO often reacts by unilaterally making decisions in isolation, further exacerbating the fragmentation of the team. In addition, the members of the executive committee themselves can systematically seek to evade conflict, as vividly captured by Frisch (2012: 13):

> [According to] Elly McColgan, former president and chief operating officer of Morgan Stanley's Global Wealth Management Group, 'once you get to the highest level, the point of the meeting is to get out of the room without saying anything controversial, without raising an issue, and certainly not asking for help. Your job is to make your three minutes of airtime positive and good and then leave. That means that decision-making happens somewhere else.'
>
> (Frisch, 2012: 13)

A third problem is that a great number of senior executives have risen to the top of organizations because they have achieved results by adopting assertive, non-consultative, and individualistic styles, which could be inappropriate for the collective work performed by an executive committee. In the future, perhaps new generations of top managers will be promoted to upper levels of their organizations because of their efficiency at teamwork.

Fourth, many executive committee members lack appropriate professional competencies, because most of them secure these positions during mature stages of their careers, after dealing with bygone contexts. One of the paradoxes of executive careers in rapidly changing contexts is that the knowledge, styles, and attitudes required for a successful ascent in the hierarchy may not be useful once an individual secures a seat on the executive committee.

The fifth typical problem affecting executive committees is rivalry for the boss's position, as most CEO candidates are members of the senior management team. This competition may undermine collaboration, both before a succession decision is made, and afterwards, due to potential resentment among those not selected for the top job. CEO succession struggles are especially intense because they are zero-sum games in which the 'winner takes all', and where coming in second often means leaving the firm and looking for opportunities elsewhere, where the waiting list could be shorter.

The intense political climate at organizational apexes gives rise to rivalries like those just mentioned, as well as natural professional differentiation between managers with different backgrounds and responsibilities. Liu et al. (forthcoming) list, classify, and analyse the different tactics of influence that senior committee members may employ. What Lawrence and Lorsch (1967a) said about conflict between different functional orientations also applies to leaders of business units on executive committees who act primarily as representatives of their units. Moreover, because top managers are usually experienced and savvy political operators (otherwise, they would not have reached upper echelon positions), conflicts can play out through highly sophisticated, assertive, and conniving political manoeuvring. Highly politicized dynamics could lead to negative consequences such as delayed decision-making (Eisenhardt and Bourgeois, 1988) and risk aversion to protect the reputations of team members. Although power tends to flow to those who better reduce uncertainty in the critical interface between organizations and their most relevant environments, this is not always necessarily so. In fact, it could be said that one function of corporate governance is to prevent executive entrenchment. Because organizational politics is not a perfect market (i.e. a meritocracy of the most capable), outcomes of conflicts may be detrimental to organizations, especially if the CEO does not take special care with team processes.

The sixth problem on executive committees is 'groupthink' (Janis, 1982), or the search for consensus in group decision-making, even at the expense of rationality, and the tendency to dismiss divergent opinions or the views of minorities. This problem manifests specifically on highly united teams.

Thus far, we have described the characteristics, benefits, and challenges of the group context (the top management team) in which CXOs operate. Traditionally, the CEO has determined the structure, composition, and processes of senior executive teams, at least until the implementation of corporate governance reforms, whereby some of these decisions have come under the purview of boards of directors. In any case, due to the lack of clear and strong rules for the design of executive committees, they have tended to become political arenas where conflicts are played out as a contact sport, fitting well with the social and political styles of CXOs.

In the subsequent sections, we show how the above universal conceptualization of executive committees has special meaning and potentially also consequences for 'teamness', as well as the interplay between competition and collaboration between CXOs. In particular, we describe the vocabularies of 'teamness', competition, and collaboration in role-based reports, thereby providing a glimpse into some of the intricacies and dynamics of CXOs as a senior leadership team. We do so by paying attention to concepts from the literature which we reviewed in the first part of the chapter (e.g. common purpose, interdependences, sharing, and added value of working together). While we distinguish CXO interactions in terms of competition and collaboration, we recognize that the nature of these is much more complex, intertwined, and ambiguous, as suggested by the title of an Ernst & Young (EY) (2014) report, 'Competition, coexistence or symbiosis?'.

6.2 Competing in the C-suite

As we noted in earlier chapters, over the years, the expanded ecology of roles has led to the emergence of role 'families' revolving, for example, around information and technology (Chief Information Officer, Chief Technology Officer, Chief Data Officer), talent (Chief Human Resources Officer, Chief Talent Officer, Chief People Officer, Chief Leadership Officer), or customers (Chief Marketing Officer, Chief Sales Officer, Chief Customer Officer). Overall, incumbents of CXOs roles 'have more in common with their executive peers than they do with the people in the functions they run' (Groysberg et al., 2011: 62). Such similarity is also undoubtedly a source of competition. Below, we illustrate two manifestations of competition in top teams: one related to executive expertise, that is, competition over areas of responsibility, and the other one related to executive identity, that is, competition for status and the top job.

Competition over areas of responsibility. The definitions and discussions of roles in the reports produced by consultancies and executive search firms reveal overlapping responsibilities and domains of action among a number of roles, particularly those operating at the intersection of customers and markets. There is also ambiguity in the language used to describe the 'closeness of orbits', whereby two or more roles 'gravitate' towards the same task(s): 'The current importance of digital factors in changing industry models and business models potentially brings the CSO's orbit closer to the CIO's' (Raskino, 2015: 1). Overlaps and close orbits enhance the possibility for 'collisions' and 'jockeying for power', bringing about power volatility.

For example, the uniqueness of the CSO's jurisdiction is often contested by an increasingly powerful and central for the strategic management of the organization CFO, which creates 'creative tension' between the two roles, as revealed in this quote from an Accenture article (London and Lowitt, 2008: 7):

This close relationship is not without friction, of course. Despite—or perhaps because of—such close and frequent interaction, CFOs and CSOs may find themselves at odds over strategic direction and priorities. The greatest point of tension can come when horizon-one activities like budgeting (the CFO's domain) blur into horizon-two efforts like strategic planning (the CSO's bailiwick).

Here's how the CFO of one Fortune 500 company described this process: 'I own the next 18 months, and our CSO owns the next 18 months to five years. And those two [periods] have to be integrated. Sometimes you want to make long-term investments, and we can't afford them in the short term. Sometimes we want to do short-term things that don't make sense for the long term. So it definitely has been a learning experience.'

(London and Lowitt, 2008: 7)

In contrast, frictions between CFOs and CIOs are attributed to their different backgrounds, rather than jurisdictional overlaps:

Many organizations have experienced friction between CFOs and CIOs. Much of it stems from these two executive roles having different backgrounds and not completely understanding the challenges and complexities of each other's world. When projects experience difficulties, for example, return on investment is affected and frustrations rise. This often causes CFOs and CIOs to 'grow apart'. On the other hand, there have been times where CFOs and CIOs have had to forge a better union—think Y2K—and they have done so effectively.

(Deloitte CFO Insights, 2012: 1)

Overlaps also frequently occur between CMOs and CIOs.

CMOs' and CIOs' focus and aspirations are surprisingly similar in scope. With the explosive change each function is experiencing, and the urgent call for transformation across many enterprises, it would seem the advantages of working together would be obvious. But as Marketing becomes more reliant on technical solutions for customer engagement, and IT's mandate becomes broader to include front-office enablement,

both functions are deep in their own transitions and looking for solutions. Despite common ambitions, their initiatives are often not as
integrated as one might expect.

(Baird and Ban, 2012: 1)

Likewise, Kaneshige (2014) described a 'traditionally strained CIO-CMO
relationship', which needs to be resolved, going so far as to call it a 'Battle
in the C-Suite'.

One could ask how frictions related to such overlapping action domains
are resolved. In some cases, it is suggested that the fault lines and arenas
of collaboration are bridged under a joint role, such as the Chief Marketing and Technology Officer, the Chief Commercial and Digital Officer,
Chief Ethics and Compliance Officer, or Chief Talent and Culture Officer, resulting in double-hatting. In addition to such cases of job crafting
(Wrzesniewski and Dutton, 2001), CXOs may engage in role delimitation
through ongoing boundary work (Stjerne and Svejenova, 2016) and/or es-
calate disagreements for resolution by the CEO as a C-suite top designer
and 'political broker' (March, 1962). They could also experience task conflict and/or role stress, if their role boundaries are ambiguous (Ebbers and
Wijnberg, 2017). Lastly, consultants and academics as ongoing role theo-
rizes may clarify distinctions between such roles. For example, in defining
the Chief Digital Officers' role, Singh and Hess (2017: 2) distinguish its core
area of responsibility – digital transformation – from the mandates of the
Chief Information Officer, the Chief Data Officer, the Chief Innovation Officer, and the Chief Strategy Officer which they consider 'adjacent C-level
executive positions that might at first glance have similar responsibilities'.

Competition for status and the top job. As Tushman (1977a) affirmed, the
distribution of power and status in organizations is inherently unstable.
The authors of role-centred reports not only discuss a role's evolution and
the needs for new capabilities or expertise, but also construct (and thereby
influence) the significance, status, and standing of a CXO by engaging in
comparisons with other CXO roles and particularly with the top chief, the
CEO. This competition also unfolds in forums provided by professional
associations (i.e. conferences) as well as in the media when CXO roles are
discussed in terms of who they aspire to be.

Whereas the leading role and position of the CEO has thus far remained
essentially unchallenged, the CFO has substantially strengthened its standing in the top team and as a strategic partner of the CEO. Paradoxically,

although the word 'strategy' is in the role's title, the Chief Strategy Officer is rarely considered part of the 'inner circle' of strategizing and 'despite its endurance as a C-suite title, the CSO role is still often treated with suspicion—sometimes bordering on cynicism' (Gartner, 2015: 1): 'Though the CSO role can carry considerable power, the CFO role will usually still outrank it. Our 2013 CEO survey found that CFOs are by far the most important executive the CEO turns to when considering business strategy issues' (Gartner, 2015: 5).

The construction of distinctiveness from and superiority over other CXOs is also visible in this depiction of the 'average CCO' (i.e. Chief Commercial Officer):

> The commercial chief is more academically qualified than the average CSO or CMO, with more than half having a master's degree. They hold senior roles, with 80% on the executive board. The CCO is interested in the big picture, getting their greatest satisfaction from strategic management and being involved in the direction of the company. They keep up with external trends: 71% believe they add value by 'exploiting in-depth knowledge of the market and competition'.
>
> (EY, 2014: 3)

The potential for obtaining the top job is not only a self-perception. Other surveyed members of the C-suite also think 'the CCO is significantly more likely to become CEO within five years than either the sales or marketing chief' (EY, 2014: 6).

Overall, the aspiration for the top job is a prominent aspect of competition dynamics among CXOs on top teams, and involves framing as to why specific CXO roles are the (best) paths to the top (CEO) job (e.g. *Harvard Business Review*'s 2014 article, 'Why Chief Human Resources Officers Make Great CEOs' or the *Wall Street Journal*'s 2014 article, 'CIOs Eye the Corner Office'). A case in point is a Russell Reynolds Associates' article, where the Chief Digital Officer was referred as being 'in the queue for CEO succession' (Grossman and Rich, 2012: 2). Likewise, Spencer Stuart (2015) published a report with the straightforward title 'From Chief Marketing Officer to CEO: The Route to the Top'. The report focused on the barriers to CMOs in getting the top job, explaining these vis-à-vis the CFO as a preferred candidate:

The legacy of the 'silo' corporate structure and the perception of marketing as a cost centre rather than an engine of growth and profitability means that board members and shareholders may feel more comfortable promoting a CFO than a former head of marketing. As one executive explained: 'CFOs are perceived as more pragmatic, with a clear understanding of the financial management of the company.' By contrast, CMOs will have to work hard to ensure that the company doesn't construe them solely as a driving creative force, a trend-changing marketer who is frustrated with financial and other limitations set on them. 'You've got to be seen as a highly commercial individual with a track record of delivering significant growth.'

(Spencer Stuart, 2015: 12)

Similarly, an Egon Zehnder (2016: 7) report provided empirical evidence that in terms of their competence profile, 'outstanding CMOs resemble CEOs', particularly in results' orientation, team leadership, influencing, organizational development, and change management. In a Korn Ferry report, Ulrich and Filler (2014: 8) argued that CEOs and CHROs are 'cut from the same cloth' along dimensions of emotional competencies, demographics, as well as styles of leadership and thinking. Guarino (2016) went even further, producing a report with the title 'Why CHROs Really are CEOs'. Data from a survey of Chief Commercial Officers (EY, 2014: 3) confirm that 'the commercial chief is ambitious: one in three thinks they will be CEO within five years'.

Aspirations for the top job are supported by the previously discussed claims that CXOs' expertise supports value, strategy, and transformation (Chapter 4), closely mimicking that of the CEO. In addition, claims of a role's rising value for the organization support the argument that a given role holds promise for providing a successor to the CEO. This may create further tensions in the already contested C-suite. As examined in Chapter 4, strategy is claimed by and is part of the jurisdiction of a wide variety of CXO roles. While CFOs 'have seen their strategic influence grow over the years' (Accenture, 2014: 50), the best CIOs are 'chief strategists' who 'help define and execute forward-looking business strategies', which 'clears the path for more strategic value' (PricewaterhouseCoopers, 2008: 3). The claimed significant contributions to strategy by multiple CXO roles imply a growing diversity of interests and perspectives involved in strategizing.

However, they can also be interpreted as sources of overlap, competition, and conflict, as well as opportunities for collaboration.

6.3 Collaborating in the C-suite

It is well recognized that inter-unit collaboration is essential for senior managers (Ibarra and Hansen, 2011) and that it involves taking on a collaborative leadership style (Hansen, 2009) as well as cultivating T-shaped capabilities, where the vertical part of the letter T captures the focus on one's area, whereas the horizontal cap of the letter T represents cross-unit work (Hansen and von Oeztinger, 2001). This is even truer for executive committee members. Recently, role-centered reports have emphasized the increasing importance of collaboration between CXOs, and revealed different forms of partnership which are essential to the effective functioning of the top team. First, these reports tend to recognize the significance of dyadic collaboration between the CEO and a specific CXO (with the CEO as a hub), due to a particular area of expertise possessed by the CXO which could support the performance of the CEO's job. In such cases, collaboration is vertical, as there is a power differential between the CXO and the CEO. Second, increasing attention is being given to collaboration among CXOs, both across 'fault lines' (i.e. unintegrated domains that need to be brought together to ensure the enterprise's success) and in contexts involving overlapping 'orbits'. Such forms of collaboration are horizontal when the CXO roles are of similar status, but could also be vertical, as we illustrated in Chapter 2, when some CXOs are N-1 from the CEO, whereas others are N-2 and report to other CXOs. Third, collaboration can be enabled through a CXO role that is either specifically created for the purpose (as we will show below) or forced to bridge different domains due to changes in organizational pressures. We illustrate these three cases of collaboration and briefly touch upon potential challenges and/or implications for the executives involved in such partnerships.

Collaboration between the CEO and CXOs. Reports emphasize the importance of and need for direct collaboration between the CEO and specific CXOs to fulfil a common enterprise-oriented purpose. This collaboration (or partnership, as some sources refer to it) has implications not only for the organization, but also for the CEO and for the relative standing of CXO roles as they compete for status, resources, and not least,

CEO attention. Collaborative relationships consist of individual CXOs reporting to the CEO as a hub, and thus reflect a non-team approach (Katzenbach and Smith, 1993; Katzenbach, 1998), as described earlier in this chapter.

The reports emphasize a number of different CEO–CXO structures and partnerships that have different consequences for the work of the CEO, and complement the role in very different ways. Some roles, such as the CFO and COO (described in detail in Chapter 1), have a long history of collaboration with the CEO, and have traditionally been considered strategic partners and members of the CEO's 'inner circle'. Yet, the contributions of each of these roles to fulfilling the demands of the CEO's job are rather different. For example, Dobbin et al. (2001: abstract) summarized that a 'CEO–COO structure implied a top executive focused on financial strategy with a sidekick focused on operational matters', whereas a 'CEO–CFO structure implied the opposite, a top executive focused on core operational matters and a sidekick focused on financial strategy'. Whereas the COO role and its collaborative relationship with the CEO have weakened, the CFO role and its relationship with the CFO has strengthened: 'the chief of finance has stepped up to become the CEO's partner in making ambitious but rational choices on a wide range of issues. A once-obscure discipline, risk management has squarely hit the executive agenda, and CFOs had better be ready for it' (Groysberg et al., 2011: 64).

In recent years, the relationship between the Chief Human Resources Officer (CHRO) and the CEO has become highly visible. The strategic significance of the CHRO has increased to the point where some have even proposed a so-called G3 structure at the top of the organizational hierarchy (Charan et al., 2015) comprising the CHRO, CEO, and CFO. As we discussed at length in Chapter 4, the CHRO role is an example of an anxious role whose strategic importance and knowledge distinctiveness have been challenged over time; as a result, incumbents are eager to be invited to sit at the so-called 'strategy table'. Their strategic importance seems to be on the rise; for example, Ulrich and Filler (2014: 5) noted that 'CEOs increasingly seek insights from their CHROs to help them succeed'. In a web article by Heidrick and Struggles, a consultancy dedicated to building leadership teams, Rassam (2018) discussed some keys to successful CEO–CHRO partnerships. Specifically, a confident CHRO can add value to an organization in multiple ways, not least as a counsel to the CEO and a master of engagement:

The role of contemporary CHROs continues to evolve as rapidly as the organizations they serve. Strategic partner. Culture leader. Counsel to the CEO. Analytics visionary. Chief engagement officer. CHROs today must be more than functional experts; they must be able to generate business value. And to bring the highest value to the company, they must partner closely with their CEOs.

(Rassam, 2018: no pagination)

Based on interviews as well as their own vast practice in evaluating and recommending CHRO candidates for CEO and other executive positions, Heidrick and Struggles identified three important practices for the success of the CEO–CHRO collaboration, which are so general that they could possibly also be fulfilled by other CXOs: 'be a practical strategist', 'have a perspective—and share it', and 'offer an aerial view of the business' (Rassam, 2018: no pagination). Rassam (2018) also claimed that the partnership between the CHRO and the CEO is unique because:

[As CHRO,] you are in a prime position to advise your CEO on the impact certain decisions will have on employees throughout the organization. You can use your knowledge to engage with the CEO on not only where the business is now but also where it should be in one or multiple business cycles.

(Rassam, 2018: no pagination)

Other roles are also considered important partners for the CEO, but on different grounds. For example, leadership advisory firm Egon Zehnder reported results from a study of German CEOs (Fritton, Fleischmann, and Will, 2011) regarding the significance of corporate communication in and for their work, their participation in wider social debates, and their expectations of Chief Communications and Public Affairs Officers. The CEO's partnership with the Chief Communication Officer (CCO) is described in several different terms, including a characterization of the CCO as the CEO's alter ego. The data show that a typical German CEO expects the CCO to serve not only as a sparring partner, but also as 'a spokesperson, minister of external affairs and adviser'. The partnership with the CCO is also considered valuable for the CEO in terms of the CCO's internal and external networks, which can be 'the basis for reporting moods, trends and emerging issues to the CEO'. Beyond specialist expertise and management and strategic competencies, the CEO–CCO collaboration is based on personal chemistry. The relationship is expected to be a very close one, based on trust.

Collaboration between CXOs. Collaboration between CXOs is discussed in reports particularly with regard to interdependencies between specific roles and their respective areas of responsibility. One commonly discussed collaboration is that between the Chief Marketing Officer (CMO) and the Chief Information Officer (CIO), which we use as an illustration. As summarized in a McKinsey & Company article (Ariker, Harrysson, and Perrey, 2014: 1–2), the interdependence between the two roles involves shared responsibility for growth, and not least, mutual respect for each other's strategic importance:

> CMOs, who are responsible for promoting growth, need the CIOs' help to turn the surfeit of customer data their companies are accumulating into increased revenue. CIOs, obliged to turn new technology into revenue, need the CMOs to help them with better functional and technical requirements for big data initiatives. . . . It may be a marriage of convenience, but it's one that CMOs and CIOs need to make work—especially as worldwide volume of data is growing at least 40 percent a year, with ever-increasing variety and velocity. That's why many CMOs are waking up to the fact that IT can't be treated like a back-office function anymore; rather, the CIO is becoming a strategic partner who is crucial to developing and executing marketing strategy.

Whereas this interdependence may sound obvious, reports also suggest a disconnect between the CIO and CMO:

> Both functions agree on the need for greater collaboration, but further digging reveals a much different picture. Globally, 77% of CIOs agree they need to be aligned with CMOs, whereas only 56% of CMOs feel this way about CIOs . . . CMOs are beginning to see alternative ways to buy technology capabilities wrapped by services, such as partnering with outside vendors rather than with the CIO.
>
> (Accenture Interactive, 2013: 4)

Working together more does not necessarily involve working better together; for example, Ariker et al. (2014) noted that 'tensions may arise about the CMO's and CIO's decision rights and budget authority'. The nature of the interdependence and existing disconnects requires clarifying resources and responsibilities, as well as partnering beyond exchanges of information and working closely to achieve a common outcome, as Baird and Ban's (2012: 15) data seem to suggest:

> The overriding characteristic of successful CMO/CIO relationships is their unwavering commitment to collaborate for the common good, as well as their own benefit. It is important to note that the pairs we interviewed do not view collaboration simply as an information exchange. Each pair is invested in rolling up their sleeves and working together with shared responsibility for the outcome.

An IBM study (Baird and Ban, 2012: 3) confirmed the importance of common goals for the success of the CMO–CIO partnership: 'CMOs and CIOs need to rely on one another to meet these common goals, rather than pursuing their own charters independently within legacy silos generated by corporate culture or organizational barriers.'

The reports also tend to offer advice as to how inter-role collaborations could be improved, some of which involves changed mind-sets, improved partnering capabilities, better awareness of the work of the other, and not least 'a frank discussion about the CMO–CIO relationship and how to strengthen and sustain it' (Ariker et al., 2014: 7). One potential obstacle could be the lack of a shared vocabulary that enables a shared understanding of what is expected (Ariker et al., 2014). In addition, as in the example below, shared leadership is expected to be motivated by having shared accountability for performance improvements:

> It's easy to say that the CMO and CIO, and sometimes the CTO, should share leadership of the overall analytics effort and a mutual definition of its success. But that agreement needs to be followed quickly by the next stage: having shared accountability for business-performance improvement based on specific key performance indicators such as revenue generation, usage, and retention.
>
> (Ariker et al., 2014: 4)

The need for collaboration is also discussed in reference to other role combinations, such as the Chief Supply Chain Management Officer's ability to partner with the CIO to ensure better interactions with customers and suppliers (Groysberg et al., 2011). Another partnership that is considered 'natural' and needs to be fostered is between the CHRO and the Chief Digital Officer. Their collaboration involves getting 'CHROs, who are focused on the employee experience, and CDOs, who are more invested in the customer experience, to embrace the symbiotic relationship between their goals and work together for the common good', which is to serve the organization's digital transformation and, in particular, the 'cultural and talent implications of digitizing legacy processes' (Zielinsky, 2019). Taken together, these multiple dyadic and triadic interdependences and partnerships suggest much more connected and collaborative top teams than ever before.

Collaboration among CXOs, as well as between functions and divisions across the entire organization sometimes requires the involvement of another CXO (aside from the CEO) as an integrator of other roles that may have difficulties engaging in direct collaboration. Some have come to suggest that functioning as such an integrator requires both dedicated effort and a proper title, for example Chief Collaboration Officer, and that a range of roles (e.g., CHRO, CSO, Chief Information Officer, CFO, COO) are all suitable bridges for cross-CXO collaboration (Hansen and Tapp, 2010).

Below, we further illustrate this integration work with some examples. The quote below, for instance, points to the CIO role in leading cross-functional collaboration:

Barriers between functions and divisions need to be dismantled—along with many of their systems, processes and norms—to enable groups that have not encountered each other to work together towards a common goal, exploring new solutions and learning from each other. . . . In many of the most successful, agile organisations, there is a shift away from highly formalised structures and towards more informal, flatter networks, where 'teams of teams' are encouraged to iterate, come up with ideas and solutions and then share what they learn across the entire organisation. CIOs are in a unique position when it comes to leading cross-functional collaboration and, while they're at it, increasing their influence in the business.

(Spencer Stuart, 2018a: 3)

Furthermore, a 2014 Accenture Interactive report on the CMO-CIO divide suggests the creation of a specific CXO role that is able to bring together the CMO and the CIO. The report qualifies this new role and its bridging function:

> In fact, there is a strong argument for going further and creating a new position at the top level of businesses: a Chief Experience Officer (CeXO). This executive would be charged with facilitating greater collaboration and integration between the marketing and IT functions, and driving relevant customer experiences across all channels and touch points.
>
> (Accenture Interactive, 2014: 1)

It also explains how this bridging function is fulfilled by leveraging knowledge across marketing and IT as essential functions.

> At the same time, the CeXO could leverage the knowledge held by marketing and IT, as well as their own expertise and strategies, to take a human-centred approach to designing customer experiences. The CeXO could act as adjudicator in difficult areas that bridge IT and marketing.
>
> (Accenture Interactive, 2014: 3)

Not all occupants of CXO roles see relationships with other C-level executives as relevant. For example, an Accenture (2014: 7) study reported that more than half of Chief Digital Officers 'see no need to focus on integration between the Marketing and IT functions', and 'are consistently less likely than their colleagues to see relationships with other C-level individuals and departments as important to their business priorities and strategic objectives'. This could be explained by the new approaches this role brings to the digital transformation of businesses.

Overall, however, in the words of an executive recruiter, 'the C-level person today needs to be more team-oriented, capable of multitasking continuously and leading without rank, and able to resist stress and make sure that . . . subordinates do not burn out' (quoted in Groysberg et al., 2011: 68). This team orientation is perhaps more easily wished for than achieved, in terms of both the demands imposed on executives' individual competences and the steering of their team-based interaction by the CEO.

As stated earlier in the chapter, we have distinguished CXO interactions in terms of competition and collaboration for analytical purposes. In practice, competitive and collaborative dynamics are closely intertwined and ambiguous, posing challenges to making the C-suite work as a (top) team. They also go beyond dyadic interactions to constitute a much more interconnected C-suite. Yet, as we also discussed in the introduction, increasing pressures call for a new configuration and operational paradigm at the top, which demands new roles and competences for CXOs, as well as for the CEO as chief designer and orchestrator of the top team.

6.4 The changing C-suite model

As we discussed in Chapter 4, a shared vocabulary of executive expertise revealed in role-centred reports produced by consultancies and executive search firms is used to make claims about CXOs' organizational contributions in terms of value creation, business strategy, and transformation. At the field level, this shared vocabulary of expertise creates a basis for constructing CXO roles into a distinctive category of 'executive roles'. At the organizational level, it may be interpreted as a more distributed form of collective leadership (Denis et al., 2001) or of multiple leadership whereby power in organizations driven by multiple goals is 'shared by two or three groups to the extent that no one is able to control all or most of the actions of the others' (Perrow, 1961: 861). However, as revealed in the previous sections, in these role-centred reports, references to the C-suite's 'teamness' and collaboration among a variety of CXOs are less frequent than mentions of specific dyadic collaborations between roles. In addition, there are references to division and competition (e.g., for resources, status, and CEO attention) among CXOs due to overlapping or inter-related arenas of attention and respective domains of expertise. This, we argue, creates an opportunity for the CEO, as chief strategist and chief designer of role games, to exercise even greater control over the organization's strategic direction; control that is fashioned to their style and preferences, as we noted in the overview of top teams at the outset of this chapter.

However, in recent years, the evolution of the overall C-suite configuration has drawn the attention of several consultancies and executive search firms. They have pointed out that the current C-suite structure and model of operation are outdated and due for reinvention. For example, an EY Performance article posed the question 'New change, new roles, new C-suite?' (Driggs and Strier, 2014), arguing for new roles and a new leadership model, as well as new capabilities that involve the 'ability to lead into the future'. The authors also lamented that certain aspects of executive boards, such as the universal outnumbering of women on top teams, 'are proving stubbornly resistant to change' (Driggs and Strier, 2014: 31).

In a Deloitte Insights article, Kelly (2014b) discussed the nature of the C-suite 1.0 and 2.0, and questioned whether the time is ripe for a C-suite 3.0:

> If the 1.0 era is now easy to dismiss as 'command and control', it might be time to also fault the 2.0 C-suite's tendency to 'divide and conquer'. It has created challenges of alignment and coherence, as different forms of functional expertise—and their associated worldviews, priorities, and language systems—have been brought together at the cost of the natural integration once provided by a small team of general managers. . . . The need for greater coherence and alignment across multiple geographies and functions is matched by the need for agility, adaptation, 'localiza-tion', openness, and fast learning. C-suite 3.0 should address both—and master the inevitably growing tensions this balancing act will create.
>
> (Kelly, 2014b: 115–16)

Relatedly, in an article published as part of EY's CEO Imperative series, de Yonge (2019: 1) suggested a need 'to take a hard look at the structure of the C-suite and how it operates', as the C-suite model does not fit current—and more importantly, future—demands. De Yonge (2019) posed a number of important questions that should be asked when rethinking C-suite config-urations, particularly with regard to implementing policies and structures that enable agility, ensuring that input from a broader set of stakehold-ers is included into corporate decision-making, and just as importantly, considering the demands of the future, arguing:

> CEOs can no longer rely on the old excuses to remain on the sidelines of global challenges, such as income inequality, the ethics of AI, cyberse-curity, and climate change. Nor must they ask permission to be at the forefront of solutions—it's an expectation and a new growth imperative.
>
> (De Yonge, 2019: 1)

When asked about their views on the suitability of the C-suite to address these global challenges, the majority of 200 global CEOs responded that the C-suite needs to be transformed. Different sources confirm that solutions to new challenges have been 'patchy', mostly involving adding new CXO titles to the C-suite to address arising new arenas or problem domains; however, these new C-suite members do not automatically 'jell' into the top team, necessitating special intervention from the CEO and the other C-suite executives. For example, Lahiri, Schwartz, and Volini (2018) called for a 'symphonic C-suite', that is, 'team leading teams', as 'the next stage in the ongoing evolution of leadership models', using the visual imagery of orchestras. (It should be noted, though, that ideas connecting leadership, teams, and orchestras have had a much longer trajectory; e.g. see Hackman, 2002 for a framework.) They argued that executive roles:

> must collaborate in what we call the 'symphonic C-suite', in which an organisation's top executives play together interdependently as a team while also leading their own functional teams. This approach enables the C-suite to understand the many impacts that external forces have on and within the organisation—not just on single functions—and plot co-ordinated, agile responses.
>
> (Lahiri et al., 2018: 25)

In a survey of executives in South African C-suites, 39 per cent of respondents reported that 'CXOs manage their functions independently but collaborate to share ideas or troubleshoot problems as part of their organisation's C-suite leadership', whereas 28 per cent of respondents 'regularly collaborate on long term interdependent work' (Lahiri et al., 2018: 25, 26).

Overall, such proposals highlight the need for and importance of further articulating visions of and experimenting with what executive power structures, the CEO's role, and executive expertise in general could become in a context of significant global challenges. Pointing in that direction, De Yonge (2019) affirmed:

> Reassessing the C-suite must go beyond roles and responsibilities and consider more fundamental issues of hierarchy, agility and organizational silos. The C-suite structure must reflect a point of view on possible futures, including global challenges, megatrends and disruptive innovation.
>
> (De Yonge, 2019: 21)

Such developments suggest the importance of opening up executive power design to an ever demanding, yet exciting new phase of working with possible futures. For example, the role of Microsoft's first Chief Environmental Officer is at the nexus of environmental issues and technology, integrating perspectives on distant futures with executive attention to complexity in the institutional arena (i.e. responding to stakeholder pressure with regard to climate responsiveness) and perspectives on near futures regarding the dynamic information arena (i.e. implementing new solutions based on artificial intelligence). Conceiving, theorizing, and empirically investigating top management teams and their dynamics as *a nexus of possible futures* opens up a new research agenda requiring new theoretical lenses to bridge extant psychological insights on executives' temporal dispositions and temporal leadership (Mohammed and Nadkarni, 2014; Chen and Nadkarni, 2017) with insights from scenario planning (Scoblic, 2020) and more recent inter-temporal approaches to sustained and sustainable organization and strategy (Bansal and DesJardine, 2014; Schultz and Hernes, 2020).

6.5 Conclusion

We began this chapter by showing how diverse carriers of practices across top teams, such as consulting and executive search firms, are increasingly expressing concerns about the inadequacy of the top team model and calling for a new structure that is more integrated and horizontally coordinated in the pursuit of shared goals and collective outcomes. We also recognized the unique role of the CEO as a chief designer and sensegiver who shapes individual CXO roles and the C-suite model as a whole (Gioia and Chittipeddi, 1991; Maitlis and Sonenshein, 2010) by framing and transforming elements of organizational experience, aspirations, and concerns into a focus of attention for executive action (Smircich and Morgan, 1982). In that, we noted that the top team is a very important structure for CEOs that helps them overcome loneliness at the top and can morph depending on their individual style and preferences due to a lack of strong institutional prescriptions.

In addition, we noted the importance of 'teamness' among CXOs, and areas of competition and collaboration. Although a radically new C-suite model has yet to emerge, what is visible in the field is an overall consensus among theorizers of CXO roles that simply expanding the C-suite by adding new CXO roles is an inadequate response to ever-changing organizational pressures and evolving complexity arenas, especially as these need to be prioritized or aligned. Widespread experimentation with new formats by both theorizers of C-suite practices and organizational actors themselves seems to suggest a more open model of top teams, a 'multi-stakeholder suite' with a 'rotational' CEO, as the following quote from an EY report illustrates:

> 'It can no longer be just about the CEO,' Mohapatra says. 'Boards are going to get more and more involved in talking to investors, and with the CEO and the management. As a result, the C-suite is going to become at a minimum a hybrid C-and-B-suite. But eventually it will become a multi-stakeholder suite where the investor has a say, the customer has a say, along with the board and CEO. You may have a rotational CEO.
>
> (de Yonge, 2019: 5)

Such changes will have implications for how CEOs manage their collaboration with CXOs, suggesting a shift away from a hub-and-spoke model, with the CEO as the hub, to a much more dynamic executive constellation. The changes are also expected to have implications for executive expertise. As we discussed in previous chapters, given the proliferation of chief officer roles and the latitude in their tasks, they do not fit clearly into well-differentiated organizational top slots. Rather, as noted in this chapter in Section 6.2 on competition, CXOs may have overlapping areas of responsibility and thereby compete to serve a specific domain of organizational attention. At the same time, the nature of work at the top demands 'collective judgement', which stems from horizontal integration and close collaboration among CXOs. Examining the nature and sources of this inter-role contestation and the consequent needs for conflict resolution and coordination enables a better understanding of how power structures are designed within organizations as dynamic and collective responses to institutional complexity and multiple logics in operation.

7
Executive Power in Transformation

In previous chapters, we used the most relevant theoretical lenses available to describe and explain the expansion of CXO roles, a phenomenon that is transforming the composition and functioning of senior management teams, or the 'government' of organizations. As is the case with many social and organizational changes, those affecting the structure, composition, and processes of senior management teams are not the uniform consequence of a solitary, forceful factor, and cannot be fully explained by a single theory. The simultaneous self-reinforcing macro, mezzo, and micro dynamics of such changes must be considered to comprehend a phenomenon like this one, as, for example, Abbott (1988) did in his influential work on professions. The need to consider a theory of personality and other micro foundations to develop upon them mezzo or macro propositions is also illustrated by Talcott Parsons in his general theory of action, and more recently, by Fligstein and McAdam (2012a, 2012b) in their theory of fields as well as by Thornton et al. (2012) in their institutional logics perspective. However, not all theories are equally relevant to this particular phenomenon.

In this concluding chapter, we review the principal distinctions of CXOs as an executive role category, evaluate the efficacy of different theoretical explanations, identify the contributions of this work to those theories, and reflect on the appeal, success, and limits of the CXO label. We also tease out *why* the CXO phenomenon appeared and became so widespread and (thus far) not much objected; *what* its essential nature is, both as a category and as a professionalization project; *where* CXOs operate, both in and between organizations; *how* they operate, in terms of the distinct tasks they perform and behaviours they exhibit; and *who* CXOs are, from an executive identity perspective. We argue that studying the spread of executive roles favours a better understanding of the importance of roles in re-shaping executive power for organizational adaptation and of the role of the CEO, the quintessential chief officer, and thereby, the essence of what it means to be

The Changing C-Suite. José Luis Alvarez and Silviya Svejenova, Oxford University Press.
© José Luis Alvarez and Silviya Svejenova (2022). DOI: 10.1093/oso/9780198728429.003.0007

an executive. We conclude by proposing the ideal type of contemporary executives in complex organizations.

7.1 Categorizing executive roles

We argued in Chapter 3 that a robust way to categorize senior executives' roles is to think of them as responses to environmental complexities, which warrants applying contingency theory in combination with other perspectives, such as neo-institutional theory. Although these two theories are quite different—the former is functionalist, the latter is not—both adopt an open systems perspective on organizations, which is also the fundamental assumption behind political studies of organizations (Weber and Waeger, 2017).

Some CXOs, especially new and hybrid roles such as the Chief Platform Officer and the Chief Marketing Technology Officer, which typically are N-2s and not members of the top executive committee, are difficult to pin to one single cluster because they are specifically designed to aid organizational integration by bridging different groups. Nevertheless, most of the CXOs discussed in this book can be classified into role clusters based on the four categories (institutional, information, primary task, and administration) presented in Table 3.3 in Chapter 3.

Because the institutional cluster is particularly revealing with regard to how organizations react to meaningful increases in environmental complexity, we summarize it in a bit more detail than we do for the others. Moreover, together with the information group, the institutional cluster is where a number of highly relevant innovations are emerging at this time. Overall, the dynamics of novelties within this clique of roles, which could also be labelled the 'legitimacy' cluster, can be explained by combining the structural design focus of contingency theory with the legitimacy and diffusion foci of neo-institutionalism.

We identified institutional complexity as stemming from demands on organizations related to their alignment with societal value systems. Some of these requirements are so fundamental that they are inscribed in the law. Without satisfying the most fundamental of them, the very right to legal organizational actorhood does not exist. In his hierarchy of organizational structures, Parsons (1956a, 1956b) placed the institutional system above the managerial layer, which in turn sits above the technical system. Adding to the requirement of being a subordinate entity within the higher order societal system, companies also need to be publicly accountable for their activities; for instance, being perceived as acting responsibly and transparently (Power, 1997) on a fast-growing list of issues: for example diversity, climate change, gender equality, social justice, and recently even political speech and voting laws. An example is corporate reactions to climate change, arguably the most enduring and intense of the currently emerging legitimacy contingencies. Reflecting on this particular new reality, Sir Christopher Hohn, director of the activist hedge fund TCI, was recently quoted in the *Financial Times* as saying, 'investing in a company that doesn't disclose its pollution is like investing in a company that doesn't disclose its balance sheet' (Thompson, 2020). Investors, non-finance activists, and other constituents are pushing for more corporate transparency and initiatives on climate change, resulting in a proliferation of Chief Sustainability Officers and related positions. A quite recent and telling novelty is the rise of the Chief Climate Change Officer role, appearing first in organizations such as the Inter-American Development Bank, that because of type of ownership, purpose, etc., are intensely affected by public opinion, and afterwards expanding to all types of firms. In the United States, incumbents in this new role have already launched the Association of Climate Change Officers (ACCO), which issues credentials, offers courses, organizes events, etc., quite similarly to what other CXO 'communities of practice' do. Chief Digital Officers are some of the most active in this regard.

As these examples illustrate, new external contingencies prompt firms to respond with new specialized and differentiated units and roles. In turn, incumbents engage with the customary panoply of initiatives to further their own identity, legitimation, expansion, field control, and institutionalization. The CXO industry, discussed in Chapter 2, helps actively in this endeavor. New roles in this cluster often take on the CXO mantle, particularly in situations involving executive turnover. For instance, in early 2021, L'Oreal's Executive Vice-president of Communication and Public Affairs left the company and was replaced by a Chief Communication and Public Affairs Officer (L'Oréal press release, 2021). Yet not all institutional top roles are CXOs. A case in point from the same period is Facebook, who had a Vice President of Civil Rights, a role that could have easily adopted a CXO title.

Similar to doubts about the ultimate identification of personnel managers—whether they are more committed to the values and interests of employees than to those of managers or owners (Watson, 1977; Foulkes, 2015)—it is interesting to question whether the leaders of emergent legitimacy units are more identified with their companies or with external constituencies, and whether they are unabated activists, a sort of 'fifth column', or, using the term popularized by Meyerson and Scully (1995), just 'tempered' radicals—that is, co-opted social actors. Weber and Waeger (2017) highlighted these potentially conflicting loyalties as a fruitful avenue for research in political theories of organizations. Although this must be investigated on a case-by-case basis, it seems reasonable to tentatively entertain the possibility that executives in the institutional cluster would have an overriding external loyalty, that their 'outsiderness' is stronger than their 'insiderness', to use Nigam, Sackett, and Golden's (2021) terms.

Overall, the roles addressing institutional complexity seek to facilitate organizational legitimacy in the face of continuously evolving, conflicting, and intertwined societal demands and institutional pressures. They are all specialized engagement executives. In fact, the Chief Engagement Officer is another role on the rise, one with a wide and varying contingent focus, sometimes vis-à-vis employees, and other times vis-à-vis external constituencies. A similarly ample or general role is the Chief Stakeholder Officer, as at The Leonardo Group, an Italy-based global high-tech company in the Aerospace, Defence and Security sectors (Leonardo, 2018). When a constituency is especially relevant, a fully focused role is created, such as Ford's Chief Government Relations Officer (Ford press release, 18 February 2019).

The current intensity of institutional complexities is exacerbated by the increased scrutiny and coverage of corporate moves by the media, as was advanced in Chapter 2. The need to proactively and promptly address the media's interpretations of what constitutes legitimate and reputable organizational behaviour has given rise to a range of roles, some of which are already quite well established, such as Chief Communications, Reputation, and Public Relations or Public Affairs Officers. These roles are expected to provide a rapid and coordinated response in the event of a conflict, crisis, or act of organizational or managerial misconduct. A most recent and rather interesting role, the Chief Resilience Officer, adopted by cities ranging from Paris to Miami Beach, is intended to help municipalities react to crises, and in all likelihood, to protect city leaders from the consequences of unforeseen events. In this way, they function as guardians of organizational image and legitimacy, portraying and conveying the 'virtues' of their organizations and leaders to the media and relevant constituents in order to pre-empt crises or to prevent these from causing irreparable harm, whether reputational or financial. At the same time, they offer the CEO options for responsiveness through, for example, the public scapegoating of designated chiefs in cases of malpractice and misconduct (Power, 2007).

Given the surge of new institutional 'necessities' for organizations, such as addressing climate change, another interesting research question has arisen on whether companies' policies on this subject are really substantial or just symbolic. This interrogation in fact has a long tradition in the new institutional school, as discussed in Chapter 5, and we can venture that there seems to be quite a non-surprising amount of what is being called 'greenwashing' and developing a 'glorified marketing position' (Talman, 2020), 'cheap talk' (Whittington and Yakis-Douglas, 2020), and more generally, 'window dressing' (Kanashivo and Rivera, 2019) or 'lip service'. Merely symbolic responses, or to put it in fashionable parlance, 'non-authentic' reactions to new growing pressures, are much more easily found, of course, in domains of activity that are difficult to measure quantitatively, or for which metrics are still not fully developed and proven, such as those related to environmental issues and institutional contingencies in general.

Rhetorical adaptation may be accompanied by 'co-optation', a process well studied in classic sociology, whereby activists in the external environment are internalized within the organization—that is, as full-time employees. Activists profit from the material advantages of being under a corporate umbrella, and provide legitimacy and social peace in exchange. These are the actors with dubious loyalty referred to a few lines earlier. Interestingly, further supporting the symbolic argument to explain the spread of these roles, Fu, Tang, and Chen (2020) showed how roles highly prone to symbolism, such as the Chief Sustainability Officer, do not bolster corporate social responsibility much, and that on senior teams, rather than 'doing more good', at most they do 'less bad'.

Role proliferation in the institutional cluster has left incumbents jostling for intra-cluster space and struggling to impose their areas of responsibility—a phenomenon common to all organizational clusters, as well as to occupations and professions of all sectors. The demarcations between roles do not correspond to neat boundaries between differentiated and well-hierarchized knowledge spaces, but rather are the result of struggles for hegemony over a field of practice. For instance, the specific differences between the already established Chief Sustainability Officer and the up-and-coming Chief Climate Change Officer role cannot be determined *a priori*, or just by paying attention to labels or what one might imagine to be standard content.

Contingency theory effectively accounts for the expansion of this cluster, in that a more changing and varied environment prompts new specializations in units and leading roles. Corporate incursions on issues such as race, migration, and even politics (e.g. Twitter cancelling Trump's account in the last days of his presidency) which signal the decline of nation-states and the public common domain as well as the strengthening of corporations and individual actors, create a need for specialization within firms. This sparks an organizational design challenge with regard to how to set up a structure that effectively integrates the growing number of differentiated departments with diverse foci of attention, each with its own CXO serving as a unit head. Empirical studies have shown that a small and stable group of senior executives, that is, the core management team, tends to be involved in all decisions and is supported by members of a dynamic periphery who contribute selectively to specific issues (Roberto, 2003). The most important team integration device available to companies is the CEO's executive committee, where CXO members should, ideally, act in the best interest of the entire organization, and not as advocates of their own units (Roberto, 2005). Of course, in turn, the integrator of the executive committee is the CEO.

If contingency theory explains how organizations adapt to the environment via structures, institutional theory—with its emphasis on legitimacy—contributes to an understanding of the activities performed by the new roles in this cluster. Moreover, institutional arguments that emphasize diffusion help explain the success of these new roles.

The increasing variety of roles in the second grouping, the information cluster, can be explained by the increasing significance and number of Information and Communication Technologies (ICTs) in servicing the primary tasks of organizations. Digitalization, artificial intelligence, data, 3-D, robotics, and other proliferating, ongoing innovations make competitive environments more uncertain as, despite an abundance of data and information, there is little clarity regarding the implications of such information for competitiveness. Rapid innovation also decreases stability, as the accelerated speed of change leads to more dynamic fields with shorter lifespans. The range of new technologies and their relatively short shelf lives spark a structural reaction through the creation of new internal units and their corresponding leadership roles, as well as wide variations in nomenclature. Widespread experimentation ensues, and if successful, roles are imitated by other organizations as they grapple with technological uncertainty. An example of the rapid emergence of roles in this clique, as well as of a predictable short life, is the 'Chief Remote Officer', created to help companies organize widespread teleworking as a result of the Covid-19 epidemic (*The Economist*, 30 January 2021: 53–4). Whereas the evolution of the information cluster exhibits the expected contingency dynamics, the spread of labels follows the mimicking waves suggested by neo-institutionalists, in a pattern quite similar to that for the institutional cluster. That both clusters are spiking in growth and impact at about the same time is one of the reasons for the current transformation of executive structures at the top.

The primary task cluster, which consists of traditional functions (e.g., R&D, marketing, operations) that predate other clusters and roles, as well as of some newer ones related directly to product and service offerings (e.g., design, procurement, customer service), can also be explained by the contingency perspective on how organizations deal with complexity. Increased complexity in products or services and market competition necessitate increased differentiation in units. Traditionally, these departments were led by managers bearing director or vice-president titles. Given the success of the CEO title and early CXO manifestations (the COO and CFO), organizations began to adopt the Chief Officer title for traditional functions. The Chief Marketing Officer was one of the first of these new CXO titles to be adopted in the 1990s (Fleit, 2017). It could be argued that the Chief Marketing Officer label and other chief function officers spread through imitation, rather than for performance reasons. Interestingly, the presence of Chief Marketing Officers on executive committees has sparked an interesting debate, pitting scholars arguing that the role does not impact positively the bottom line (Nath and Mahajan, 2008, 2011) against others trying to prove the opposite (Germann, Ebbes, and Grewal, 2015.)

The primary cluster also offers examples of N-2 role proliferation. For instance, increased differentiation within the marketing function has spawned a range of roles, such as Chief Branding, Customer, and Product Officers. Sometimes these roles are like matryoshkas dolls in terms of specialization: some companies such as Mastercard have Chief Experience Officers, whereas other companies, such as MCC Insurance, have Chief Customer Experience Officers. Intra-role fission is not incompatible with overall expansion attempts by the cluster itself. The following quote from a Heidrick and Struggles report titled 'The Evolved Chief Marketing Officer' (Pattek, Moorehead, and Abele, 2016: 1) captures how expanding marketing roles may lead to inter-role conflict: 'Winning in the age of the customer requires a fundamental reset of a company's operating model. Evolved CMOs [Chief Marketing Officers] are championing and taking on the challenges of culture and talent management, process redesign, and data and business technology realignment.'

Beyond the ambitions of individual leaders, role 'expansionism', or in some instances, even role 'imperialism', is facilitated by the very tasks performed by senior executives when sitting on executive committees. As explained in Chapter 6, N-1s' duties are twofold: they are dedicated full-time to their units (i.e. a differentiation task) and simultaneously serve part-time for a few hours per week (typically, early in the week) as members of the highest organizational team, where they are expected to act not as representatives of their units, but as senior executives with the purview of and responsibility for the entire organization (i.e. an integration task). Nevertheless, their very membership on the senior team, and the cross-functional perspective it brings, provides them with information on other parts of the organization. If opportunities arise, they can use this information to claim rights to more organizational territory.

The administration cluster reveals dynamics similar to those of the primary task group. As the former is comprised mostly of shared services, it is ancillary to the later. In the 1990s, personnel directors were re-labelled Chief Human Resources Officers in an effort to stress that employees ought to be deemed strategic assets. More recently, aligned with the evolution of the motivations linking employees to their organizations, the human resources lead role has either adopted a label denoting a less instrumental notion of personnel, such as Chief People Officer, or undergone a cladogenesis, whereby the role has been divided amongst a number of N-2 specialties (e.g., Chief Talent Officer, Chief Learning Officer, Chief Culture Officer, Chief Leadership Officer, etc.)

The administration cluster contains a range of additional roles that are important for the operation of an enterprise, such as Chief Administrative Officer and Chief Accounting Officer. Because roles in this cluster provide support to those engaged in the primary task, they do not directly add easy-to-identify value to products or services, and thus are most often situated at lower levels of the organizational hierarchy, predominantly at N-2 from the CEO. Because their roles differ from N-1 roles and from those of direct relevance to addressing institutional and informational complexity, executives who are responsible for these more fragile functions, such as human resources and strategy, may experience the role anxiety described in Chapter 4.

Finally, although they do not constitute a proper cluster, the original CXO roles (i.e., CEO, COO, CFO) remain those which other CXO roles seek to emulate. Notably, the CFO remains the most powerful N-1 role, a true *primus inter pares*, and should be considered apart from the administrative cluster. Without exception, CFOs are members of executive committees, and when boards of listed companies include internal executives besides the CEO, the CFO is among them (Tricker, 2015). In fact, CFOs are ten times more likely to be board members than other CXOs. An article in the 'CFO Journal' section of the *Wall Street Journal* on 20 March 2020 titled 'Boards are Likely to Review Temporary Succession Plan Amid Pandemic' stated that, in the event of a sudden unplanned need to replace the CEO, the CFO is the person best positioned to do so, because the individual in that role has the best and most comprehensive understanding of a firm's complex inner workings. So close CFOs are to CEOs, that even psychological complementarity between the incumbents of the two roles raises the chances of successful mergers and acquisitions (Chen and Shi, 2019).

The main lenses we set out to use at the beginning of this study have proven useful. As a mezzo-level theory, contingency theory enables us to understand the designs of organizational structures that arise in response to complexity. As a macro- or field-level theory, neo-institutionalism enables us to comprehend symbolic reasons for role adoption, as well as the content legitimating an increasing number of roles. Although we do not contribute to the refinement of these theories, we propose that senior teams, because of their power and integrative function, constitute a particularly productive yet underexplored site for their continuous development.

A particular point about neo-institutional theory is that our study offers additional confirmation of the two-step explanation of the adoption of new organizational practices offered early on by Tolbert and Zucker (1983). Specifically, the adoption of new practices by organizations is initially driven by functional needs, whereas fads and fashions increase velocity and reach, thereby contributing to the spread of a practice (in this case, units, roles, and labels) during a second phase. A new label or role structure may not add value to a firm, and may even be irrelevant or absurd but, in a competitive field, it will not survive for long if it detracts substantially from performance or puts an organization's continuity at risk. Because companies operate with a degree of slack (Katz and Khan, 1978), non-value-adding structures, processes, and roles may be present in corporations with the economic capacity to subsidize them. The organizational stupidity described by Alvesson and Spicer (2016) may persist because such organizations can afford it; those who cannot afford it simply do not survive. Of course, in areas of activity where competitiveness and adaptation are less disciplining or punished, such as the public sector, there is even more room for non-value-added management fads and trends. Revealingly, the public sector is precisely the setting in which many neo-institutionalists have performed a good deal of their empirical work, which probably explains the school's emphases on mimetic dynamics. In summary, the spread of isomorphism posed by neo-institutional scholars does not contradict Ross Ashby's 'only variety absorbs variety' law underlying contingency theory. The capacity to adopt fads and fashions is limited, and for-profit organizations in particular have a built-in reality check in the form of the bottom line and its consequences for managers' careers, as well as for their material incentives indexed to results.

7.2 Contesting expertise

A fascinating aspect of the phenomenon we are studying is the competition between clusters, or even intra-cluster units of expertise, for the limited number of positions available on TMTs, particularly the executive committee. Limits on the size of executive committees stem from group dynamics, by which, beyond a certain number of members, process costs exceed the benefits brought by the team. Whereas expertise benefits drive team expansion, group dynamics constrain it, and the limit is already being reached for most extant executive teams. The very existence of this inter-specialization competition aligns with the basic tenet of political theories of organizations, which conceives of organizations as bundles of collectives engaged in ongoing friction as they opportunistically strive to gain autonomy, secure incentives, control organizational activities, set priorities, and remain in influential positions (Heinze and Weber, 2016; Weber and Waeger, 2017). It is no coincidence that the two main stylistic features of CXOs—which we propose are networking skills and political savvy—fit well the behaviour required for executives in non-unitary systems.

The degree of formalization and abstraction of the knowledge on which these differentiated units rely is the key to predicting which ones are more likely to emerge triumphant. To understand the nature of the communities of practice based on specialized business knowledge within both non-profit and not-for-profit organizations, we need to distinguish between 'occupations' and 'professions'. Anteby, Chan, and DiBenigno (2016) affirmed that a scholarly reappraisal of occupations and professions in the workplace is overdue. The C-suite, with the proliferation of occupations, competition among them, and their continuous adjustment to substantive and symbolic demands, is a splendid setting for rekindling that research.

Professions are based on formal knowledge. Access to praxis is regulated by the state. Professional practice must follow protocols that serve as reference points for performance evaluations, and compliance is enforced by fellow members of the profession (i.e. leaders of professional associations) or members of ethics committees, not by clients. The basis for remuneration is knowledge, not production levels. An interesting aspect of professions is that they often require a solemn declaration of purpose. Some of these covenants have religious origins or are born out of an explicit commitment to some public good. In contrast, efforts thus far to inject moral motives into business accreditations to further the professionalization of management—for example the Hippocratic oath for MBAs upon graduation promoted by Khurana and Nohria (2008)—have not been successful. How is it feasible to professionalize leadership, entrepreneurship, innovation, boundary-spanning, and even strategizing? What would an executive 'calling' be, exactly? (see Byrkjeflot and Nygaard, 2018, for a thorough review of the sceptical arguments about the professionalization of management). The very curricula of the most prestigious MBA programmes are based on the assumption, stated or implicit, that management is neither a science nor a profession, as the more academic aspects of economics and business are covered by undergraduate studies, whereas MBA curricula are mostly aimed at the transmission of working knowledge. Significantly, MBA programmes are open to candidates from all undergraduate disciplines, which is an implicit recognition that the knowledge imparted in these programmes does not require, and does not build on, any specific formal knowledge foundation provided by undergraduate studies.

There is an exception, though. Studies in the sociology of professions tend to single out one particular management function as a profession: accounting. Yet, accounting is only a profession when exercised by accredited accountants working for tax and auditing professional services firms. That is, executives in the accounting or internal auditing departments of private or listed companies are not accounting professionals in the strict sense of the term. Chief Accounting Officers are no more 'professionals' than Chief Marketing Officers, although they may need to comply with more state-issued regulations or even with the norms of international organizations like the EU on topics such as data protection (Data Protection Officers specialize in these norms) or combatting money laundering. There is, however, some professionalization of accountancy in the area of corporate governance, as there is increasing pressure to require audit committee members to possess accredited formal accounting knowledge, experience, and certification, as they are obligated to endorse the financial and tax statements of firms, along with CEOs and CFOs, with legal consequences in the event of misinformation, ineptitude, etc.

Senior executive roles, whether in businesses or non-profit organizations, are just occupations. In action, managers apply working knowledge, not formal, codified knowledge (Whitley, 1989). At most, we may call management a 'weak profession' (Fligstein and McAdam, 2012b), an 'occupational profession' (Freidson, 1986), an 'expertise' (Eyal, 2013), an 'occupational order' or 'skilled occupation' (Bechky, 2020), or a 'semi-profession' (Kellogg, 2019). Nonetheless, although management is not a full-fledged profession, concepts and arguments drawn from the sociology of professions are helpful for analysing the competition between new and traditional managerial specializations over seats at the executive committee table. Managers develop a jousting instinct to establish dominance and erect confines around their tasks and units, much like 'strong' professionals. Scholars have baptized this sort of behaviour as a 'corporatist guild mood' (White, 1992: 224), an 'upward mobility project' (Armstrong, 1985: 132), a project aimed at closing a slice of the labour market (Larson, 1977), and an attempt to establish 'occupational cartels' (Freidson, 1986: 63). In the pursuit of closure around specific areas of expertise, communities of occupational practices become as much political bodies as professions. White (1992) affirmed that jurisdiction is the obsession of professions. Likewise, the texts we have examined point out that it is also the obsession of those in senior executive roles (and their advisors, e.g. consulting and executive search firms)—probably even more so, as their practice boundaries are weaker and more porous than those of classic professionals, and the potential political games more numerous and varied, as there are fewer restrictions on them.

A CXO label is, undoubtedly, both an inter-role competitive advantage, and for incumbents and aspirants, a coveted status prize.

Our research confirms, then, the ongoing validity of one of the main insights of contingency theory: functional or subunit differentiation introduces the possibility of conflict. Sometimes it may remain latent, other times it may erupt, fuelled, among other possibilities, by competition over an influential seat on a TMT, or a desire to gain proximity or direct access to the CEO. Senior leadership teams are highly charged political settings, composed of savvy and experienced operators, where it does not take much to spark sophisticated political competition (Nadler et al., 1998). Particularly when a CEO's succession process is underway, jousting among candidates and the occupations they represent can be intense (Ocasio, 1994). Further, the ongoing adding, removal, renaming, or transforming of CXO mandates can create a context of uncertainty and exacerbate this competition. As we explained in Chapter 6, the search for a balance between collaboration and competition in executive committees is one of the most difficult and consequential tasks encountered by CEOs (Roberto, 2005). Under the CEO's leadership, executive committees are the main integration devices of organizations, and the CXOs serving in them ought to behave according to that logic.

According to Abbott (1988: 102), 'knowledge is the currency of competition'. In a piece on the power of accounting vis-à-vis engineering and other functions, Armstrong (1985) articulated one of the best arguments available, detailing how knowledge affects the competition between domains of managerial expertise. He argued that for functional specialists to have exclusive rights over a domain and to have a chance at preventing others from entering and operating in their territory, 'the knowledge base needs to contain sufficient indeterminacy to debar outsiders from professional practice' (Armstrong, 1985: 132). That is, the more routine and operational an activity, the more feasible it is to break its requisite knowledge base into easy-to-learn tasks, thereby making it difficult to erect barriers of entry against new actors. However, when the knowledge base of a specialization is vague, lacks abstract components, and does not require a lengthy period of formal education, it is categorized as 'craft knowledge'—common sense plus experience—without further differentiating elements. In this case, aspirants and claims to its legitimate possession will also proliferate. This is the grievance that Whittington et al. (2011) expressed regarding the strategy task: because strategy is not sufficiently differentiated as a knowledge set and as a practice, it is difficult to develop a monopoly, or even just credible boundaries, around it. As a consequence, Chief Strategy Officers are frail roles.

The CFO is the CXO role that exhibits the best balance between, on the one hand, the indeterminacy of its practice, and on the other hand, the formalization of its knowledge base to ensure its jurisdiction remains unchallenged, thereby strengthening the role's position at the top of the N-1 layer. In addition, CFOs play a key role in interfacing between firms and shareholders, financial analysts, and other suppliers of financial resources, further strengthening their indispensability. CFOs' 'functional centrality' (for more on this concept, see Hickson et al., 1971; Ibarra, 1993; Gresov and Razin, 1997) continues to be unsurpassed. CFOs not only speak the universal, boundary-spanning language of numbers, but also have internal connections with all units, as well as external ties with boards of directors and the investor community. As Cappelli and Hamori (2005) argued, while suppliers of financial resources continue to brandish their influence, the CFO role will be secured in its solid number two position. White (2008: 113) wrote that a credible style needs a combination of relations and discourse, and CFOs are the strongest CXOs in both dimensions. Similar to Bechky (2020), who in her study of forensic occupations played with a Freudian pun and used the expression 'DNA Envy', we can speak of 'CFO Envy' among those in other CXO roles. The CFO role is the source of the 'evaluative spillovers' (for more on this concept, see Bechky, 2020) on lesser status roles, who are judged by the techniques, values, and institutional pathways of CFOs. In that, CFOs are the yardsticks of other N-1 roles.

In the competition between functions for territory and access to the CEO, enjoying a good brand is key, as in any such contest. In turn, an attractive label is key to a successful brand. Beyond convincing arguments (i.e. a strong 'intellectual position'; Fligstein, 1987), an appealing name for a function or role increases the likelihood of prevailing in a jurisdictional struggle. The attractiveness of the CXO label, and of what could be called widespread 'chief-ing', comes from sharing two words with the Chief Executive Officer title, signalling that CXOs share some defining characteristics with the superordinate executive. Often, obtaining the CXO label indicates power and ownership over a piece of strategic adaptive action and signals for incumbents that they are on the fast track to the top. The very fact that in formally classifying senior managers for compensation policies, personnel administrators typically do not use CXO titles, but the more hierarchical titles of Executive Vice-presidents, Senior Vice-presidents, Vice-presidents, Group Vice-presidents, Managing Directors, etc., further bolsters the attractiveness of the label. CXOs are not, primarily, formal slots in the hierarchy, but rather distinct *ad personam* appointments. Implied by the CXO title is that the functions of the role have a major impact on the entire organization or on an autonomous part of it. CXOs deserve this motivating and appealing name because the very adjective 'chief' implies an integrative focus and strategic viewpoint. For instance, Grewal and Wang (2009: 32) investigated if CMOs and VP Marketing are different species', concluding that: 'we are witnessing not only a change in the nomenclature, from Marketing VP to CMOs . . . [but] a transformation in the expectations of the head of marketing and of the function', according to which 'the modern CMO becomes responsible for a long-term vision of the firm and is held accountable for all organizational stakeholders'. CXOs have the same responsibilities as CEOs on a smaller and local scale, hence the two-thirds similarity in their titles. The analogy CXO/CEO is explicitly posed in reports on roles such as CMOs, claiming to be the best lesser version of CEOs, and even more fancifully, in claims by CHRO advocates of access to the peak role.

The need to classify employees, including senior managers, for payroll purposes, further complicates comprehension of the CXO phenomenon. As just mentioned, CXOs are often formally classified with the hierarchical titles listed above, rungs that are easily identifiable on a formal organizational chart. For instance, all twelve members of the Coca-Cola Company's senior team are CXOs who simultaneously hold vice-president or senior vice-president titles. In this case, in the rapidly fading American tradition of corporate governance, the only exceptions are the CEO, who also serves as the Chair of the Board of Directors, and the COO, who also holds the title of President. The only other exception is a vice-president who is not a CXO, as he runs the McDonald's Division, which is a profit centre, in line with our arguments. Although a CXO may also simultaneously be classified as holding a hierarchical title of, for instance, vice-president, executives with the VP title who run business units focused on clients, territories, technologies, etc. (as opposed to shared services or functions) almost never simultaneously bear the CXO label, as in the Coca-Cola case described in the previous paragraph. The same phenomenon, which is quite general, can be illustrated at Cargill, a very different type of company in a completely different sector with a highly differentiated portfolio of businesses. With only one exception (the Chief Risk Officer, who also leads the Protein & Salt division), none of the members of the executive committee who run business units have the CXO title, which is reserved for corporate senior managers.[1]

In *Distinction*, Bourdieu (1984) argued that fashions are class-markers of imitation and aversion. It can be said that CXO titles signal status and differences in organizational hierarchies. The three CXO letters are not equal in appeal, though. The X word, the one in the middle, is used for inter-functional competitive purposes, to carve out territories. It is employed to signal claims on horizontal spaces. It is the one that mutates almost *ad infinitum*, as it follows the whim of fashions and the twists and turns in organizational attention. In contrast, there is permanence and stability in the first and third letters. The 'officer' badge signals that its holder is in a management position in the hierarchy (i.e. has subordinates), but it does not specify more than that. It indicates that the role is not rank and file, but not what it specifically and essentially is. The lack of universal and enforceable rules for assigning standard titles to senior executive roles fuels their proliferation and variety. In the United States, this latitude is even legally protected by the Model Business Corporation Act, which strictly regulates boards of directors, but not executive committees.

Etzioni's (1965) taxonomy of managers according to their power sources further clarifies the differences between 'officer' and 'chief'. In a two-by-two table, he combined positional power (the influence executives may draw from the relevance, uniqueness, centrality, autonomy, and visibility of their formal role) and personal power (the influence that executives obtain from their autonomy, energy, and impetus). A manager who has neither positional nor personal power is a 'follower'; one that only shows personal power is an 'informal leader'; one that only possesses positional power is an 'officer'; and, finally, one with both personal and positional power is, in Etzioni's lexicon, a 'formal leader', perhaps not a very appealing denomination. The word 'Chief' would, in fact, be more appropriate for those who wield both positional and personal power. 'Chief' is much more defining, as it signals responsibility and authority in the leadership of a strategically relevant piece of organizational action. Of the two permanent locutions in the CXO title ('chief', always requiring appealing personal power) and 'officer'

---

[1] https://www.cargill.com/about/executive-team, accessed on 23 March 2020.

(purely a formal role) the former is the most attractive, by far. Yet, it is precisely the formality of the latter, signalling both the transcending nature of the role and the ethics of 'office' (du Gay, 2017), that has an important role in re-balancing, at least in aspiration, the appeal of the personal power.

As stable elements of the label, Cs and Os are 'customs', not fleeting and fragile 'fashions', to use Lieberson's (2000) terminology. When the word 'Chief' is combined with the word 'Officer', the lure generated becomes ravishing and patent. If expertise is composed of specialized knowledge and pragmatics or working knowledge (see Chapter 4), X represents the specialized and differentiated knowledge, while C represents the pragmatics, the ways and means of getting things done, the style, which therefore holds much more weight than the knowledge ingredient in composing senior executive roles' expertise. To be credible, aspirants to the highest superordinate role need to overcome their identification with a particular X, and identify themselves with the formal knowledge-stripped, pure action orientation of the C.

In this and other chapters, we have discussed how classic organization theories, such as neo-institutional and contingency theories, are useful for understanding the spread of CXO roles. Although both are open systems perspectives, institutional theory has been less systematic and focused on considering the role of boundary processes and inter-unit conflicts. Political theories of organizations, the ultimate open systems perspective, are useful for studying CXOs as well. Despite a less coherent body of work than contingency theory, or even than the ununified neo-institutional school (Alvesson and Spicer, 2018; Ocasio and Gai, 2020), political theories continue to hold great scholarly promise (Weber and Waeger, 2017). Our arguments endorse a characterization of senior managers as more 'opportunistic, calculating, and dispassionate' (terms used by Weber and Waeger, 2017: 45) than the one explicitly or implicitly acknowledged by neo-institutionalism, not dissimilar to those pragmatic artisans, studied by Anteby and Holm (2021), who (to gain legitimacy) rapidly and deliberately shift the presentation of their expertise, depending on the expectations of their audiences. The curation of role identities via associations, magazines, and events, as well as the careful search for appealing X labels illustrated in this book, imply that executives are very self-conscious about their influence, aware of political dynamics internal to their organizations and their fields, and mindful of status and reputation as power sources. Executives are also attentive to opportunity structures, such as new legislation, for boosting role legitimacy and enhancing their career trajectories, as shown in Dobbin's (2009) study of human resources managers. We argue that similar dynamics are unfolding for roles in the institutional cluster as new soft and hard norms are being established with regard to diversity, climate, etc. Increasing obligatory reporting by companies on policies and initiatives being undertaken in those fields 'institutionalizes' the new legitimacy roles.

Our examination of the CXO phenomenon recognizes that the executive committee is the most important 'government' structure with regard to political dynamics in organizations, the most important figure on them, of course, being the CEO, who is served by all of the other roles. CEOs and their executive committees are the ultimate boundary spanners of organizations, integrating the vast array of organizational functions. Importantly, the new legitimacy contingencies originating from both institutional and corporate governance demands can only be satisfied by those at the very apexes of organizations. Organizations' incremental political, social, and cultural responsibilities (Meyer and Bromley, 2013) are requiring the creation of organizational units led by CXO roles. The heightened relevance to organizations of the technological and external institutional environments and their corresponding internal clusters, as well as the resulting increasing differentiation between units in structures and roles on executives committees, make organizations and their upper layers fit the assumptions of political theories of organizations which frame them as shifting coalitions of diverse units with ongoing collaborative/competitive relationships under the escalating influence of actors in external environments. This political work can only be sustained by pragmatic leaders.

7.3 The changing essence of executive power

While manifestations of CXO roles are immensely varied, they have several defining traits in common, but these are not easy to unravel and identify. The very fact that management is an occupation without universal, homogenous, and obligatory norms for behaviour, status, or titles prevents arguments on CXOs from being uniformly and universally valid across organizations and business systems. There will always be exceptions or uncommon practices in the spread of CXO roles and in the composition of executive committees. The dynamics of most senior management teams are very different from those of boards of directors. Corporate governance reforms enacted since the early 2000s have sought to render the structures, compositions, and processes of boards of directors as homogenous, controllable, and reliable as possible across contexts—that is, more institutionalized. The goal of these reform measures was to make corporations more responsive to the interests of shareholders, and to guarantee safe and predictable global flows of capital and investments. The transparency and publicity demanded of corporate governance bodies, especially boards of directors, makes the work of researchers easier. As a result, 'governance' bodies have been studied much more, and more quantitatively, than executive committees, the 'governments' of organizations.

There is a pattern, though, in the functions and labels of 'government' roles. The essential characteristic of CXOs, the *what* of their function, whether oriented toward product and technological environments, or institutional environments and people, is to serve CEOs as instruments for organizational adaptation. The flexibility of CXO roles and executive committee structures enables organizations to adapt to rapidly changing and more numerous contingencies, as the following quote by Vancil and Green (1984: 73) recognizes: 'The primary advantage of top management committees is that they are flexible, personal tools for enhancing leadership effectiveness. Committees are easy to form and continue to exist only at the pleasure of the CEO. Their agendas are totally in the CEO's hands.' Even practitioner-oriented publications recognize the adaptive task of senior roles (Russell Reynolds, 2020a). This is the main function of CXOs who are members of TMTs, and even of those positioned below the N-1 level. Most CXOs fulfil boundary spanning roles and exhibit transversal brokerage behaviours, both inside and outside organizations. External and internal interface roles are more in demand today than decades ago due to the integration mechanisms required by increasingly complex structures.

As findings in the literature on spanning roles and integrators examined in this book confirm, these CXO roles are designed to cut across structures and boundaries—horizontal, and sometimes vertical—to induce transformative action. This is the behavioural characteristic of what neo-institutionalists have termed 'institutional entrepreneurship' (DiMaggio, 1988; Battilana, Leca, and Boxenbaum, 2009), and of what sociologists such as White (1992) and authors of innumerable practice-oriented works have called 'leadership'. CXO is the role and the title assigned to leaders in today's organizations.

Because they fulfil an adaptive function, TMTs adopt a variety of configurations, depending on location, industry, predicaments, etc., and include
different roles and titles depending on the labelling preferences of CEOs,
as well as of CXO candidates and incumbents themselves. The latitude for
CXO naming has motivational benefits for incumbents. Scholars such as
Baron and Bielby (1986), Miner (1987, 1990), Barley (1990), and Miner
and Akinsanmi (2016) who have examined idiosyncratic jobs (a concept
that applies more to CXO roles than to Profit & Loss executive jobs), and
scholars who have explored autonomous role labelling (Berg, Grant, and
Johnson, 2010) and job crafting (Wrzesniewski and Dutton, 2001) have
highlighted the motivating potential of title and role crafting by incumbents, especially those operating under the conditions of ambiguity and
uncertainty often faced by members of senior management teams.

What Cohen (2013) called the processes of 'assembling jobs'—the deter-
mination of tasks to be executed by a role—are malleable, rather indeter-
minate, and subject to the negotiation between superiors and subordinates.
A great deal of role and label crafting, what Sandhu and Kulik (2019)
expressively described as 'shaping and being shaped', occurs at senior management levels between superiors and incumbents. We may hypothesize
that even more than at lower levels. Titles are not standardized across firms,
even those operating in the same business context or industry. The CXO
label *per se* does not ensure unequivocal and predictable membership in
any of the possible configurations of the CEO's top team, whether formal (executive committee) or informal (kitchen cabinet, etc.), or a certain
position in the hierarchy (e.g. a vice-president). A CXO could be an N-
1, an N-2 reporting to an N-1, an N-2 who occasionally has a seat at the
table or reports directly to the CEO, or even an N-3. This polysemy is due,
as argued above, to the fact that management functions are not true professions, but merely occupations, or at most 'weak professions' in areas such as
accounting. The feebler their positions, the more CXOs need to erect barriers to protect their territories. The CXO designation does not unequivocally
signal status or position, but rather a particular type of manager: an adaptive and integrating executive who performs boundary work (*what* they do)
by capitalizing on strong sociability and political prowess (*how* they do it).

Accountancy vocabulary, in its quest for precision in measuring and
evaluating the contributions of different structural units and their leading
roles, helps us to understand the core nature of CXO roles. Most CXOs
do not have profit and loss responsibility, and are not at the helm of profit

centres, like most vice-presidents or senior vice-presidents of business units are. CXO roles are ontologically different from, for example, country or market managers or executives who lead units specialized in relevant clients or differentiated products, as such roles entail bottom line responsibilities accounted for as revenue or profit centres. Most often, the units headed by CXOs are 'shared services' or 'functional' departments treated in accounting as 'discretionary expenses' or 'cost centres'. The literature on control systems acknowledges the difficulties involved in establishing objective metrics for these types of units and, therefore, for their evaluation and compensation. Although a variety of qualitative and even quantitative key performance indicators have been developed and fined tuned to monitor expense centres (e.g. in terms of operational excellence, relationships with stakeholders, service to internal and external clients, strategic support for business units, etc.), these are still much more difficult to monitor and measure than profit and revenue centres (Kaplan and Norton, 2006). This is true of both for-profit and not-for-profit organizations, as well as rating agencies and governance intermediaries (see, for instance, 'Environment, Sustainability and Governance [ESG] Investing: Poor Scores', *The Economist*, 7 December 2019). The challenges in gathering, analysing, and evaluating performance data remain higher in institutional domains, such as social value (Mulgan, 2010: 38–43).

Roles such as the Chief Diversity Officer, Chief Communications Officer, Chief Transformation Officer, and even Chief Data Officer are either directly accountable to the CEO, or indirectly accountable through other CXOs. Because the CEO's evaluation is the ultimate yardstick of CXO performance, CEOs have discretionary power of the highest order over CXOs. Thus, another defining facet of CXOs (N-1s or lower) has to do with their relationship with the figure who fully embodies 'chiefdom' and 'officership': the Chief Executive Officer (N). The expansion of CXOs at the service of CEOs illustrates the new ways whereby executive power in organizations is being organized and exercised, with a stronger nucleus of loyal executives close to the CEO to help with adaptation tasks. The CXO phenomenon reveals a greater breadth of control by the CEO and, therefore, more centralization of power. Executive committees are organizational political bodies.

Identifying *where* these CXO roles operate further clarifies their essence. Most CXO roles operate from headquarters and are responsible for the widening array of different functions. Chandler (1962) classified these into two basic types: value-creating/entrepreneurial, and loss-preventing/administrative. Goold, Pettifer, and Young (2001) and Collis, Young, and Goold (2012) proposed two basic types: 'parent' functions (e.g. general management, legal, finance, public relations, etc.) and 'shared services' functions (e.g. research and development, business intelligence, information technology, marketing, etc., depending on the particular needs of the company). CXOs, who could be of either type, depending on the company pertaining to the primary or secondary cluster, operate from organizational headquarters because their essential function is to serve the 'centre of the centre', or the 'ground zero' of executiveness—the CEO. They need to be close to the superordinate executive in order to provide responsive service.

These senior executive groups could be organized by CEOs in an 'infinite and immense variety of ways, in a bewildering array of situational practices' (Vancil, 1987: 106). This variety exists not only because organizations need to adapt to ever-changing and increasingly variegated external contingencies, but also because executive committees exist only as teams serving at the pleasure of the CEO, a service that cannot be standardized. What Mansfield (1989: 296) affirmed about the executive branches of democracies and how they should be studied also applies to the CEO as the top organizational executive: 'the executive stands for what is singular, individual, and particular. Any science that does not recognize those qualities, but insists on counting, aggregating, and formalizing will not comprehend executive power.' Above all, CXOs collectively serve the singularity of the CEO in ways that cannot be protocolled. CEOs' styles in managing their upper teams constitute the supreme contingency in explaining the design and dynamics of executive committees, and, therefore, of CXOs' roles, tasks, labels, and hierarchical status.

Using the vocabulary of White's (1992, 2008) theory of action, it may be said that corporate governance is a system of control in search of predictability, acting mostly in a surveillance and disciplinary mode based on a mistrust of internal executives, particularly CEOs. Corporate governance is primarily intent on thwarting autonomous executive action. The CEO and the executive branch, in contrast, aim for fresh action, adaptation, and change. This is *why* CXO roles are so pervasive and indispensable: CEOs need to enable flexibility of the structures, compositions, and processes of the most important tool for external adaptation and organization-wide integration: executive committees. As White (1992: 240) pointed out, the system of senior teams is a 'flexible lattice of constraints' that makes action possible. This flexibility is especially required when limitations on the power of CEOs and their executive committees are being increasingly imposed from the top by boards of directors. For CEOs to be efficient drivers of change, they need to rely on loyal CXOs, whose careers depend on them, and operate as much as possible without predetermined protocols and strict definitions of responsibilities in order to preserve enough adaptive ability, as suggested by White (1992). Scholars from other academic traditions also recognized that changes at the top constitute an adaptation mechanism that aligns an organization with its environment (Mitsuhashi and Greve, 2004). Such changes are justified, because structures and roles produce inertia (i.e. institutionalization of strategy) and entrenchment (vested interests in the preservation of favourable resource allocation schemes) that impede alignment with environmental changes. White (1992: 256) pointed out that getting action manifests without fixed patterns, featuring a constant variation of roles and names, a rapid selection of appealing titles, and an uneven and fragile retention of novel structural forms. The flows of divergence and convergence of the strategic leadership constellation studied by Ma and Seidl (2018) are a good illustration. CEOs compensate for regulation and control from governance bodies, as well as from new legitimacy-demanding groups in the external environment, by establishing senior teams with flexible and constantly changing compositions staffed by officers with high levels of ambition, energy, and commitment. This liability in the composition of executive committees, whether proactive or reactive, helps to disguise senior executives' motives and actions from corporate governance oversight, and makes it challenging for external observers to fathom the true nature of executive power.

This is another manifestation of the fundamental drivers of any political action: the search for autonomy and a desire to escape from constraints (Emerson, 1962). The more corporate governance restricts CEOs, the more these crave and seek autonomy. In fact, as Bebchuk and Tallarita (2020) suggested, given how difficult it is for boards to monitor and evaluate performance in those areas, initiatives on matters of the institutional cluster could be one way superordinate executives free themselves from board interference. CXOs would be CEO's instruments in those tactics.

Therefore, the essential function of CXOs and the executive committees they comprise is to help CEOs pursue adaptive, value-adding strategies by leading cross-boundary initiatives. Collectively, their efforts are transformative and help companies respond to new contingencies or logics. This is why most new CXOs do not have profit and loss responsibilities. The essence of positions accountable for profit and loss (non-CXO roles, typically bearing titles such as Vice-president, Senior Vice-president, etc.) is to produce results through discipline while working under predictable conditions that preserve the status quo. Vice-presidents are not typically tasked with innovation or adaptation, but rather are expected to efficiently achieve recurrent or predefined objectives. Incumbents in such positions require less impetus and personal power, and do not need to engage in as much role crafting as CXOs, as expectations about them are quite established. The existence of the CXO role makes explicit the separation at the upper levels of organizations between 'change' agents and 'performance' agents, between 'efficacy' roles (CXOs) and 'efficiency' roles, and, we suggest, between the classic dichotomy of 'leadership' and 'management'. CXOs are the current role specification of leadership.

Having summarized the *what* of the CXO phenomenon (roles that direct attention and facilitate adaptation to new or relevant environmental factors), the *where* (corporate headquarters with close dependence on the CEO), and the *why* (the CEO's need for a 'personal', trusted team in a context of constraints imposed by governance bodies and new political and social environments, and accelerated by technological changes), it is now time to summarize the main characteristics of CXO actors—that is, the *how* or behaviour, and the *who* or identity. The *who* is determined by the *how*, since what Han (2019) affirmed about power applies as well to executiveness: it is a phenomenon of form.

To break inertias in the pursuit of strategic value-added adaptation (see Chapters 4 and 5), CXOs need to be able to exercise a distinctive social and political style that enables them to establish connections, alliances, coalitions, etc. Executive expertise at the top is primarily about bridging and aligning external and internal groups, and only secondarily about applying formal knowledge. Therefore, CXOs need to have and/or develop social skills (Fligstein, 1997, 2001). White (1992) argued that more than norms (either hard, in the form of formal structures, or soft, in the form of corporate values or culture) or unbridled personal characteristics, such as charisma, style is the best resource available to social actors for working across boundaries, because, as White conceptualized it, style offers a good balance between flexibility and reliability. CXOs have a signature style that makes them identifiable, similar to the one proposed for boundary spanners, discussed in detail in Chapter 5. The *how*, therefore, is the application of a pragmatic style defined by social and political skills to the *what* of adaptive tasks geared toward organizational transformation. Personal traits such as energy (Mansfield, 1989; Eastland, 1992; Bruch and Ghoshal, 2004), autonomy (Vancil, 1978), and impetus (Bower, 1986) sustain the *how* of CXOs. Senior management's expertise is high on pragmatic style and low on formal knowledge. The *who*, thus, are action-oriented, skilled actors whose collective identity is based on a style of executiveness, made feasible by their psychological traits. The personality foundations of 'executiveness' give only a fraction of the population significant chances for success.

7.4 Conclusion

Top team structures have been explored by scholars from a variety of angles. Led by Don Hambrick, upper echelon theorists have been shedding light on the 'black box' of TMTs, particularly on the impact of CEOs on organizations' strategies. Scholars in different traditions have highlighted the notable increase in the size of executive committees: Medcof, Medcof, Menz, Medcof, and Cannella (2015) employed the word 'revolution' in the title of their *Academy of Management* symposium to call attention to the sharp increase in top team size and the heightened presence of functional and shared services roles in it; Guadalupe et al. (2014) corroborated the spike in top team membership; and Menz (2012) has already supplied the first exhaustive compilation and classification of CXOs. A slew of reports, mostly by professional services firms, but also, increasingly, scholarly works, zero in on specialized roles at the top. Our purpose in this book has been to examine and explain, by illustrating and theorizing, the ongoing transformation of executive committees, and the unceasing proliferation of CXOs, which we consider to be the most important and revealing manifestation of the continuing transformation in executive power.

Our book has detailed how the social construction of executive roles and the discourses about them, their executive expertise, identity, and style, is a collective enterprise, not only by interested CEOs as well as executive roles' incumbents and aspirants, but also by other actors: executive search firms, consultancies, the media, role associations and networks, etc. These actors go about role building, legitimation, institutionalization, and expansion of the executive roles' nomenclature, aware of their resources—organizational and ideological—and the vocabulary available to them, tactically mindful and pro-active in the quest for attaining superiority in the contests for a seat at the executive committee table. In sum, CXOs are manifestations of 'agentic' search for power and strategic use of the organizing potential of executive roles as political resources. That is, we show the resourcefulness of executive roles for governance, communication, focusing of the organizational attention and efforts and, not least, as means for creativity in designing and transforming executive power to acknowledge demands by relevant stakeholders and their diverse (and at times conflicting) time horizons and expectations for actionable futures.

The increasing presence of CXO roles in the composition of top management teams shows the mounting influence of 'parent' units (i.e. headquarters) over business units and, consequently, of the corporate executives who lead 'shared services', as well as of what traditionally have been called 'functions', over the managers who lead profit and loss units. Larger executive committees with shifting membership provide more resources for CEOs to support organizational adaptation. Also, the rapid institutionalization of the CXO institutional cluster provides resources for CEOs to grapple with a novel type of contingency, for which they lack much experience. New CXOs may be willing actors in promoting a much more plural and less predictable model of organizational control, one that could be well theorized from the tenets of political theories of organizations. The growth of this institutional cluster of executive roles, which is signalling organizations' expanded actorhood as a result of what Meyer and Bromley (2013) identified as the triumph of a liberal global society, should be the focus of heightened scholarly attention. The resolution of the competition between, on one side, corporations trying to reduce the sources of uncertainty by controlling external activists and, on the other side, external activists trying to sway organizations into accepting their priorities, will impact the future political and economic character of firms and society. With regard to the strategy-making process, Whittington and Yakis-Douglas (2020) highlighted global networks of strategy professionals (whom we argue are not really professionals) as emergent actors in the opening up of firms to non-elite organizational actors and to external groups. As mentioned earlier, the final loyalty of some CXO institutional roles will be one of the deciding factors in the resolution of this confrontation, where corporate legitimacy is being challenged in ways that have not been seen since the pre-World War II economic crises.

Executive roles in general, and those in the institutional arena in particular, should then be considered as political resources. These roles constitute such resources for CEOs, as they are moving parts in the puzzle of power balance at their organizations' upper echelons. Furthermore, to the extent that executive roles are interface roles, i.e. boundary spanners, they also influence the way organizations are embedded in the wider society. That influence is bi-directional, not just in the organization-to-society direction, but also from society to organizations, as creators of and incumbent CXOs infuse these with their own ideologies and identities.

The 'everybody-is-a-chief' phenomenon, fuelled by status envy and label imitation, may at first glance seem too shallow or too easily dismissed as a management fad to warrant propositions about power structures in organizations, or perhaps just another manifestation of what Alvesson and Spicer (2016) called 'stupidity'. However, the spread of innumerable CXO titles reveals a long-term transformation in executive power that continues to unfold. A new era of technological advancement and societal pressure exerted on corporations to engage in non-commercial areas (e.g., equality, climate, diversity, migration, etc.) are exacerbating top team design challenges spawned by globalization and new technologies. As external environments change, so must the structures, compositions, and processes of executive committees. The law of isomorphism reigns unchallenged in structural design with regard to both horizontal and vertical structures, and the internal environments of corporations, including executive committees, are becoming increasingly complex. Flexible executive committees contribute to organizations' readiness to adapt, as highlighted by White (1992: 256): 'Getting action must invoke changing concrete patterns, attaining new varieties and the combination of discipline, role, and position, and the changing must always continue.'

Incumbents in CXO roles share a common nature that is probably best captured by the word 'energy', which Alexander Hamilton considered the distinguishing characteristic of executive powers (Mansfield, 1989). An understated fact of senior executive life is that not all personality types provide the psychological traction required to confront the frictions sparked by adaptation tasks. Therefore, the pool of candidates with the energy to be successful in senior positions is limited. The fact that the fundamental component of the expertise of senior executives is not formal knowledge (which is widely accessible and attainable), but rather action skills, confirms that management is an occupation, not a profession.

Because TMTs in general, and CXOs in particular interface with external and internal environments, CXOs must exhibit the strong networking skills and political savvy necessary in boundary spanning roles. We have used White's (1992) concept of style to account for these behavioural capacities. Most certainly, authors such as Mintzberg (1973), Kotter (1982, 1985, 1990), and Cohen and Bradford (1989), among others, noted time ago the importance of social and political aptitudes for senior managers. Preceding them all, Philip Selznick (1957) asserted that that for 'administrators' (his word for senior executives of both for-profit and not-for-profit organizations), the 'profession is politics' (1957: 61) Yet, because today's senior executives must engage more actively and decisively with a proliferation of environments and a plurality of players in them, a social and political style is even more essential, distinctive, and defining.

Not all existing roles with the CXO title fit the profile we have been describing in this book. This is a testimony to the popularity and attraction of the Chief X Officer label: in many cases it has become a floating signifier, a label that may be attached to almost any management role (and even beyond business). The name's very success makes the essence and impact of the roles on executive power difficult to unveil and gauge. At first glance, CXOs may seem to be specialists. Amongst the vast collection of second words in CXO titles, a majority refer to areas of knowledge (e.g., Chief Marketing Officer, Chief Supply Chain Officer, Chief Cybersecurity Officer, etc.). Very few CXO titles bear an action-oriented 'X' (e.g., Chief Operating Officer, Chief Performance Officer, Chief Impact Officer, and a few others). But knowledge expertise is not the essence of CXOs. There is a role with a pure action-oriented second letter in the acronym that is not subject to the fugacity of fashions: the Chief Executive Officer, the superordinate, for whom signifier and signified are in full correspondence. The fact that the top role is precisely the one that expurgates from its label any pretence of formal knowledge or specialization-based expertise, signals that non-'E' CXO roles are just approximations of 'executiveness'. Max Weber wrote that an ideal type is not the average manifestation of a phenomenon, but a construct that facilitates the methodical capture of its essence. The ideal type of CXOs we have been contouring in these pages is a role defined by a style of social and political pragmatism. It already exists and is called CEO, the Chief Executive Officer.

Factiva[1] Mentions of C-Suite and CXO Titles, 2000–2020

[1] Factiva contents include business information from 1,200 newspapers, 6,500 journals and trade magazines, and 350 news agencies as well as financial information of about 23,000 listed companies worldwide. Covers 118 countries and 22 languages. (https://www.cbs.dk/en/library/databases/factiva). The search has included only unique articles, having duplicates switched off.

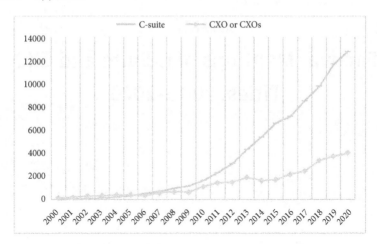

Fig. A.1 Factiva mentions of the terms C-suite and CXO or CXOs, 2000–2020

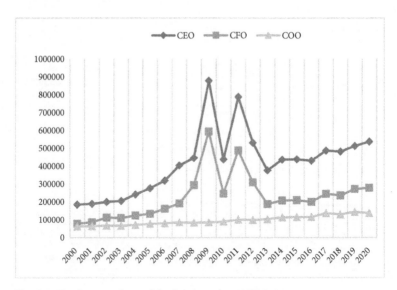

Fig. A.2 Factiva mentions of the C-suite core, 2000–2020

*Search was performed with full titles: Chief Executive Officer, Chief Financial Officer, Chief Operating Officer.

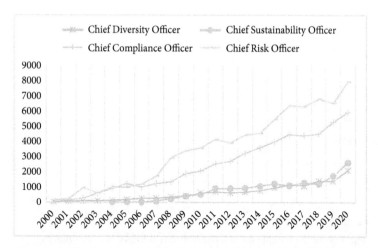

Fig. A.3 Factiva mentions of CXOs from the institutional complexity cluster, 2000–2020

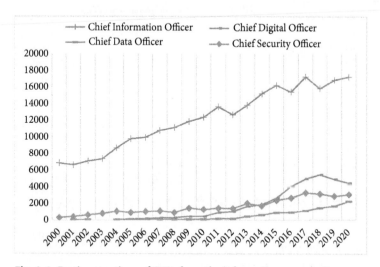

Fig. A.4 Factiva mentions of CXOs from the information complexity cluster, 2000–2020

Fig. A.5 Factiva mentions of CXOs from the primary task complexity cluster, 2000–2020

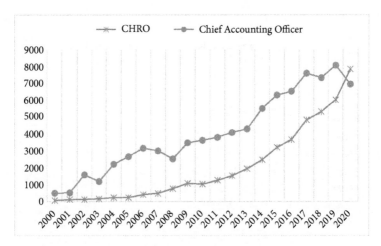

Fig. A.6 Factiva mentions of CXOs from the administrative complexity cluster, 2000–2020

*CHRO—Chief Human Resources Officer.
**Only two roles were selected for the comparison due to there being less following in the media of other CXO roles from this cluster.

Top 40 CXO Titles in Companies Featured in The Official Board Database, 2020

#	Title	Firms/# titles	Geographical distribution*	Industry distribution**	Role domain	Mother/daughter firm	Reporting level
1	Chief Executive Officer	62,247/ 141,015	Africa: 1,758 Asia: 12,023 Europe: 23,485 N. America: 24,864 Oceania: 2,019 S. America: 1,098	Agriculture: 402 Transportation: 3,365 Consumer goods: 3,439 Leisure: 2,424 Finance: 12,071 Health care: 4,729 Technology: 9,176 Manufacturing: 14,570 Media: 1,718 Service: 13,353	Board: 68 CEO: 53,973 Corporate: 149 Development: 741 Finance: 633 Management: 9,023 People: 73 Technical: 572	Mother: 37,876 N-1: 18,406 N-2: 6,821 N-3+: 2,144	CEO: 54,244 Board: 179 N-1: 9,326 N-2: 1,483
2	Chief Financial Officer	30,867/ 31,818	Africa: 639 Asia: 4,526 Europe: 8,514 N. America: 15,812 Oceania: 1,035 S. America: 341	Agriculture: 209 Transportation: 1,338 Consumer goods: 1,241 Leisure: 1,139 Finance: 6,022 Health care: 2,684 Technology: 4,666 Manufacturing: 6,942 Media: 729 Service: 5,897	Board: 6 CEO: 260 Corporate: 15 Development: 3 Finance: 29,542 Management: 1,025 People: 6 Technical: 8	Mother: 21,501 N-1: 6,703 N-2: 2,113 N-3+: 550	CEO: 235 Board: 6 N-1: 30,210 N-2: 414

3	Chief Operating Officer	15,963/ 17,490	Africa: 334 Asia: 2,102 Europe: 4,153 N. America: 8,809 Oceania: 457 S. America: 108	Agriculture: 70 Transportation: 757 Consumer goods: 506 Leisure: 769 Finance: 3,771 Health care: 1,189 Technology: 2,315 Manufacturing: 2,663 Media: 415 Service: 3,508	Board: 6 CEO: 194 Corporate: 11 Development: 104 Finance: 419 Management: 14,712 People: 8 Technical: 509	Mother: 10,762 N-1: 3,660 N-2: 1,190 N-3+: 351	CEO: 302 Board: 6 N-1: 15,162 N-2: 493
4	Chief Information Officer (Count includes Chief Technology Officer)	11,290/ 12,219	Africa: 174 Asia: 1,151 Europe: 2,771 N. America: 6,840 Oceania: 289 S. America: 65	Agriculture: 33 Transportation: 399 Consumer goods: 273 Leisure: 409 Finance: 2,102 Health care: 766 Technology: 3,236 Manufacturing: 1,479 Media: 324 Service: 2,269	Board: 6 CEO: 30 Corporate: 2 Development: 27 Finance: 50 Management: 679 People: 2 Technical: 10,494	Mother: 8,168 N-1: 2,340 N-2: 645 N-3+: 137	CEO: 34 Board: 8 N-1: 10,512 N-2: 736

Continued

Table *Continued*

#	Title	Firms/# titles	Geographical distribution*	Industry distribution**	Role domain	Mother/daughter firm	Reporting level
5	Chief Human Resources Officer (Count includes Chief HR, People, and Talent Officers)	3,965/ 4,002	Africa: 52 Asia: 456 Europe: 797 N. America: 2,547 Oceania: 90 S. America: 23	Agriculture: 13 Transportation: 136 Consumer goods: 184 Leisure: 207 Finance: 770 Health care: 355 Technology: 704 Manufacturing: 552 Media: 90 Service: 954	CEO: 4 Corporate: 8 Development: 1 Finance: 12 Management: 103 People: 3,836 Technical: 1	Mother: 2,832 N-1: 841 N-2: 223 N-3+: 69	CEO: 4 N-1: 3,874 N-2: 87
6	Chief Marketing Officer	3,770/ 3,820	Africa: 44 Asia: 399 Europe: 726 N. America: 2,510 Oceania: 74 S. America: 17	Agriculture: 12 Transportation: 64 Consumer goods: 227 Leisure: 267 Finance: 663 Health care: 160 Technology: 1,072 Manufacturing: 271 Media: 106 Service: 928	Board: 1 CEO: 5 Development: 3,519 Finance: 2 Management: 238 People: 3 Technical: 2	Mother: 2,620 N-1: 837 N-2: 262 N-3+: 51	CEO: 5 Board: 1 N-1: 3,607 N-2: 157

#	Role	Count	Region	Industry	Function	Reporting	Level
7	Chief Commercial Officer (Count includes Chief Sales and Business Officers)	3,394/ 3,589	Africa: 63 Asia: 388 Europe: 1,296 N. America: 1,518 Oceania: 97 S. America: 32	Agriculture: 14 Transportation: 305 Consumer goods: 132 Leisure: 427 Finance: 663 Health care: 663 Technology: 607 Manufacturing: 494 Media: 97 Service: 499	Board: 2 CEO: 17 Development: 2,745 Finance: 27 Management: 601 Technical: 2	Mother: 2,257 N-1: 797 N-2: 260 N-3+: 80	CEO: 18 Board: 2 N-1: 3,275 N-2: 99
8	Chief Risk Officer	2,008/ 2,143	Africa: 97 Asia: 475 Europe: 599 N. America: 798 Oceania: 103 S. America: 16	Agriculture: 3 Transportation: 15 Consumer goods: 9 Leisure: 3 Finance: 1,875 Health care: 6 Technology: 35 Manufacturing: 62 Media: 1 Service: 79	Board: 1 CEO: 5 Corporate: 37 Development: 4 Finance: 1,906 Management: 132 People: 2 Technical: 1	Mother: 1,193 N-1: 633 N-2: 228 N-3+: 34	CEO: 5 Board: 1 N-1: 1,850 N-2: 232

Continued

Table *Continued*

#	Title	Firms/# titles	Geographical distribution*	Industry distribution**	Role domain	Mother/daughter firm	Reporting level
9	Chief Compliance Officer (Count includes Chief Governance Officer)	1,903/ 1,906	Africa: 23 Asia: 241 Europe: 205 N. America: 1,410 Oceania: 14 S. America: 10	Agriculture: 2 Transportation: 27 Consumer goods: 22 Leisure: 19 Finance: 1,178 Health care: 196 Technology: 101 Manufacturing: 173 Media: 10 Service: 175	Board: 1 CEO: 4 Corporate: 1,609 Development: 4 Finance: 124 Management: 147 People: 8 Technical: 6	Mother: 1,348 N-1: 400 N-2: 125 N-3+: 30	CEO: 4 Board: 1 N-1: 1,563 N-2: 335
10	Chief Investment Officer	1,671/ 2,038	Africa: 29 Asia: 248 Europe: 402 N. America: 919 Oceania: 63 S. America: 10	Agriculture: 2 Transportation: 12 Consumer goods: 4 Leisure: 32 Finance: 1,219 Health care: 15 Technology: 15 Manufacturing: 48 Media: 13 Service: 310	Board: 4 CEO: 130 Corporate: 7 Development: 2 Finance: 1,286 Management: 241 Technical: 1	Mother: 1,018 N-1: 408 N-2: 199 N-3+: 46	CEO: 142 Board: 5 N-1: 1,396 N-2: 128

| 11 | Chief Strategy Officer | 1,651/ 1,584 | Africa: 21 Asia: 246 Europe: 321 N. America: 1,000 Oceania: 54 S. America: 9 | Agriculture: 7 Transportation: 39 Consumer goods: 42 Leisure: 63 Finance: 239 Health care: 139 Technology: 370 Manufacturing: 125 Media: 61 Service: 566 | Board: 12 CEO: 5 Development: 1,488 Finance: 12 Management: 128 People: 1 Technical: 5 | Mother: 1,044 N-1: 341 N-2: 162 N-3+: 104 | CEO: 5 Board: 7 N-1: 1,567 N-2: 72 |
| 12 | Chief Legal Officer | 1,340/ 1,350 | Africa: 13 Asia: 98 Europe: 214 N. America: 975 Oceania: 19 S. America: 21 | Agriculture: 4 Transportation: 61 Consumer goods: 47 Leisure: 78 Finance: 312 Health care: 164 Technology: 198 Manufacturing: 204 Media: 19 Service: 253 | CEO: 1 Corporate: 1,257 Development: 7 Finance: 13 Management: 58 People: 4 | Mother: 1,052 N-1: 238 N-2: 40 N-3+: 10 | CEO: 1 N-1: 1,322 N-2: 17 |

Continued

Table *Continued*

#	Title	Firms/# titles	Geographical distribution*	Industry distribution**	Role domain	Mother/daughter firm	Reporting level
13	Chief Revenue Officer	1,331/ 1,354	Africa: 1 Asia: 38 Europe: 143 N. America: 1,138 Oceania: 10 S. America: 1	Transportation: 17 Consumer goods: 15 Leisure: 76 Finance: 112 Health care: 52 Technology: 603 Manufacturing: 37 Media: 106 Service: 313	CEO: 1 Development: 1,244 Finance: 1 Management: 85	Mother: 1,084 N-1: 200 N-2: 36 N-3+: 11	CEO: 1 N-1: 1,278 N-2: 52
14	Chief Accounting Officer	1,227/ 1,238	Asia: 89 Europe: 82 N. America: 1,049 Oceania: 2 S. America: 5	Agriculture: 2 Transportation: 41 Consumer goods: 26 Leisure: 56 Finance: 233 Health care: 107 Technology: 124 Manufacturing: 313 Media: 32 Service: 293	Corporate: 3 Finance: 1,177 Management: 46 People: 1	Mother: 1,018 N-1: 183 N-2: 25 N-3+: 1	N-1: 265 N-2: 962

15	Chief Product Officer	1,195/ 1,210	Africa: 3 Asia: 60 Europe: 296 N. America: 817 Oceania: 17 S. America: 2	Agriculture: 2 Transportation: 24 Consumer goods: 22 Leisure: 54 Finance: 164 Health care: 36 Technology: 498 Manufacturing: 42 Media: 53 Service: 300	Board: 1 CEO: 1 Development: 1,099 Finance: 1 Management: 77 Technical: 16	Mother: 923 N-1: 195 N-2: 67 N-3+: 10	CEO: 2 Board: 1 N-1: 1,158 N-2: 34
16	Chief Administrative Officer	1,187/ 1,202	Africa: 2 Asia: 90 Europe: 92 N. America: 989 S. America: 14	Agriculture: 4 Transportation: 45 Consumer goods: 34 Leisure: 32 Finance: 421 Health care: 86 Technology: 121 Manufacturing: 170 Media: 22 Service: 252	CEO: 1 Corporate: 53 Development: 2 Finance: 987 Management: 135 People: 6 Technical: 3	Mother: 884 N-1: 240 N-2: 55 N-3+: 8	CEO: 1 N-1: 1,133 N-2: 53

Continued

Table *Continued*

#	Title	Firms/# titles	Geographical distribution*	Industry distribution**	Role domain	Mother/daughter firm	Reporting level
17	Chief Medical Officer	1,152/ 1,215	Africa: 2 Asia: 52 Europe: 174 N. America: 902 Oceania: 21 S. America: 1	Agriculture: 1 Transportation: 2 Consumer goods: 9 Leisure: 5 Finance: 56 Health care: 1,024 Technology: 36 Manufacturing: 5 Media: 14 Service: 928	CEO: 7 Development: 3 Management: 102 Technical: 1,040	Mother: 879 N-1: 200 N-2: 65 N-3+: 8	CEO: 8 N-1: 1,102 N-2: 42
18	Chief Digital Officer	987/ 1,000	Africa: 12 Asia: 132 Europe: 434 N. America: 363 Oceania: 41 S. America: 5	Agriculture: 1 Transportation: 28 Consumer goods: 60 Leisure: 31 Finance: 210 Health care: 41 Technology: 111 Manufacturing: 142 Media: 75 Service: 288	CEO: 4 Corporate: 14 Development: 836 Finance: 1 Management: 101 Technical: 31	Mother: 605 N-1: 245 N-2: 96 N-3+: 41	CEO: 4 N-1: 814 N-2: 169

19	Chief Customer Officer (Count includes Chief Experience Officer)	804/826	Africa: 9 Asia: 39 Europe: 175 N. America: 516 Oceania: 63 S. America: 2	Agriculture: 1 Transportation: 22 Consumer goods: 36 Leisure: 31 Finance: 121 Health care: 29 Technology: 272 Manufacturing: 29 Media: 17 Service: 246	CEO: 5 Development: 737 Finance: 1 Management: 61	Mother: 574 N-1: 159 N-2: 58 N-3+: 13	CEO: 1 N-1: 2,492 N-2: 46
20	Chief Creative Officer	602/698	Africa: 9 Asia: 72 Europe: 120 N. America: 359 Oceania: 21 S. America: 21	Consumer goods: 28 Leisure: 34 Finance: 3 Health care: 4 Technology: 15 Manufacturing: 10 Media: 32 Service: 476	Board: 2 CEO: 24 Development: 515 Management: 61	Mother: 195 N-1: 124 N-2: 158 N-3+: 125	CEO: 24 Board: 2 N-1: 522 N-2: 54

Continued

Table *Continued*

#	Title	Firms/# titles	Geographical distribution*	Industry distribution**	Role domain	Mother/daughter firm	Reporting level
21	Chief Development Officer	581/ 591	Africa: 6 Asia: 39 Europe: 107 N. America: 404 Oceania: 23 S. America: 2	Agriculture: 1 Transportation: 6 Consumer goods: 9 Leisure: 93 Finance: 77 Health care: 155 Technology: 40 Manufacturing: 81 Media: 11 Service: 108	Board: 1 CEO: 2 Corporate: 4 Development: 518 Finance: 2 Management: 45 People: 2 Technical: 7	Mother: 424 N-1: 118 N-2: 32 N-3+: 7	CEO: 2 Board: 1 N-1: 564 N-2: 14
22	Chief Credit Officer	577/ 594	Africa: 7 Asia: 51 Europe: 30 N. America: 481 Oceania: 8	Transportation: 1 Finance: 556 Health care: 1 Technology: 1 Manufacturing: 2 Service: 16	CEO: 1 Finance: 536 Management: 40	Mother: 407 N-1: 146 N-2: 22 N-3+: 2	CEO: 2 Board: 1 N-1: 522 N-2: 52

23	Chief Technical Officer	564/575	Africa: 23 Asia: 76 Europe: 229 N. America: 211 Oceania: 24 S. America: 1	Transportation: 37 Consumer goods: 9 Leisure: 8 Finance: 40 Health care: 58 Technology: 221 Manufacturing: 127 Media: 5 Service: 59	CEO: 1 Finance: 4 Management: 33 Technical: 526	Mother: 370 N-1: 136 N-2: 49 N-3+: 9	CEO: 1 N-1: 541 N-2: 22
24	Chief Innovation Officer	409/413	Africa: 3 Asia: 29 Europe: 107 N. America: 263 Oceania: 7	Agriculture: 3 Transportation: 10 Consumer goods: 20 Leisure: 9 Finance: 54 Health care: 39 Technology: 91 Manufacturing: 44 Media: 15 Service: 124	Board: 1 Development: 2 Management: 35 Technical: 371	Mother: 281 N-1: 91 N-2: 30 N-3+: 7	CEO: 1 N-1: 376 N-2: 32

Continued

Table *Continued*

#	Title	Firms/# titles	Geographical distribution*	Industry distribution**	Role domain	Mother/daughter firm	Reporting level
25	Chief Growth Officer	382/ 390	Africa: 3 Asia: 31 Europe: 51 N. America: 287 Oceania: 6 S. America: 4	Transportation: 6 Consumer goods: 21 Leisure: 11 Finance: 52 Health care: 47 Technology: 69 Manufacturing: 16 Media: 7 Service: 153	CEO: 1 Development: 341 Finance: 1 Management: 39	Mother: 229 N-1: 99 N-2: 33 N-3+: 21	CEO: 1 N-1: 364 N-2: 17
26	Chief Security Officer (Count includes quality and health positions)	317/ 322	Africa: 3 Asia: 58 Europe: 62 N. America: 193 Oceania: 1	Agriculture: 4 Transportation: 6 Consumer goods: 7 Leisure: 9 Finance: 45 Health care: 55 Technology: 104 Manufacturing: 40 Media: 4 Service: 43	CEO: 1 Corporate: 1 Development: 3 Management: 32 People: 253 Technical: 17	Mother: 242 N-1: 52 N-2: 16 N-3+: 7	CEO: 1 N-1: 249 N-2: 67

| 27 | Chief Communications Officer | 297/299 | Africa: 1
Asia: 19
Europe: 69
N. America: 203
Oceania: 4
S. America: 1 | Agriculture: 2
Transportation: 14
Consumer goods: 20
Leisure: 34
Finance: 48
Health care: 22
Technology: 48
Manufacturing: 38
Media: 22
Service: 49 | Corporate: 2
Development: 270
Finance: 2
Management: 18
People: 2
Technical: 3 | Mother: 215
N-1: 61
N-2: 17
N-3+: 4 | N-1: 254
N-2: 43 |
| 28 | Chief Procurement Officer | 279/282 | Africa: 6
Asia: 30
Europe: 121
N. America: 117
Oceania: 4
S. America: 1 | Agriculture: 2
Transportation: 21
Consumer goods: 27
Leisure: 12
Finance: 15
Health care: 22
Technology: 36
Manufacturing: 105
Media: 4
Service: 35 | CEO: 1
Corporate: 3
Development: 252
Management: 18
Technical: 5 | Mother: 165
N-1: 92
N-2: 19
N-3+: 3 | CEO: 1
N-1: 189
N-2: 89 |

Continued

Table *Continued*

#	Title	Firms/# titles	Geographical distribution*	Industry distribu-tion**	Role domain	Mother/daughter firm	Reporting level
29	Chief Trans-formation Officer	258/ 261	Africa: 3 Asia: 26 Europe: 98 N. America: 113 Oceania: 16 S. America: 2	Agriculture: 2 Transportation: 9 Consumer goods: 20 Leisure: 10 Finance: 59 Health care: 15 Technology: 40 Manufacturing: 33 Media: 9 Service: 61	Development: 1 Finance: 2 Management: 29 People: 233 Technical: 3	Mother: 161 N-1: 69 N-2: 19 N-3+: 9	N-1: 228 N-2: 30
30	Chief Science Officer	240/ 243	Africa: 1 Asia: 21 Europe: 38 N. America: 174 Oceania: 6	Agriculture: 3 Consumer goods: 18 Leisure: 1 Finance: 18 Health care: 86 Technology: 36 Manufacturing: 21 Media: 2 Service: 55	Board: 1 CEO: 3 Management: 41 Technical: 195	Mother: 191 N-1: 38 N-2: 9 N-3+: 2	CEO: 3 Board: 1 N-1: 217 N-2: 19

Appendix **215**

| 31 | Chief Research Officer | 240/243 | Africa: 1
Asia: 21
Europe: 38
N. America: 174
Oceania: 6 | Agriculture: 3
Consumer goods: 18
Leisure: 1
Finance: 18
Health care: 86
Technology: 36
Manufacturing: 21
Media: 2
Service: 55 | Board: 1
CEO: 3
Management: 41
Technical: 195 | Mother: 191
N-1: 38
N-2: 9
N-3+: 2 | CEO: 3
Board: 1
N-1: 217
N-2: 19 |
| 32 | Chief Data Officer | 235/235 | Africa: 5
Asia: 19
Europe: 86
N. America: 119
Oceania: 2
S. America: 4 | Agriculture: 1
Transportation: 5
Consumer goods: 4
Leisure: 3
Finance: 87
Healthcare: 12
Technology: 29
Manufacturing: 9
Media: 14
Service: 71 | Development: 71
Management: 29
People: 1
Technical: 134 | Mother: 126
N-1: 68
N-2: 33
N-3+: 8 | N-1: 172
N-2: 63 |

Continued

Table *Continued*

#	Title	Firms/# titles	Geographical distribution*	Industry distribution**	Role domain	Mother/daughter firm	Reporting level
33	Chief Supply Chain Officer	175/ 176	Africa: 3 Asia: 18 Europe: 48 N. America: 100 Oceania: 4 S. America: 2	Agriculture: 2 Transportation: 3 Consumer goods: 64 Leisure: 7 Finance: 1 Health care: 8 Technology: 10 Manufacturing: 40 Media: 3 Service: 37	Development: 1 Management: 13 Technical: 161	Mother: 129 N-1: 38 N-2: 7 N-3+: 1	N-1: 170 N-2: 5
34	Chief Sustainability Officer	99/ 100	Africa: 1 Asia: 16 Europe: 25 N. America: 53 Oceania: 4	Agriculture: 5 Transportation: 4 Consumer goods: 14 Leisure: 4 Finance: 10 Health care: 3 Technology: 6 Manufacturing: 33 Media: 3 Service: 18	Board: 1 CEO: 1 Corporate: 1 Finance: 3 Management: 13 People: 78 Technical: 2	Mother: 79 N-1: 17 N-2: 3	CEO: 1 Board: 1 N-1: 71 N-2: 26

35	Chief Brand Officer	97/103	Asia: 12 Europe: 12 N. America: 72 S. America: 1	Transportation: 1 Consumer goods: 18 Leisure: 11 Finance: 11 Health care: 3 Technology: 11 Manufacturing: 10 Media: 10 Service: 22	CEO: 1 Development: 81 Management: 14 People: 1	Mother: 80 N-1: 13 N-2: 3	CEO: 2 N-1: 89 N-2: 6
36	Chief Privacy Officer	94/94	Asia: 7 Europe: 7 N. America: 80	Transportation: 1 Consumer goods: 2 Leisure: 2 Finance: 25 Health care: 13 Technology: 15 Manufacturing: 4 Media: 2 Service: 30	Corporate: 62 Finance: 2 Management: 29 Technical: 1	Mother: 75 N-1: 10 N-2: 8 N-3+: 1	N-1: 61 N-2: 33

Continued

Table *Continued*

#	Title	Firms/# titles	Geographical distribution*	Industry distribution**	Role domain	Mother/daughter firm	Reporting level
37	Chief Analytics Officer	93/ 93	Asia: 7 Europe: 13 N. America: 72 Oceania: 1	Transportation: 2 Consumer goods: 2 Leisure: 1 Finance: 29 Health care: 7 Technology: 13 Manufacturing: 1 Media: 4 Service: 34	Development: 86 Management: 7	Mother: 63 N-1: 22 N-2: 6 N-3+: 2	N-1: 84 N-2: 9
38	Chief Diversity Officer	78/ 80	Asia: 1 Europe: 4 N. America: 72 Oceania: 1	Transportation: 3 Consumer goods: 4 Leisure: 6 Finance: 20 Health care: 1 Technology: 6 Manufacturing: 11 Media: 3 Service: 24	CEO: 1 Corporate: 3 Management: 19 People: 55	Mother: 64 N-1: 12 N-2: 2	CEO: 1 N-1: 39 N-2: 38

| 39 | Chief Design Officer | 75/73 | Asia: 8
Europe: 17
N. America: 49
Oceania: 2 | Consumer goods: 8
Leisure: 1
Finance: 10
Health care: 2
Technology: 13
Manufacturing: 15
Media: 2
Service: 25 | Development: 72
Management: 4 | Mother: 62
N-1: 9
N-2: 2
N-3+: 3 | N-1: 59
N-2: 17 |
| 40 | Chief Tax Officer | 50/50 | Asia: 1
N. America: 49 | Transportation: 2
Consumer goods: 3
Leisure: 3
Finance: 18
Health care: 1
Technology: 3
Manufacturing: 12
Media: 3
Service: 5 | Finance: 49
Management: 1 | Mother: 38
N-1: 11
N-2: 1 | N-1: 5
N-2: 45 |

Source: The Official Board (www.theofficialboard.com/). Data collected 5–8 March 2020 based on search across 77,426 companies listed in the database in 89 industries and 244 countries

* Listed companies by geography: Africa(1,906); Asia (14,475), Europe (27,441); North America (29,926); Oceania (2,219); South America (1,459).

** Listed companies by industry: Agriculture (468); Transportation (3,981); Consumer Goods (3,971); Leisure (2,795); Finance (14,918); Health Care (5,680); Technology (10,532); Manufacturing (17,037); Media (2,077); Service (15,967).

Papers and Reports on CXOs by Consulting and Executive Search Firms (2000–2020)

	Firms	Papers and reports on CXOs			
		2000–2010	2011–2020	Year unspecified	Total
1	Accenture	3	61	—	64
2	Bain	4	15	—	19
3	BCG	6	14	1	21
4	Capgemini	4	10	—	14
5	Deloitte	2	81	2	85
6	Egon Zehnder	—	15	8	23
7	Ernst & Young	1	29	2	32
8	Heidrick & Struggles	1	17	2	20
9	IBM	13	28	—	41
10	Korn Ferry	4	24	4	32
11	KPMG	3	28	—	31
12	McKinsey	7	29	1	37
13	PwC	4	38	—	42
14	Russell Reynolds	2	47	4	53
15	Spencer Stuart	2	44	—	46
	Total	56	480	24	560

References

Abbatiello, A., Bécotte, P., and Handcock, T. 2020. *The End of Expertise? Rethinking the C-suite*. Russell Reynolds Associates, https://www.russellreynolds.com/insights/thought-leadership/the-end-of-expertise-rethinking-the-c-suite.

Abbott, A. 1988. *The System of Professions: An Essay on the Division of Expert Labor*. Chicago, IL: The University of Chicago Press.

Abbott, A. 1991. "The Future of Professions: Occupation and Expertise in the Age of Organizations", *Research in the Sociology of Organizations*, 8: 17–42. Bingley: Emerald Group Publishing Limited.

Abrahamson, E. 1991. "Managerial Fads and Fashion: The Diffusion and Rejection of Innovations", *Academy of Management Review*, 16(3): 586–612.

Abrahamson, E. 1996. "Management Fashion", *Academy of Management Review*, 21(1): 254–285.

Accenture, 2011. Chief Procurement Officer Circular, December.

Accenture, 2013. The Agility-Creating Strategy Officer: Bringing Speed to Change. Accenture. Retrieved from: https://www.accenture.com/mz-en/~/media/Accenture/Conversion-Assets/DotCom/Documents/Global/PDF/Strategy_1/Accenture-The-Agility-Creating-CSO.pdf

Accenture, 2014. The CFO as Architect of Business Value, Accenture. Retrieved from: https://www.accenture.com/t20150523t035018z__w__/us-en/_acnmedia/accenture/conversion-assets/dotcom/documents/global/pdf/dualpub3/accenture-2014-high-performance-finance-study-cfo-architect-business-value.pdf

Accenture Interactive, 2013. The CMO–CIO Disconnect: Bridging the Gap to Seize the Digital Opportunity. Accenture. https://insuranceblog.accenture.com/wp-content/uploads/2013/11/Accenture-2040-CMO-CIO.pdf.

Accenture Interactive, 2014. Disrupting the C-suite: The Emergence of the Chief Experience Officer to Bridge the CMO-CIO Divide (2014 CMO-CIO Alignment Survey – Australia). Accenture.

Aldrich, H. and Herker, D. 1977. "Boundary Spanning Roles and Organizational Structure", *Academy of Management Review*, 2(2): 217–30.

Alexander, W., Anterasian, C., Doshi, P., and Welch, G. 2015. Do We Need a CXO? Evolving the Senior Management Team. Spencer Stuart Point of View. Retrieved from: https://www.spencerstuart.com/-/media/2020/january/pov15_cxo-2020-newimage.pdf

Allen, J. 2013. CHRO 3.0: The New Chief Human Resources Officer. Founder's Mentality Blog. Bain & Company, 7 Oct, https://www.bain.com/insights/chro-30-the-new-chief-human-resources-officer-fm-blog/

Alvarez, J.L. 1997. "The Sociological Tradition and the Spread and Institutionalization of Business Knowledge". In Alvarez, J.L. (ed.), *The Diffusion and Consumption of Business Knowledge* (pp. 13–57). London: Macmillan.

Alvarez, J.L. and Svejenova, S. 2005. *Sharing Executive Power: Roles and Relationships at the Top*. Cambridge: Cambridge University Press.

Alvesson, M. 2013. *The Triumph of Emptiness: Consumption, Higher Education, and Work Organization*. Oxford: Oxford University Press.

Alvesson, M. and Spicer, A. 2016. *The Stupidity Paradox: The Power and Pitfalls of Functional Stupidity at Work*. London: Profile Books.

Alvesson, M. and Spicer, A. 2018. "Neo-Institutional Theory and Organizational Studies: A Mid-Life Crisis?", *Organization Studies*, 40(2): 199–218.

Amason, A. 1996. "Distinguishing the Effects of Functional and Dysfunctional Conflict on Strategic Decision Making: Resolving a Paradox for Top Management Teams", *Academy of Management Journal*, 39(1): 123–48.

Ancona, D. and Nadler, D. 1989. "Top Hats and Executive Tales: Designing the Senior Team", *MIT Sloan Management Review*, Fall: 19–28.

Anteby, M. 2010. "Markets, Morals, and Practices of Trade: Jurisdictional Disputes in the US Commerce in Cadavers", *Administrative Science Quarterly*, 55: 606–38.

Anteby, M., Chan, C., and DiBenigno, J. 2016. "Three Lenses on Occupation and Professions in Organizations", *Academy of Management Annals*, 10(1): 183–244.

Anteby, M., and Holm, A. 2021. "Translating Expertise across Work Contexts: US Puppeteers Move from Stage to Screen", *American Sociological Review*, 86(2): 310–40.

Anthony, P. and Crichton, A. 1969. *Industrial Relations and the Personnel Specialists*. London: Batsford.

Ariker, M., Harrison, M., and Perrey, J. 2014. Getting the CMO and CIO to work as partners. McKinsey Digital. Retrieved from: https://www.mckinsey.com /business-functions/mckinsey-digital/our-insights/getting-the-cmo-and-cio-to-work-as-partners

Armstrong, P. 1985. "Changing Management Control Strategies: The Role of Competition between Accountancy and Other Organizational Professions", *Accounting, Management and Society*, 10(2): 129–48.

Artho, S., Mijnarends, H., Siebeke, S., Warburton, D. and Wilhelm, B. 2020. *CHRO 2025. How Leaders Are Preparing for Change (updated edition, 2020)*. Spencer Stuart. https://www.spencerstuart.com/research-and-insight/chro-2025

Ashby, W.R. 1968. "Variety, Constraint, and the Law of Requisite Variety". In Buckley, W. (ed.), *Modern Systems Research for the Behavioral Scientist* (pp. 129–36), Chicago, IL: Aldine Publishing Co.

Ashforth, B.E. and Kreiner, G.E. 1999. "'How Can You Do It?': Dirty Work and the Challenge of Constructing a Positive Identity", *Academy of Management Review*, 24(3): 413–34.

Awazu, Y. and Desouza, K. 2004. "The Knowledge Chiefs: CKOs, CLOs and CPOs", *European Management Journal*, 22(3): 339–44.

Aziz, A. 2020. How Chief Is Building a Network to Create More Women C-Suite Leaders—and Keep Them There. Forbes, 29 July. Retrieved from: https://www.forbes.com/sites/afdhelaziz/2020/07/29/how-chief-is-building-a-network-to-create-more-women-c-suite-leadersand-keep-them-there/#8edd0b55fe35

Bacharach, S. and Lawler, E. 1980. *Power and Politics in Organizations*. San Francisco, CA: Jossey-Bass.

Baird, C.H. and Ban, L. 2012. CMOs and CIOs: Acquaintances or Allies? C-Suite Studies, IBM Global Business Services report, IBM Institute for Business Value. IBM Corporation. Retrieved from: https://www.ibm.com/downloads/cas/KBVR2VLY

Baker, W. and Faulkner, R. 1991. "Role as Resource in the Hollywood Film Industry", *American Journal of Sociology*, 97(2): 279–309.

Banker, R., Hu, N., Pavlou, P., and Luftman, J. 2011. "CIO Reporting Structure, Strategic Positioning, and Firm Performance", *MIS Quarterly*, 35(2), 487–504.

Bansal, P. and DesJardine, M. 2014. "Business Sustainability: It Is About Time", *Strategic Organization*, 12(1): 70–8.

Barley, S. 1990. "The Alignment of Technology and Structure through Roles and Networks", *Administrative Science Quarterly*, 35: 61–103.

Barley, S. 2011. "Signifying Institutions", *Management Communications Quarterly*, 25: 200–6.

Battilana, J., Leca, B., & Boxenbaum, E. 2009. "How Actors Change Institutions: Towards a Theory of Institutional Entrepreneurship". *Academy of Management Annals*, 3(1): 65–107.

Barnard, Ch. 1938. *The Functions of the Executive*. Cambridge: Cambridge University Press.

Barnes, W. 2019. The Evolving Role of the CFO: The Chief 'Future' Officer. Deloitte private blog. 18 July, Retrieved from: https://www2.deloitte.com/au/en/blog/deloitte-private-blog/2019/evolving-role-of-CFO-chief-future-officer.html#

Baron, J. and Bielby, W. 1986. "The Proliferation of Job Titles in Organizations", *Administrative Science Quarterly*, 31: 561–86.

Baron, J., Dobbin, F., and Jennings, P. 1986. "War and Peace: The Evolution of Modern Personnel Administration in US Industry", *American Journal of Sociology*, 92(2): 350–83.

Barret, A. 2019. Should Your Board Include a CHRO? KPMG. https://board-leadership.kpmg.us/content/dam/boardleadership/en/pdf/2019/should-your-board-include-a-chro.pdf

Battilana, J. and D'Aunno, T. 2009. "Institutional Work and the Paradox of Embedded Agency". In Lawrence, T., Suddaby, R., and Leca, B. (eds), *Institutional Work: Actors and Agency in Institutional Studies of Organizations* (pp. 31–58). Cambridge: Cambridge University Press.

Bebchuk, L. and Tallarita, R. 2020. "The Illusory Promise of Stakeholder Governance", *Cornell Law Review*, 106: 91–178.

Bechky, B. 2020. "Evaluative Spillovers from Technological Change: The Effects of 'DNA Envy' on Occupational Practices in Forensic Science", *Administrative Science Quarterly*, 65(3): 606–43.

Beckman, C. and Burton, M. 2011. "Bringing Organizational Demography Back in: Time, Change, and Structure in Top Management Team Research". In Carpenter M. (ed.), *Handbook of Top Management Team Research*: pp. 49–70. Cheltenham: Edward Elgar.

Beechler, S., Søndergaard, M., Miller, E.L., and Bird, A. 2004. "Boundary Spanning". In Lane, W. et al. (eds), *The Blackwell Handbook of Global Management: A Guide to Managing Complexity*: pp. 121–33. Malden, MA: Blackwell.

Bendix, R. 1974. *Work and Authority in Industry*. Berkeley, CA: University of California Press.

Benko, C., Gorman, T., and Steinberg, A. 2014. "Disrupting the CHRO: Following into the CFOs' Footsteps", *Deloitte Review*, 14: 48–63.

Bennett, N. and Miles, S. 2006a. *Riding Shotgun: The Role of the Chief Operating Officer*. Stanford, CA: Stanford University Press.

Bennett, N. and Miles, S. 2006b. "Second in Command: The Misunderstood Role of the Chief Operating Officer", *Harvard Business Review*, May: 71–8.

Berg, J., Grant, A., and Johnson, V. 2010. "Perceiving and Responding to Challenges in Job Crafting of Different Ranks When Proactivity Requires Adaptability", *Journal of Organizational Behavior*, 31: 158–.186.

Berger, P.L. and Luckmann, T. 1966 [1991]. *The Social Construction of Reality* (reprint), London: Penguin Books.

Besharov, M. and Khurana, R. 2015. "Leading among Competing Technical and Institutional Demands: Revisiting Selznick's Conception of Leadership, Research in the Sociology of Organizations, 44: 53–88, Bingley: Emerald Group Publishing Limited.

Biddle, B. 1986. "Recent Developments in Role Theory", *Annual Review of Sociology*, 12: 67–92.

Birkinshaw, J., Ambos T., and Bouquet, C. 2017. "Boundary Spanning Activities of Corporate Headquarter Executives: Insights from a Longitudinal Study", *Journal of Management Studies*, 54: 422–54.

Boltanski, L. (translated by A. Goldhammer) 1987 [1982]. *The Making of a Class: Cadres in French Society*. Cambridge and Paris: Cambridge University Press and the Maison des Sciences de l'Homme.

Bonet, R., Cappelli, P., and Hamori, M. 2020. "Gender Differences in Speed of Advancement: An Empirical Examination of Top Executives in the Fortune 100 Firms", *Strategic Management Journal*, 41(4): 708–37.

Bontis, N. 2001. "CKO Wanted — Evangelical Skills Necessary: A Review of the Chief Knowledge Officer Position", *Knowledge and Process Management*, 8(1): 29–38.

Bontis, N. 2002. "Rising Star of the Chief Knowledge Officer", *Ivey Business Journal*, March–April, retrieved from: https://iveybusinessjournal.com/publication/rising-star-of-the-chief-knowledge-officer/

Boorman, S. 2011. "A Memo on Style: Reflections on 'Style' as a Sociological Concept", *Yale Journal of Sociology*, 8: 181–94.

Bottger, P. (ed.). 2008. *Leading in the Top Team: The CXO Challenge*. Cambridge: Cambridge University Press.

Boudreau, J. 2015. "Avoiding the 'Profession' Trap by Reaching Out". In Ulrich, D., Schiemann, B. and Sartain, L. *The Rise of HR* (pp. 355–60). Alexandria, VA: HR Certification Institute.

Boudreau, J. and Rice, S. 2015. "Bright, Shiny Objects and the Future of HR", *Harvard Business Review*, 93(7/8): 72–8.

Bourdieu, P. 1984. *Distinction: A Social Critique of the Judgement of Taste*. Cambridge, MA: Harvard University Press.

Bower, J. 1986. *Managing the Resource Allocation Process*. Boston, MA: Harvard Business School Press Classics.

Boyden. 2015. "Chief Digital Officer", *Executive Monitor*, 2(3): 1–24.

Boxenbaum, E. and Jonsson, S. 2017. "Isomorphism, Diffusion and Decoupling: Concept Evolution and Theoretical Challenges". In Greenwood, R., Oliver, C., & Lawrence, T. B. *The SAGE Handbook of Organizational Institutionalism* (pp. 77–97). SAGE Publications Ltd.

Bramante, J., Pillen, G., and Simpson, D. 2003. CFO Survey: Current State and Future Direction. IBM Business Consulting Services. Sommers, NY: IBM Corporation. Retrieved from: https://www.ibm.com/downloads/cas/DGWPVLPX

Breene, T., Nunes, P., and Shill, W. 2007. "The Chief Strategy Officer", *Harvard Business Review*, October: 84–93.

Brinker, S. and McLelland, L. 2014. "The Rise of the Chief Marketing Technologist", *Harvard Business Review*, 92(7/8): 82–5.

Bromley, P. and Meyer, J. 2015. *Hyper-Organization: Global Organizational Expansion*. Oxford: Oxford University Press.

Bromley, P. and Meyer, J. 2021. "Hyper-Management: Neo-Liberal Expansions of Purpose and Leadership". Organization Theory, doi:10.1177/26317877211 020327.

Brown, W. 1960. *Exploration in Management*. London: Heinemann.

Brown, W. 1965. *Informal Organization?* In Brown, W. and Jaques, E., *Glacier Project Papers* (pp. 144–62). London: Heinemann Educational Books.

Bruch, H. and Ghoshal, S. 2004. *A Bias for Action: How Effective Managers Harness Their Willpower, Achieve Results, and Stop Wasting Time*. Boston, MA: Harvard Business School Publishing.

Brynjolfsson, E. and McAfee, A. 2016. *The Second Machine Age: Work, Progress, and Prosperity in a Time of Brilliant Technologies*. New York: W. W. Norton & Company, Inc.

Bryson, J., Crosby, B., and Bloomberg, L. (eds). 2015. *Public Value and Public Administration*. Georgetown, Washington, DC: Georgetown University Press.

Burnham, J. 1941. *The Managerial Revolution*. New York: John Day.

Business Insurance. 2009. How to Choose, and Be the Best Chief Risk Officer Possible, p. 2.

Byrkjeflot, H. and Nygaard, P. 2018. "How and Why Management has not Become a Profession". In Ortenblad, A. (ed.), *Professionalizing Leadership* (pp. 49–68). Cham, Switzerland: Palgrave Macmillan.

Byrne, R. and Whiten, A. 1988. *Machiavellian Intelligence*. Oxford: Oxford University Press.

Byrnes, S. 2014. What Are the Differences Between Assigning VP-Level Titles Vs. CXO Titles in a Startup? Forbes, 18 April. https://www.forbes.com/sites/quora/2014/04/18/what-are-the-differences-between-assigning-vp-level-titles-vs-cxo-titles-in-a-startup/#59f5b4f08bcd, accessed on 6 November 2019.

Callero, P.L. 1994. "From Role-Playing to Role-Using: Understanding Role as a Resource", *Social Psychology Quarterly*, 57(3): 228–43.

Canales, R. and Greenberg, J. 2016. "A Matter of (Relational) Style: Loan Officer Consistency and Exchange Continuity in Micro Finance", *Management Science* 62(4): 1202–24.

Cappelli, P. 2015. "Why We Love to Hate HR . . . and What HR Can Do about It?", *Harvard Business Review*, July–August: 55–61.

Cappelli, P. and Hamori, M. 2005. "The New Road to the Top", *Harvard Business Review*, March: 25–32.

Cappelli, P., Hamori, M., and Bonet, R. 2014. "Whose Got Those Top Jobs?", *Harvard Business Review*, March: 75–9.

Carruthers, C. and Jackson, P. 2018. *The Chief Data Officer's Playbook*. London: Facet Publishing.

Chandler, A. 1962. *Strategy and Structure: Chapters in the History of the American Industrial Enterprise*. Cambridge, MA: MIT Press.

Chandler, A. 1976. "The Chief Executive's Office in Historical Perspective". In Glover, J. and Somon, G. (eds), *Chief Executive's Handbook* (pp. 38–49), Homewood, IL: Dow Jones-Irwin, Inc.

Chandler, A. 1977. *The Visible Hand: The Managerial Revolution in American Business*. Cambridge, MA: Harvard University Press.

Chandler, A. 1984. "The Emergence of Managerial Capitalism", *Business History Review*, 58(4): 473–503.

Chandler, D. 2014. "Organizational Susceptibility to Institutional Complexity", *Organization Science*, 25(6): 1722–43.

Charan, R. 2014. "It's Time to Split HR". *Harvard Business Review*, July–August.

Charan, R., Barton, D., and Carey D. 2015. "People Before Strategy: A New Role for the CHRO", *Harvard Business Review*, July–August: 63–71.

Chen, G. and Shi, W. 2019. "The CEO and CFO Pairing that Makes Mergers More Successful", *Harvard Business Review*, 12 August. https://hbr.org/2019/08/the-ceo-and-cfo-pairing-that-makes-mergers-more-successful.

Chen, J. and Nadkarni, S. 2017. "It's about Time! CEOs' Temporal Dispositions, Temporal Leadership, and Corporate Entrepreneurship", *Administrative Science Quarterly*, 62(1): 31–66.

Chief Medical Officers Summit. 2020. http://theconferenceforum.org/conferences/chief-medical-officer-summit/overview/, accessed 16 August 2020

Chreim, S., Williams, B., and Hining, B. 2007. "Interlevel Influences on the Reconstruction of Professional Role Identity", *Academy of Management Journal*, 50(6): 1515–39.

Clinton Foundation. 2019. https://www.clintonfoundation.org/about/leadership-team, accessed on 22 May 2019.

CNN. 2020. Trump's Pardon Spree Deepens Crisis Gripping American Justice. 19 February, https://www.cnn.com/2020/02/19/politics/donald-trump-pardons/index.html

Cohen, A. and Bradford, D. 1989. *Influence without Authority*. New York: John Wiley and Sons.

Cohen, L. 2013. "Assembling Jobs: A Model of How Tasks Are Bundled Into and Across Jobs", *Organization Science*, 24(2): 432–54.

Cole, J. 2017. Startups: When to Hire a CXO. The Startup, 2 August. https://medium.com/swlh/startups-when-to-hire-a-cxo-fd1d1ce7fb87, accessed on 20 June 2019.

Collis, D., Young, D., and Goold, M. 2012. "The Size and Composition of Corporate Headquarters in Multinational Companies: Empirical Evidence", *Journal of International Management*, 18: 260–75.

Crilly, D., Zollo, M., and Hansen, M. 2012. "'Faking It' or 'Muddling Through'? Understanding Decoupling in Response to Stakeholders Pressures", *Academy of Management Journal*, 55(6): 1429–48.

Crilly, D., Hansen, M., and Zollo, M. 2016. "The Grammar of Decoupling: A Cognitive-Linguistic Perspective on Firms' Sustainability Claims and Stakeholders' Interpretation", *Academy of Management Journal*, 59(2): 705–29.

Crozier, M. 1964. *The Bureaucratic Phenomenon: An Examination of Bureaucracy in Modern Organizations and Its Cultural Setting in France*. Chicago, IL: The University of Chicago Press.

De Waal, F. 1982. *Chimpanzee Politics: Power and Sex Among Apes*. Baltimore, MD: The John Hopkins University Press.

De Yonge, J. 2019. "For CEOs, are the days of sidelining global challenges numbered?" *EY CEO Imperative Study*. EYQ, EY's Think Tank, 8 July, retrieved from: https://www.ey.com/en_gl/growth/ceo-imperative-global-challenges

Delmar, D. 2003. "The Rise of the CSO", *Journal of Business Strategy*, 24(2): 8–10.

Delmestri, G. and Greenwood, R. 2016. "How Cinderella Became a Queen: Theorizing Radical Status Change", *Administrative Science* Quarterly, 61(4): 507–50.

Delmestri, G., Wezel, F.C., Goodrick, E., and Washington, M. 2020. "The Hidden Paths of Category Research: Climbing New Heights and Slippery Slopes", *Organization Studies*, 41(7): 909–20.

Deloitte. 2016. 3 CIO Profiles Create Lasting Enterprise Value. CIO Insights and Analysis from Deloitte. The Wall Street Journal. Retrieved from: https://deloitte.wsj.com/cio/2016/01/19/3-cio-profiles-create-lasting-enterprise-value/

Deloitte. 2018. Chief Data Officers 2.0. Deloitte LLP. Retrieved from: https://www2.deloitte.com/content/dam/Deloitte/ca/Documents/deloitte-analytics/ca_EN_CDO_POV_2018.pdf

Deloitte CFO Insights, 2012. Data-driven: The New CFO/CIO Dynamic. Deloitte Development LLC. Retrieved from: https://www2.deloitte.com /content/dam/Deloitte/us/Documents/finance-transformation/us-cfo-data-driven-102412.pdf.

Deloitte CFO Insights, 2014. Why Globalization Demands Chief Frontier Officers. Deloitte Development LLC. Retrieved from: https://www2.deloitte. com/us/en/insights/focus/business-trends/2014/cfo-as-chief-frontier-officer.html.

Deloitte Canada. 2015. CMO 2.0: How Chief Marketing Officers Will Succeed in the Omnichannel Era. Deloitte. Retrieved from: https://www2.deloitte.com /content/dam/Deloitte/ca/Documents/consumer-business/ca-en-cmo-2-0-takes-charge.pdf

Deloitte Johannesburg. 2016. Deloitte Executive Institute: C-suite Impact that Matters. Creative Services at Deloitte, Johannesburg, South Africa.

Denis, J., Lamothe, L., and Langley, A. 2001. "The Dynamics of Collective Leadership and Strategic Change in Pluralistic Organizations", *Academy of Management Journal*, 44(4): 809–37.

DiMaggio, P. J. 1988. "Interest and Agency in Institutional Theory". In L. G. Zucker (Ed.), *Institutional patterns and organizations: Culture and environment* (pp. 3–21). Cambridge, MA: Ballinger.

DiMaggio, P. 1991. "The Micro–Macro Dilemma in Organizational Research: Implications of Role-System Theory". In Huber, J. (ed.), *Macro–Micro Linkages in Sociology* (pp. 76–98), Newbury Park, CA: Sage.

DiMaggio, P. and Powell, W. 1983. "The Iron Cage Revisited: Institutional Isomorphism and Collective Rationality in Organizational Fields", *American Sociological Review*, 48: 147–60.

Dobbin, F. 2009. *Inventing Equal Opportunity*. Princeton, NJ: Princeton University Press.

Dobbin, F., Dierkes, J., Kwok, M., and Zorn, D. 2001. The Rise and Stagnation of the COO: Fad and Fashion in Corporation Titles. Working Paper, Princeton University.

Doh, J., Lawton, T., Rajwani, T., and Paroutis, S. 2014. "Why Your Company May need a Chief External Officer: Upgrading External Affairs Can Help Align Strategy and Improve Competitive Advantage", *Organizational Dynamics*, 43: 96–104.

Doliva, L. 2014. *Transforming the Future. The CHRO as Chief Change Officer*. Heidrick & Struggles International, Inc. https://www.heidrick.com/Knowledge-Center/Publication/Transforming-the-Future-The-CHRO-as-Chief-Change-Officer.

Dörrenbächer, Ch. and Geppert, M. (eds). 2011. *Politics and Power in the Multinational Corporation: The Role of Institutions, Interests and Identities*. Cambridge: Cambridge University Press.

Driggs, W. and Strier, K. 2014. "New Change, New Roles, New C-suite?", *Performance*, 6(4): 24–31. EY, Ey.com/performance.

Drori, G. 2020. "Hasn't Institutional Theory Always Been Critical?!". *Organization Theory*, 1: 1–9.

Drucker, P. 1954. *The Practice of Management*. New York: Harper and Brothers.

Drucker, P. 1973. *Management: Tasks, Responsibilities, Practices*. New York: Harper & Row.

du Gay, P. 2017. "Introduction: Office as a Vocation", European Journal of Cultural and Political Sociology, 4(2): 156–65.

du Gay, P. and Vikkelsø, S. 2017. *Formal Organization: The Past in the Present and Future of Organizational Theory*. Oxford: Oxford University Press.

Dunn, M. B. and Jones, C. 2010. "Institutional Logics and Institutional Pluralism: The Contestation of Care and Science Logics in Medical Education, 1967–2005". *Administrative Science Quarterly*, 55(1): 114–49.

Durkheim, E. 2014, first edition 1893. *The Division of Labour in Society*. New York: Free Press.

Dyer, A., Dyrchs, S., Bailey, A., Bürkner, H.-P., and Puckett, J. 2020. Why It's Time to Bring Learning to the C-Suite. BCG, July 14, https://www.bcg.com/publications/2020/why-it-is-time-to-bring-learning-to-the-c-suite

Eastland, T. 1992. *Energy in the Executive: The Case for the Strong Presidency*. New York, NY: The Free Press.

Ebbers, J.J. and Wijnberg, N.M. 2017. "Betwixt and Between: Role Conflict, Role Ambiguity and Role Definition in Project-Based Dual-Leadership Structures". *Human Relations*, 70(11): 1342–1365.

Eccles, R. and Nohria, N. 1992. *Beyond the Hype*. Boston, MA: Harvard Business School Publishing.

Edelman, L. 1990. "Legal Environments and Organization Governance: The Expansion of Due Process in the American Workplace", *American Journal of Sociology*, 95(6): 1401–40.

Edelman, L. 1992. "Legal Ambiguity and Symbolic Structures: Organization Mediation of Civil Rights Law", *American Journal of Sociology*, 97(6): 1531–76.

Edmondson, A., Roberto, M., and Watkins, M. 2003. "A Dynamic Model of Top Management Team Effectiveness: Managing Unstructured Task Streams", *The Leadership Quarterly*, 14(3): 297–325.

Egon Zehnder. 2016. The CMO Redefined. Egon Zehnder International, Inc. Retrieved from: file:///C:/Users/ssve.ioa/Downloads/cmo_redefined_updated_version_2016%20(3).pdf

Eisenhardt, K. and Bourgeois, L. 1988, "Politics of Strategic Decision Making in High-Velocity Environments: Toward a Midrange Theory", *Academy of Management Journal*, 31(4): 737–70.

Eisenhardt, K., Kahwaji, J., and Bourgeois, L. 1997. "How Management Teams Have a Good Fight", *Harvard Business Review*, 75(4): 77–85.

Eisenhardt, K., Kahwaji, J., and Bourgeois, L. 1998. "Conflict and Strategic Choice: How Top Management Teams Disagree". In Hambrick, D., Nadler, D., and Tushman, M. (eds), *Navigating Change: How CEOs, Top Teams, and Boards Steer Transformation* (pp. 141–69). Boston, MA: Harvard Business School Press.

Elkeles, T. and Phillips, J. 2011. *The Chief Learning Officer: Improving Human Performance*. New York: Routledge.

Elkeles, T., Phillips, J.J., and Phillips, P.P. 2017. *The Chief Talent Officer: The Evolving Role of the Chief Learning Officer*. New York: Routledge.

Elsbach, K. and Sutton, R. 1992. "Acquiring Organizational Legitimacy throughout Illegitimate Actions: A Marriage of Institutional and Impression Management Theories", *Academy of Management Journal*, 35(4): 699–738.

Emerson, R. 1962. "Power–Dependence Relations", *American Sociological Review*, 27(1): 31–40.

Engelen, A., Lackhoff, F., and Schmidt, S. 2013. "How can Chief Marketing Officers Strengthen their Influence? A Social Capital Perspective across Six Country Groups", *Journal of International Marketing*, 21(4): 88–109.

Engwall, L. and Kipping, M. 2006. "Management Education, Media and Consulting and the Creation of European Management Practice". *Innovation: The European Journal of Social Science Research*, 19(1): 95–106.

Ernst, B. and Kieser, A. 2002. "In Search of Explanations for the Consulting Explosion". In Sahlin-Andersson, K. and Engwall, L. (eds), *The Expansion of Management Knowledge: Carriers, Flows, and Sources* (pp. 47–73). Stanford, CA: Stanford Business Books.

Ernst & Young. 2010. The DNA of the CFO: What Makes a CFO?

Ernst & Young. 2013. Aiming for the Top: A Guide for Aspiring COOs and Their Organizations. EYGM Limited.

Ernst & Young. 2014. The DNA of the COO: Time to Claim the Spotlight. EYGM Limited. Retrieved from: http://www.agileleanhouse.com/lib/lib/Organizations/EY/DNA%20of%20the%20COO.pdf.

Etzioni, A. 1961. *A Comparative Analysis of Complex Organizations*. Glencoe, IL: Free Press.

Etzioni, A. 1965. "Dual Leadership in Complex Organizations", *American Sociological Review*, 30(5): 688–98.

Eyal, G. 2013. "For a Sociology of Expertise: The Social Origins of the Autism Epidemic", *American Journal of Sociology*, 118(4): 863–907.

Fairclough, N. 1989. *Language and Power*. London: Longman.

Farley, S. 2020. Twilio Just Appointed Its First Chief Social Impact Officer and She's Changing the Way Tech Companies Think about Impact. *Forbes*. 15 Jan. https://www.forbes.com/sites/fastforward/2020/01/15/twilio-just-appointed-its-first-chief-social-impact-officer-and-shes-changing-the-way-tech-companies-think-about-impact/#66feaacb274a, accessed on 11 July 2020.

Fayard, A-L, Stigliani, I., Bechky, B. 2017. "How Nascent Occupations Construct a Mandate: The Case of Service Designers' Ethos", *Administrative Science Quarterly*, 62(2): 270–303.

Finkelstein, S. and Hambrick, D. 1996. *Strategic Leadership: Top Executives and Their Effect on Organizations*. St. Paul, MN: West Publishing Company.

Finkelstein, S., Hambrick, D., and Cannella Jr., A. 2009. *Strategic Leadership: Theory and Research on Executives, Top Management Teams, and Boards*. Oxford: Oxford University Press.

Fleit, C. 2017. "The Evolution of the CMO", Harvard Business Review, July–August: 60.

Fleming, P. and Spicer, A. 2005, "Towards a Machiavellian Organizational Theory?", *Sociological Review*, 53(1): 95–105.

Fleming, P. and Spicer, A. 2014. "Power in Management and Organization Science", *The Academy of Management Annals*, 8(1): 237–98.

Fligstein, N. 1985. "The Spread of the Multidivisional Form among Large Firms, 1919–1979", *American Sociological Review*, 52(1): 44–58.

Fligstein, N. 1987. "The Intraorganizational Power Struggle: The Rise of Finance Personnel to Top Leadership in Large Corporations, 1919–1979", *American Sociological Review*, 50(3): 377–91.

Fligstein, N. 1990. *The Transformation of Corporate Control*. Cambridge, MA: Harvard University Press.

Fligstein, N. 1997. "Social Skill and Institutional Theory", *American Behavioral Scientist*, 40(4): 397–405.

Fligstein, N. 2001. "Social Skill and the Theory of Fields", *Sociological Theory*, 19(2): 105–25.

Fligstein, N. and McAdam, D. 2012a. "A Political Cultural Approach to the Problem of Strategic Action", *Research in the Sociology of Organizations*, 34: 287–316, Bingley: Emerald Group Publishing Limited.

Fligstein, N. and McAdam, D. 2012b. *A Theory of Fields*. Oxford: Oxford University Press.

Fontdevila, J., Opazo, P., and White, H. 2011. "Order at the Edge of Chaos: Meanings from Netdom Switchings across Functional Systems", *Sociological Theory*, 29(3): 178–98.

Ford press release, 2019. Ford Names New Leader of Global Government Relations. 18 February. Retrieved from: https://media.ford.com/content/fordmedia/fna/us/en/news/2019/02/18/ford-names-new-leader-of-global-government-relations.html.

Forbes. 2018. "AI: A CXO Strategy Guide", *Forbes Insights*.

Foulkes, F. 2015. "Succeeding as a CHRO: Advice from an Observer". In Ulrich; D., Schiemann, B., and Sartain, L., *The Rise of HR* (pp. 465–70). Alexandria, VA: HR Certification Institute.

Fragkos, G. 2016. The Rise of the (Chief) Data Protection Officer. Sysnet blog. https://sysnetgs.com/2016/02/the-rise-of-the-chief-data-protection-officer/

Franz, P. and Kirchmer, M. 2012. *The Chief Process Officer—A Role to Drive Value*, London, Philadelphia: Accenture Whitepapers.

Freidson, E. 1986. *Professional Powers: A Study in the Institutionalization of Formal Knowledge*. Chicago, IL: The University of Chicago Press.

Friedland, R. and Alford, R. 1991. "Bringing Society Back in: Symbols, Practices and Institutional Contradictions". In Powell, W. and DiMaggio, P. (eds.), *The New Institutionalism in Organizational Analysis* (pp. 232–67). Chicago: University of Chicago Press.

Friedrich, R., Péladeau, P., and Mueller, K. 2015. Adapt, Disrupt, Transform, Disappear: The 2015 Chief Digital Officer Study. Strategy&, PwC. Retrieved from: https://www.strategyand.pwc.com/gx/en/insights/2015/adapt-disrupt-transform-disappear/the-2015-chief-digital-officer-study.pdf

Frisch, B. 2012. *Who's in the Room? How Great Leaders Structure and Manage the Teams Around Them*. San Francisco, CA: John Wiley and Sons.

Fritton, M., Fleischmann, P., and Will, M. 2011. Communication from the CEO's perspective – an Underestimated Challenge? Egon Zehnder, August 31, https://www.egonzehnder.com/what-we-do/ceo-search-succession/insights/communication-from-the-ceos-perspective-an-underestimated-challenge

Fu, R., Tang, Y., and Chen, G. 2020. "Chief Sustainability Officers and Corporate Social (Ir)Responsibility", *Strategic Management Journal*, 41(4): 656–80.

Gallo, M. A., Alvarez, J. L., and Ricart J. E. 1998. *Prácticas de Gobierno Corporativo en España*. Barcelona: Ediciones IESE.

Galunic, Ch. 2020. *Backstage Leadership: The Invisible Work of Highly Effective Leaders*. Cham, Switzerland: Palgrave Macmillan.

Galunic, Ch. and Eisenhardt, K. 1994. Renewing the Strategy–Structure–Performance Paradigm. *Research in Organizational Behavior*, 16: 215–55.

Gangopadhyay, S. and HomRoy, S. 2020. What Is Left to Say: CEO Social Activism as Corporate Strategy (1 June 2020). Available at SSRN: https://ssrn.com/abstract=3622605 or http://dx.doi.org/10.2139/ssrn.3622605.

Gartner. 2015. CEO Survey. CFOs Tie Tech to Growth but Downplay the CIOs Role.

Gates Foundation. 2019. Who We Are. https://www.gatesfoundation.org/Who-We-Are/General-Information/Leadership/Executive-Leadership-Team, retrieved on 22 May 2019.

Germann, F., Ebbes, P., and Grewal, R. 2015. "The Chief Marketing Officer Matters!", *Journal of Marketing*, 79(3): 1–22.

Gilliatt, N. and Cuming, P. 1986. "The Chief Marketing Officer: A Maverick Whose Time Has Come". *Business Horizons*, Jan–Feb, 41–8.

Gingiss, D. 2019. What is a Chief Experience Officer and Why Does a Company Need One? Forbes, 17 Dec, retrieved from: https://www.forbes.com/sites/dangingiss/2019/12/17/what-is-a-chief-experience-officer-and-why-does-a-company-need-one/#1d5f8cd12b69

Gioia, D.A. and Chittipeddi, K. 1991. "Sensemaking and Sensegiving in Strategic Change Initiation", *Strategic Management Journal*, 12, 433–48.

Godart, F. 2018. "Why Style Is Not in Fashion? Using the Concept of 'Style' to Understand Creative Industries", *Research in the Sociology of Organizations*, 55: 103–28, Bingley: Emerald Group Publishing Limited.

Godart, F. and Galunic, Ch. 2019. "Explaining the Popularity of Cultural Elements: Networks, Culture and the Structural Embeddedness of High Fashion Trends", *Organization Science*, 30(1): 151–68.

Goodrick, E. and Reay, T. 2010. "Florence Nightingale Endures: Legitimizing a New Professional Role Identity", *Journal of Management Studies*, 47(1): 55–84.

Goold, M., Pettifer, D. and Young, D. 2001. "Redesigning the Corporate Centre". *European Management Journal*, 19(1): 83–91.

Gordon, C. 1976. "Development of Evaluated Role Identities", *Annual Review of Sociology*, 2: 405–33.

Gordon, D. 1972. *Theories of Power and Underemployment*. Lexington, MA: D.C. Heath.

Gorter, O., Hudson, R., and Scott, J. 2016. The Role of the Chief Transformation Officer. McKinsey & Company. Retrieved from: https://www.mckinsey.com/~/media/McKinsey/Business%20Functions/Transformation%20and%20Restructuring/Our%20insights/The%20role%20of%20the%20chief%20transformation%20officer/The-role-of-the-chief-transformation-officer.pdf

Goudreau, J. 2012. C Is for Silly: The New C-Suite Titles. *Forbes*, http://www.forbes.com/sites/jennagoudreau/2012/01/10/c-is-for-silly-the-new-c-suite-titles/, accessed 29 September 2013.

Graeber, D. 2019. *Bullshit Jobs: A Theory*. London, UK: Penguin Books.

Granqvist, N., Grodal, S., and Woolley, J. 2013. "Hedging your Bets: Explaining Executives' Market Labelling Strategies in Nanotechnology", *Organization Science*, 24: 395–413.

Grant, A., Berg, J., and Cable, D. 2014. "Job Titles as Identity Badges: How Self-Reflective Titles Can Reduce Emotional Exhaustion", *Academy of Management Journal*, 57(4): 1201–25.

Greenwood, R. and Meyer, R. 2008. "Influencing Ideas: A Celebration of DiMaggio and Powell (1983)". *Journal of Management Inquiry*, 17(4):258–264.

Greenwood, R., Suddaby, R., and Hinings, C.R. 2002. "Theorizing Change: The Role of Professional Associations in the Transformation of Institutionalized Fields", *Academy of Management Journal*, 45: 58–80.

Greenwood, R., Raynard, M., Kodeih, F., Micelotta, E., and Lounsbury, M. 2011. "Institutional Complexity and Organizational Responses", *The Academy of Management Annals*, 5(1): 317–71.

Greenwood, R., Hinings, C.R., and Whetten, D. 2014. "Rethinking Institutions and Organizations", *Journal of Management Studies*, 51(7): 1206–20.

Gresov, Ch. and Razin, R. 1997. "Equifinality: Functional Equivalence in Organizational Design", *Academy of Management Review*, 22(2): 403–28.

Grewal, R. and Wang, R. 2009. "The Chief Marketing Officer: New Vintage, or Just Old Wine in a New Bottle?" *The Chief Marketing Officer Journal*, 1: 29–34.

Grodal, S. and Kahl, S.J. 2017. "The Discursive Perspective of Market Categorization: Interaction, Power, and Context". *Research in the Sociology of Organizations*, 51: 151–84, Bingley: Emerald Group Publishing Limited.

Gross, T. and Zilber, T.B. 2020. "Power Dynamics in Field-Level Events: A Narrative Approach", *Organization Studies*, 41(10): 1369–90.

Grossman, R. and Rich, J. 2021. The Rise of the Chief Digital Officer. Leadership & Talent series. Russell Reynolds Aassociates. https://www.russellreynolds.com /sites/default/files/leadership-and-talent-rise-of-chief-digital-officer.pdf

Groysberg, B., Kelly, K., and MacDonald, B. 2011. "The New Path to the C-Suite", *Harvard Business Review*, March: 60–8.

Guadalupe, M., Li, H., and Wulf, J. 2014. "Who Lives in the C-Suite? Organizational Structure and the Division of Labor in Top Management", *Management Science*, 60(4): 824–44.

Guarino, A. 2016. *Why CHROs Really are CEOs*. Los Angeles, CA: Korn Ferry Institute.

Gupta, Y. 1991. "The Chief Executive Officer and the Chief Information Officer: The Strategic Partnership", *Journal of Information Technology*, 6(3/4): 128–39.

Gieryn, T. 1983. "Boundary-Work and the Demarcation of Science from Non-Science: Strains and Interests in Professional Ideologies of Scientists". *American Sociological Review*, 48: 781–95.

Hacking, I. 1986. "Making Up People". In Heller, T. et al. (eds), *Reconstructing Individualism* (pp. 222–36). Stanford, CA: Stanford University Press.

Hackman, R. 1989. *Groups that Work (and Those That Don't): Creating Conditions for Effective Teamwork*. San Francisco, CA: Jossey Bass Publishers.

Hackman, R. 2002. *Leading Teams: Setting the Stage for Great Performance*. Boston, MA: Harvard Business School Publishing.

Hafenbradl, S. and Waeger, D. 2017. "Ideology and the Foundations of CSR: Why Executives Believe in the Business Case for CSR and How This Affects CSR Engagements", *Academy of Management Journal*, 60(4): 1581–606.

Hambrick, D. 1994. "Top Management Groups: A Conceptual Integration and Re-consideration of the Team Label". In Staw, B. and Cummings, L. (eds), *Research in Organizational Behavior*, 15 (pp. 171–214). Greenwood, CT: JAI Press.

Hambrick, D. 1995. "Fragmentation and the Other Problems CEOs Have with Their Top Management Teams", *California Management Review*, 37(3): 110–27.

Hambrick, D. 2007. "Upper Echelons Theory: An Update", *Academy of Management Review*, 32(2): 334–43.

Hambrick, D. and Cannella Jr., A. 2004. "CEOs Who Have COOs: Contingency Analysis of an Unexplored Structural Form", *Strategic Management Journal*, 25(10): 959–79.

Hambrick, D. and Lovelace, J. 2018. "The Role of Executive Symbolism in Advancing New Strategic Themes in Organizations", *Academy of Management Review*, 43(1): 120–31.

Hambrick, D. and Mason, P. 1984. "Upper Echelons: The Organization as a Reflection of Its Top Managers", *Academy of Management Review* 2: 193–206.

Hambrick, D., Finkelstein, S., and Mooney, A.C. 2005. "Executive Job Demands: New Insights for Explaining Strategic Decisions and Leader Behaviors", *Academy of Management Review*, 30(3): 472–91.

Han, B-Ch. 2019. *What Is Power?* Cambridge, UK: Polity Press.

Hansen, M. 2009. *Collaboration: How Leaders Avoid the Traps, Building Common Ground, and Reap Big Results*. Boston, MA: Harvard Business School Press.

Hansen, M. and Tapp, S. 2010. "The Chief Collaboration Officer", *Harvard Business Review*, 11 October, https://hbr.org/2010/10/who-should-be-your-chief-colla.

Hansen, M. and von Oetinger, B. 2001. "Introducing the T-Shaped Managers", *Harvard Business Review*, 79(3): 106–16.

Hardy, C. and Phillips, N. 2004. "Discourse and Power". In Grant, D., Hardy, C., Oswick, C., and Putnam, L. (eds), *Handbook of Organizational Discourse* (pp. 219–318). London: Sage.

Hargrave, T. and Van de Ven, A. 2009. "A Collective Action Model of Institutional Innovation". *Academy of Management Review*, 31(4): 864–88.

Harrington, B. and Seabrooke, L. 2020. "Transnational Professionals", *Annual Review of Sociology*, 46: 399–417.

Harris, T.G. 1993. "The Post-Capitalist Executive: An Interview with Peter F. Drucker", *Harvard Business Review*, May–June: 114–22.

Harrison, E. 1999. *The Managerial Decision-Making Process*. New York: Houghton Mifflin.

Haskel, J. and Westlake, S. 2018. *Capitalism without Capital: The Rise of the Intangible Economy*. Princeton, NJ: Princeton University Press.

Hegel, W.F.H. 1807/2019. The Phenomenology of Spirt. Cambridge: Cambridge University Press.

Heinrich, J., Heric, M., Goldman, N., and Cichocki, P. 2014. *A Higher Bar*. Bain & Company Inc.

Heinze, K. and Weber, K. 2016. "Toward Organizational Pluralism: Institutional Intrapreneurship in Integrative Medicine", *Organization Science*, 27(1): 157–72.

Henriksen, L. and Seabrooke L. 2016. "Transnational Organizing: Issue Professionals in Environmental Sustainability", *Organization*, 23(5): 722–41.

Hickson, D., 1966. "A Convergence in Organization Theory". *Administrative Science Quarterly*, 12: 224–37.

Hickson, D., Hinings, C., Lee, C., Schneck, R., and Pennings, J. 1971. "A Strategic Contingencies Theory of Intraorganizational Power", *Administrative Science Quarterly*, 16(2): 216–29.

Hill, A. 2016. "Chief Digital Officer—the Role that We Will all Need to Assume", *The Financial Times*, 7 March, https://next.ft.com/content/402e9c08-e223-11e5-9217-6ae3733a2cd1, accessed on 9 June 2016

Hofstadter, D. and Sander, E. 2013. *Surfaces and Essences: Analogy as the Fuel and Fire of Thinking*. New York: Basic Books.

Höllerer, M., Jancsary, D., Meyer, R., and Vettori, O. 2013. "Imageries of Corporate Social Responsibility: Visual Recontextualization and Field-Level Meaning". *Research in the Sociology of Organizations*, 39B: 139–74, Bingley: Emerald Group Publishing Limited.

Hudson, L. 2014. Your First Look at Entrepreneur Barbie, Smartphone and All. *Wired*, 18 June, https://www.wired.com/2014/06/entrepreneur-barbie/.

Ibarra, H. 1992. "Structural Alignments, Individual Strategies, and Managerial Action: Elements toward a Network Theory of Getting Things Done", in Nohria, N.

and Eccles, R. (eds), *Networks and Organizations: Structure, Form, and Action* (pp. 165–88). Boston, MA: Harvard Business School Press.

Ibarra, H. 1993. "Network Centrality, Power, and Innovation Involvement: Determinants of Technical and Administrative Roles", *Academy of Management Journal*, 36: 277–303.

Ibarra, H. and Hansen, M. 2011. "Are You a Collaborative Leader?", *Harvard Business Review*, 89(7/8): 68–74.

IBM Business Consulting Services. 2003. CFO Survey: Current State and Future Direction. IBM Corporation. Retrieved from: https://www.ibm.com/downloads/cas/DGWPVLPX.

IBM Institute for Business Value. 2015. The New Hero of Big Data and Analytics: The Chief Data Officer. IBM Institute for Business Value. IBM.

IBM Institute for Business Value. 2016. Redefining Markets: Insights from the Global C-suite Study—The CMO perspective. IBM Corporation. Retrieved from: https://www.ibm.com/downloads/cas/P5MDVY0G

IBM Institute for Business Value. 2020. The Intelligent Operations Advantage: Global C-suite Study 20th Edition Chief Operations Officer Insights from the Global C-suite Study. IBM Corporation. Retrieved from: https://www.ibm.com/downloads/cas/JPMKDBVZ

IBM Institute for Business Value. 2021. Find Your Essential: How to Thrive in a Post-Pandemic Reality. C-suite Series: The 2021 CEO Study. IBM Corporation. Retrieved from: https://www.ibm.com/thought-leadership/institute-business-value/report/ceo

Jacobs, E. 2021. 'Chief Medical Officers Are Now at the Heart of Business'. *Financial Times (online editition)*, March 28, https://www.ft.com/content/3efac481-4ed5-4619-bf65-3f61e4d2b567.

Jancsary, D., Meyer, R., Höllerer, M., and Barberio, V. 2017. Toward a Structural Model of Organizational-Level Institutional Pluralism and Logic Interconnectedness. *Organization Science*, 28(6): 1150–67.

Janis, I. 1982. *Groupthink: Psychological Studies of Policy Decisions and Fiascos*. New York: Houghton Mifflin.

Johnson, K. and Duxbury, L. 2010. "The View from the Field: A Case Study of the Expatriate Boundary-Spanning Role", *Journal of World Business*, 45: 29–40.

Jones, C. and Livne-Tarandach, R. 2008. "Designing a Frame: Rhetorical Strategies of Architects", *Journal of Organizational Behavior*, 29: 1075–99.

Jones, C., Maoret, M., Massa, F., and Svejenova, S. 2012. "Rebels with a Cause: The Formation, Contestation and Expansion of the de Novo Category Modern Architecture, 1870–1975", *Organization Science*, 23: 1523–45.

Joseph, J., Ocasio, W., and McDonnell, M. 2014. "The Structural Elaboration of Board Independence: Executive Power, Institutional Logics, and the Adoption of the CEO-Only Board Structures in U.S. Corporate Governance", *Academy of Management Journal*, 57(6): 1834–58.

Jung, J. 2014. "Political Contestation at the Top: Politics of Outsider Succession at US Corporations", *Organization Studies*, 35(5): 727–64.

Jung, J. 2016. "Through the Contested Terrain: Implementation of Downsizing Announcements by Large US Firms, 1984–2005", *American Sociological Review*, 81: 347–73.

Kachaner, N. and Stewart, S. 2013. *Understanding the Role of the Chief Strategy Officer.* Boston, MA: BCG, The Boston Consulting Group, Inc.

Kanashivo, P. and Rivera, J. 2019. "Do Chief Sustainability Officers Make Companies Greener? The Moderating Role of Regulatory Pressures", *Journal of Business Ethics*, 155(1): 687–701.

Kaneshige, T. 2014. "CIO–CMO Marriage Strained, But Can Be Saved", *CIO Magazine*, (September Issue), 23 July, retrieved from: https://www.cio.com/article/2456696/cio-cmo-marriage-strained-but-can-be-saved.html

Kaplan, R. and Norton, D. 2006. *Alignment: Using Balanced Scorecard to Create Corporate Synergies.* Boston, MA: Harvard Business School Press.

Karaian, J. 2014. *The CFO: What CFOs Do, the Influence They Have, and Why It Matters.* London: Profile Books.

Kark, K. and Vanderslice, P. 2015. CIO as a Chief Integration Officer. In Briggs, B. and Shingles, M. in collaboration with Singularity University Faculty and Leadership. *Tech Trends 2015: The Fusion of Business and IT* (pp. 5–19). Westlake, TX: Deloitte University Press.

Katz, D. and Kahn, R. 1978. *The Social Psychology of Organizations.* Second Edition. New York: John Wiley and Sons.

Katzenbach, J. 1998. *Teams at the Top. Unleashing the Potential of Both Teams and Individual Leaders.* Boston, MA: Harvard Business School Press.

Katzenbach, J. and Smith, D. 1993. *The Wisdom of Teams: Creating the High Performing Organization.* Boston, MA: Harvard Business School Press.

Kellogg, K. 2019. "Subordinate Activation Tactics: Semi-professionals and Micro-level Institutional Change", *Administrative Science Quarterly*, 64(4): 928–75.

Kellogg, K., Orlikowski, W., & Yates, J. 2006. "Life in the Trading Zone: Structuring Coordination across Boundaries in Postbureaucratic Organizations". *Organization Science*, 17: 22–44.

Kelly, E. 2014a. "Introduction: Navigating the Next Wave of Globalization". In *Business Trends 2014: Navigating the Next Wave of Globalization* (pp. i–xvii). Westlake, TX: Deloitte University Press. Retrieved from: https://www2.deloitte.com/us/en/insights/focus/business-trends/2014.html

Kelly, E. 2014b. "The C-suite: Time for Version 3.0?" In *Business Trends 2014 Navigating the Next Wave of Globalization* (pp 113–23). Westlake, TX: Deloitte University Press. Retrieved from: https://www2.deloitte.com/us/en/insights/focus/business-trends/2014.html

Khurana, R. and Nohria, N. 2008. "It is Time to Make Management a True Profession", *Harvard Business Review*, October: 71–7.

Kieser, A. 1997. "Rhetoric and Myth in Management Fashion", *Organization*, 4(1): 49–74.

Kieser, A. 2002. "Managers as Marionettes? Using Fashion Theories to Explain the Success of Consultancies". In Kipping, M. and Engwall, L. (eds), *Management*

Consulting: Emergence and Dynamics of a Knowledge Industry (pp. 167–83). Oxford: Oxford University Press.

King, M. 2020. *Social Chemistry: Decoding the Patterns of Human Connection*. New York: Dutton.

Kipping, M. and Engwall, L. (eds). 2002. *Management Consulting: Emergence and Dynamics of a Knowledge Industry*. Oxford: Oxford University Press.

Klimas, T. and Corson, M. 2016. "Do You Define Your CFO Role? Or Does It Define You?". EYGM Limited, https://assets.ey.com/content/dam/ey-sites/ey-com/en_gl/topics/cfo/cfo-agenda-pdf/ey-do-you-define-your-cfo-role-or-does-it-define-you.pdf

Knights, D. and Morgan, G. 1991. "Corporate Strategy, Organizations, and Subjectivity: A Critique", *Organization Studies*, 12(2): 251–73.

Korn Ferry Institute. 2008. The Path to the C-suite 2008 A Guide for Human Resources Executives. Korn/Ferry Institute. Retrieved from: https://www.kornferry.com/content/dam/kornferry/docs/article-migration/The%20Path%20to%20the%20C-suite%202008-%20A%20Guide%20for%20Human%20Resources%20Executives%20.pdf

Korn Ferry Institute. 2012. The Chief Communications Officer: Korn/Ferry's 2012 Survey of Fortune 500 Companies, Korn/Ferry Institute. Retrieved from: https://www.kornferry.com/insights/articles/543-the-chief-communications-officer-korn-ferry-s-2012-survey-of-fortune-500-companies

Korn Ferry Institute. 2016. Why CHROs Really Are CEOs. Korn Ferry. Retrieved from: https://www.kornferry.com/insights/articles/why-chros-really-are-ceos

Kornberger, M. 2017. "The Values of Strategy: Valuation Practices, Rivalry and Strategic Agency", *Organization Studies*, 38(12): 1753–73.

Kosminsky, F. and Cannon, K. n.d. *The Next CHRO Brand: HR's Promise of Value*. Korn/Ferry International. Retrieved from: https://www.kornferry.com/insights/this-week-in-leadership/286-the-new-chro-brand-hr-s-promise-of-value.

Kostova, T. and Zaheer, S. 1999. "Organizational Legitimacy under Conditions of Complexity: The Case of the Multinational Enterprise", *Academy of Management Review*, 24(1): 64–81.

Kostova T., Roth, K., and Dacin, T. 2008. "Institutional Theory in the Study of Multinationals: A Critique and New Directions", *Academy of Management Review*, 33(4): 994–1006.

Kotter, J.P. 1982. *The General Managers*. New York: The Free Press.

Kotter, J.P. 1985. *Power and Influence: Beyond Formal Authority*. New York: The Free Press.

Kotter, J.P. 1990. "What Leaders Really Do", *Harvard Business Review*, 68(3): 103–11.

KPMG, 2017. The Rise of the CHRO Officer, p. 10.

KPMG International. 2013. Survey Being the Best: Inside the Intelligence Finance Function

KPMG International. 2015. The View from the Top. CEOs See a Powerful Future for the CFO: Are the CFOs Ready for the Challenge?

KPMG International. 2018. Chief Tax Officer Outlook: Top-of-Mind Issues for Tax Leaders—Seventh Global Edition. KPMG International Cooperative.

Kraatz, M. 2009. "Leadership as Institutional Work: A Bridge to the Other Side". In Lawrence, T., Suddaby, R., and Leca, B. (eds), *Institutional Work: Actors and Agency in Institutional Studies of Organizations* (pp. 59–91). Cambridge: Cambridge University Press.

Kraatz, M.S. and Block, E.S. 2008. "Organizational Implications of Institutional Pluralism". In Greenwood, R., Oliver, C., Suddaby, R., and Sahlin-Andersson, K. (eds), *Handbook of Organizational Institutionalism* (pp. 243–76). London: Sage.

Krachenberg, A., Henke, J., and Lyons, T. 1993. "The Isolation of Upper Management", *Business Horizons*, July–August: 41–7.

Kruecken, G., Mazza, C., Meyer, R., and Walgenbach, P. 2017. *New Themes in Institutional Analysis: Topics and Issues from European Research.* Cheltenham: Edward Elgar.

Kunisch, S., Menz, M., and Cannella Jr., A. 2019. "The CEO as a Key Microfoundation of Global Strategy: Task Demands, CEO Origin, and the CEO's International Background". *Global Strategy Journal*, 9(1): 19–41.

Kunisch, S., Menz, M., and Langan, R. 2020. "Chief Digital Officers: An Exploratory Analysis of their Emergence, Nature, and Determinants", *Long Range Planning*, https://doi.org/10.1016/j.lrp.2020.101999

Kunisch, S., Müller-Stewens, G., and Campbell, A. 2014. "Why Corporate Functions Stumble?" *Harvard Business Review*, 92(12): 110–117.

L'Oréal press release, 2021. L'Oréal Executive Committee Nomination: Blanca Juti is appointed Chief Communications & Public Affairs Officer, 13 January. Retrieved from: https://www.loreal.com/en/press-release/group/loreal-executive-committee-nomination-blanca-juti-is-appointed-chief-communications–public-affairs/.

Laamanen, T., Lamberg, J., and Vaara, E. 2015. "Explanations of Success and Failure in Management Learning: What Can We Learn from Nokia's Rise and Fall?", *Academy of Management Learning & Education*, 15(1): 2–25.

Lahiri, G., Schwartz, J., and Volini, E. 2018. *The Symphonic C-suite: Teams Leading Teams.* Deloitte Insights, 28 March. https://www2.deloitte.com/us/en/insights/focus/human-capital-trends/2018/senior-leadership-c-suite-collaboration.html

Langley, A., Lindberg, K., Mørk, B., Nicolini, D., Raviola, E., and Walter, L. 2019. "Boundary Work among Groups Occupations and Organizations: From Cartography to Process". *Academy of Management Annals*, 13: 704–736.

Larson, M. 1977. *The Rise of Professionalism: A Sociological Analysis.* Berkeley, CA: University of California Press.

Lawrence, P. and Lorsch, J. 1967a. *Organization and Environment.* Boston, MA: Harvard Business School Press.

Lawrence, P. and Lorsch, J. 1967b. "A New Management Job: The Integrator", *Harvard Business Review*, November–December: 142–51.

Lawrence, T. and Phillips, N. 2019. *Constructing Organizational Life*. Oxford: Oxford University Press.

Lawrence, T., Suddaby, R., and Leca, B. (eds). 2009a. *Institutional Work: Actors and Agency in Institutional Studies in Organizations*. Cambridge: Cambridge University Press.

Lawrence, T., Suddaby, R., and Leca, B. 2009b. "Introduction: Theorizing and Studying Institutional Work". In Lawrence, T. B., Suddaby, R., and Leca, B. (eds), *Institutional Work: Actors and Agency in Institutional Studies of Organizations* (pp. 1–27). Cambridge: Cambridge University Press.

Leahey, C. 2011. 7 Executive Jobs in the Future C-suite. Fortune, http://money.cnn.com/galleries/2011/fortune/1106/gallery.csuite_executives_future.fortune/index.html, accessed on 29 September 2013.

Lee, A. 2020. *Machiavelli: His Life and Times*. London: Picador.

Leonardo. 2018. Sustainability and Innovation Report. Rome: leonardocompany.com. Retrieved from: https://www.leonardocompany.com/documents/20142/116025/Leonardo_2018+Sustainability+Report_Non-financial+Statement-final.pdf?t=1556644909652.

Levi Strauss. 2019. Kate Walsh Appointment. Press Release. https://www.levistrauss.com/wp-content/uploads/2019/03/Katia-Walsh_Appointment_PR_022019_FINAL.pdf

Levy, D. and Scully, M. 2007. "The Institutional Entrepreneur as Modern Prince: The Strategic Face of Power in Contested Fields", *Organization Studies*, 28(7): 971–91.

Lieberson, S. 2000. *A Matter of Taste: How Names, Fashions and Culture Change*. New Haven, CT: Yale University Press.

Light, L. 2020. It Is CMO Wake-Up Time. Forbes, 17 Feb, Retrieved from: https://www.forbes.com/sites/larrylight/2020/02/17/it-is-cmo-wake-up-time/#6ad4476d2809

Liu, F., Jarrett, M., and Maitlis, S. Forthcoming 2021. "Top Management Teams Constellations and Their Implications for Strategic Decision Making", *The Leadership Quarterly*.

Loewenstein, J., 2014. "Take My Word for It: How Professional Vocabularies Foster Organizing", *Journal of Professions and Organization*, 1: 65–83.

Loewenstein, J., Ocasio, W., and Jones, C. 2012. "Vocabularies and Vocabulary Structure: A New Approach Linking Categories, Practices, and Institutions", *Academy of Management Annals*, 6: 41–86.

Logue, D. and Clegg, S. 2015. "Wikileaks and the News of the World: The Political Circuitry of Labeling", *Journal of Management Inquiry*, 24: 394–404.

London, D. and Lowitt, E. 2008. "The CSO and the CFO: Creative Tension in the C-suite". In Breene, T., Nunes, P., and Shill, W., *Rise of the Chief Strategy Officer* (p.7), Outlook, January. Accenture.

Long Lingo, E. and McGinn, K.L. 2020. "A New Prescription for Power", *Harvard Business Review*, 98(4): 66–75.

Long Lingo, E. and O'Mahony, S. 2010. "Nexus Work: Brokerage on Creative Projects", *Administrative Science Quarterly*, 55: 47–81.

Lorange, P. 2008. "The Chief Executive Officer—Orchestrating the Whole". In Bottger, P. (ed.), *Leading in the Top Team: The CXO Challenge* (pp. 348–64). Cambridge: Cambridge University Press.

Lorsch, J. and Morse, J. 1974. *Organizations and Their Members: A Contingency Approach.* New York: Harper & Row.

Lovric, D. and Schneider, G. 2019. "What Kind of Chief Innovation Officer Does Your Company Need?", *Harvard Business Review*, November.

Lukes, S. 1974. *Power: A Radical View.* London: Macmillan.

Lundberg, A. and Westerman, G. 2020. "The Transformer CLO", *Harvard Business Review*, Jan–Feb: 84–93.

Luthans, F. and Stewart, T. 1977. "A General Contingency Theory of Management", *Academy of Management Review*, 2(2): 181–96.

Ma, S., and Seidl, D. 2018. "New CEOs and Their Collaborators: Divergence and Convergence Between the Strategic Leadership Constellation and the Top Management Team", *Strategic Management Journal*, 39(3): 606–38.

MacGregor, S. and Simpson, R. 2018. *Chief Wellbeing Officer: El Bienestar Como Herramienta Estratégica.* Madrid: LID.

Maitlis, S., and Sonenshein, S. 2010. "Sensemaking in Crisis and Change: Inspiration and Insights From Weick (1988)", *Journal of Management Studies* 47(3): 551–80.

Malik Chua, J. 2019. "Why Fashion Needs Chief Diversity Officers", *Vogue Business Talent*, 21 November, https://www.voguebusiness.com/talent/articles/chief-diversity-officers-inclusion-burberry-gucci-hm/, accessed on 11 July, 2020.

Mansfield, H. 1989. *Taming the Prince: The Ambivalence of Modern Executive Power.* New York: Macmillan.

Mantere, S. 2013. "What Is Organizational Strategy? A Language-Based View", *Journal of Management Studies*, 50(8): 1408–26.

March, J.G. 1962. "The Business Firm as a Political Coalition", *The Journal of Politics*, 24(4): 662–78.

Marshall, R., Fowler, B., and Olson, N. 2015. *The Chief Communications Officer: Survey and Findings among the Fortune 500.* Los Angeles, LA: Korn Ferry. Retrieved from: https://www.kornferry.com/content/dam/kornferry/docs/article-migration/Korn-Ferry-Institute-The-Chief-Communications-Officer.pdf

Martin, G., Currie, G., Weaver, S., Finn, R., and McDonald, R. 2017. "Institutional Complexity and Individual Responses: Delineating the Boundaries of Partial Autonomy", *Organization Studies*, 38(1): 103–27.

Mathison, D. 2020. "Salesforce Acquires The CMO Club". Newsletter email. Chief Digital Officer Club cdoclub-service@chiefdigitalofficerclub.biglist.com (6 March).

Mayo, A. and Nohria, N. 2005. *In Their Time: The Greatest Business Leaders of the XX Century.* Boston, MA: Harvard Business School Press.

Mazza, C. and Alvarez, J.L. 2000. "Haute Couture and Pret-a-Porter: The Popular Press and the Diffusion of Management Practices", *Organization Studies*, 21(3): 567–89.

Mazza, C. and Strandgaard Pedersen, J. 2015. "Good Reading Makes Good Action: Nothing So Practical as a Managerial Panacea?" In Örtenblad, A. (ed.), *Handbook of Research on Managerial Panaceas: Adaptation and Context* (pp. 338–59). Cheltenham: Edward Elgar.

McCracken, G. 2009. *Chief Culture Officer: How to Create a Living, Breathing Corporation.* New York: Basic Books.

McDonnell, M. and King, B. 2013. "Keeping up Appearances: Reputational Threat and Impression Management after Social Movement Boycotts", *Administrative Science Quarterly*, 58(3): 387–419.

McPherson, Ch.M. and Sauder, M. 2013. "Logics in Action: Managing Institutional Complexity in a Drug Court." *Administrative Science Quarterly*, 58(2): 165–96.

me too. Impact Report, 2019. https://metoomvmt.org/wp-content/uploads /2020/01/2019-12-09_MeToo_ImpactReport_VIEW_4.pdf

Mees-Buss, J. and Welch, C. 2018. "Managerial Ideologies Dividing the Corporate Elite: A Process Study of the Rise and Fall of a Counterideology", *Organization Studies*, 40(4): 563–92.

Menz, M. 2012. "Functional Top Management Team Members: A Review, Synthesis and Research Agenda", *Journal of Management*, 38(1): 45–80.

Menz, M., Kunisch, S., and Collis, D. 2015. "The Corporate Headquarters in the Contemporary Corporation: Advancing a Multimarket Firms Perspective", *Academy of Management Annals*, 9(1): 633–714.

Menz, M., Müller-Stewens, G., Zimmermann, T., and Lattwein, Ch. 2013. "The Chief Strategy Officer in the European Firm: Professionalizing Strategy in Times of Uncertainty", *European Management Review*, May–June: 5–8.

Menz, M. and Scheef, Ch. 2014. "Chief Strategy Officers: Contingency Analysis of Their Presence in Top Management Teams", *Strategic Management Journal*, 35: 461–71.

Merton, R. 1948. "The Bearing of Empirical Research upon the Development of Social Theory", *American Sociological Review*, 13(5): 505–15.

Meyer, J. 2002. "Globalization, Expansion, and Standardization of Management". In Sahlin-Andersson, K. and Engwall, L. (eds), *The Expansion of Management Knowledge: Carriers, Flows, and Sources* (pp. 33–44). Stanford, CA: Stanford Business Books.

Meyer, J. and Bromley, P. 2013. "The Worldwide Expansion of 'Organization'", *Sociological Theory*, 3(4): 366–89.

Meyer, J. and Rowan, B. 1977. "Institutionalised Organizations: Formal Structures as Myth and Ceremony", *American Journal of Sociology*, 83(2): 340–63.

Meyer, R.E. 2014. "'Re-localization' as Micro-mobilization of Consent and Legitimacy". In Drori, G. S., Höllerer, M. A., and Walgenbach, P. (eds), *Global Themes and Local Variations in Organizations and Management: Perspectives on Glocalization* (pp. 79–89). New York: Routledge.

Meyer, R.E. and Hammerschmid, G. 2006. "Changing Institutional Logics and Executive Identities", *American Behavioural Scientist*, 49(7): 1000–14.

Meyer, R. and Höllerer, M. 2010. "Meaning Structures in a Contested Issue Field: A Topographic Map of Shareholder Value in Austria", *Academy of Management Journal*, 53(6): 1241–62.

Meyer, R.E., Jancsary, D., Höllerer, M., and Boxenbaum, E. 2018. "The Role of Verbal and Visual Text in the Process of Institutionalization", *Academy of Management Review*, 43(3): 392–418.

Meyer, R.E., Sahlin, K., Ventresca, M.J., and Walgenbach, P. 2009. "Ideology and Institutions: Introduction", *Research in the Sociology of Organizations*, 27: 1–15, Bingley: Emerald Group Publishing Limited.

Meyerson, D. and Scully, M. 1995. "Tempered Realism and the Politics of Ambivalence and Change", *Organizational Science*, 6(5): 585–600.

Michels, R. 1915. *Political Parties: A Sociological Study of the Oligarchical Tendencies of Modern Democracy*. New York: Hearst International Co.

Mikes, A. Hall, M. and Millo,Y. 2013. "How Experts Gain Influence", *Harvard Business Review*, 91(7/8): 70–74.

Miles, S.A., Bennett, N., and Shill, W. 2012. "The Disappearing COO and the Evaporating Talent Pool". Bloomberg, 10 Sept, retrieved from: https://www.bloomberg.com/news/articles/2012-09-10/the-disappearing-coo-and-the-evaporating-talent-pool

Miller, K. and Serafeim, G. 2014. Chief Sustainability Officers: Who Are They and What They Do? Harvard Business School Research Paper. 9 November.

Miner, A. 1987. "Idiosyncratic Jobs in Formalized Organizations", *Administrative Science Quarterly*, 32: 327–51.

Miner, A. 1990. "Idiosyncratic Jobs: The Potential for Unplanned Learning", *Organization Science*, 1(2): 195–210.

Miner, A. and Akinsanmi, O. 2016. "Structural Evolution through Idiosyncratic Jobs, Organizational Transformation, and Career Mobility". Research in the Sociology of Organizations, 47: 61–101, Bingley: Emerald Group Publishing Limited.

Mintzberg, H. 1973. "A New Look at the Chief Executive's Job", *Organizational Dynamics*, 1(30): 20–30.

Mintzberg, H. 1979. *The Structuring of Organizations*. Englewood Cliffs, NJ: Prentice Hall.

Mishra, G. 2018. Women in the C-Suite: The Next Frontier in Gender Diversity. https://corpgovlawharvardedu/2018/08/13/women-in-the-c-suite-the-next-frontier-in-gender-diversity/,posted on 13 August.

Mitsuhashi, H. and Greve, H. 2004. "Powerful and Free: Intraorganizational Power and the Dynamics of Strategy", *Strategic Organization*, 2(2): 107–32.

Mizruchi, M. and Marshal II, L. 2016. "Corporate CEOs, 1890–2015: Titans, Bureaucrats and Saviours", *Annual Review of Sociology*, 42: 143–63.

Mobb, S. 2018. "Firm CFO Board Membership and Departures", *Journal of Corporate Finance*, 51: 316–31.

Mohammed, S. and Nadkarni, S. 2014. "Are We All on the Same Temporal Page? The Moderating Effects of Temporal Team Cognition on the Polychronicity

Diversity–Team Performance Relationship", *Journal of Applied Psychology*, 99(3): 404–22.

Moore, M. 1995. *Creating Public Value: Strategic Management in Government*. Cambridge, MA: Harvard University Press.

Moore, M. 2013. *Recognizing Public Value*. Cambridge, MA: Harvard University Press.

Morgan, B. 2020. The Case Against a Chief Customer Officer, Forbes, 5 Jan. Retrieved from: https://www.forbes.com/sites/blakemorgan/2020/01/05/the-case-against-a-chief-customer-officer/#59823f4f181c.

Mulgan, G. 2010. "Measuring Social Value", *Stanford Social Innovation Review*, Summer, https://ssir.org/articles/entry/measuring_social_value

Munir, K. 2015. "A Loss of Power in Institutional Theory", *Journal of Management Inquiry*, 24(1): 90–2.

Mylander, W. 1955. "Management by Executive Committee", *Harvard Business Review*, 33(3): 51–8.

Nadler, D., Spencer, J. and Associates. (eds). 1998. *Executive Teams*. San Francisco, CA: Jossey-Bass Publishers.

Nath, P. and Mahajan, V. 2008. "Chief Marketing Officers: A Study of Their Presence in Top Management Teams.", *Journal of Marketing*, 72: 65–81.

Nath, P. and Mahajan, V. 2011. "Marketing in the C-Suite: A Study of Chief Marketing Officers' Power in Top Management Teams", *Journal of Marketing*, 75: 60–77.

National Association of Corporate Directors (NACD). 2013. C-Suite Expectations: Understanding C-Suite Roles Beyond the Core. Washington, DC. Retrieved from: https://www.nacdonline.org/files/FileDownloads/PDF/C-Suite%20Expectations_1364247261983_2.pdf

Neilson, G. 2015. "The Decline of the COO", Forbes, May 20, https://www.forbes.com/sites/strategyand/2015/05/20/the-decline-of-the-coo/?sh=6b8a2abe7cee.

New York Public Library. 2019. https://www.nypl.org/help/about-nypl/president-and-leadership, accessed on 22 May 2019.

Nigam, A., Sackett, E., and Golden, B. 2021. "Duality and Social Position: Role Expectations of People Who Combine Outsider-ness and Insider-ness in Organizational Change", *Organization Studies*, https://doi.org/10.1177/0170840621989004.

Nohria, N. and Ghoshal, S. 1997. *The Differentiated Network: Organizations Knowledge Flows in Multinational Corporations*. San Francisco, CA: Jossey-Bass.

Nowosel, K., Terrill, A., and Timmermans, K. 2015. Procurement's Next Frontier: The Future Will Give Rise to an Organization of One. Accenture Strategy. https://www.accenture.com/_acnmedia/pdf-52/accenture-digital-procurement-next-frontier.pdf

O'Mahony, S. and Bechky, B. 2008. "Boundary Organizations: Enabling Collaboration among Unexpected Allies", *Administrative Science Quarterly*, 53: 422–59.

Ocasio, W. 1994. "Political Dynamics and the Circulation of Power: CEO Succession in U.S. Industrial Corporations, 1960-1990". *Administrative Science Quarterly*, 39(2), 285–312.

Ocasio, W. 1997. "Towards an Attention-based View of the Firm", *Strategic Management Journal*, 18 (Summer Special Issue): 187–206.

Ocasio, W. and Joseph, J. 2005. Cultural Adaptation and Institutional Change: The Evolution of Vocabularies of Corporate Governance, 1972–2003. *Poetics*, 33(3–4): 163–78.

Ocasio, W. 2011. "Attention to Attention", *Organization Science*, 22(5): 1286–96.

Ocasio, W. and Gai, S. 2020. "Institutions: Everywhere but Not Everything", *Journal of Management Enquiry*, 29(3): 262–71.

Oh, H. and Kilduff, M. 2008. "The Ripple Effect of Personality on Social Structure: Self-monitoring Origins of Network Brokerage". *Journal of Applied Psychology*, 93(5): 1155–64.

Ohl, M. (translated by E. Lauffer). 2018. *The Art of Naming*. Cambridge, MA: The MIT Press.

Oxford Learner Dictionaries. 2020. Complexity. Retrieved from: https://www.oxfordlearnersdictionaries.com/definition/english/complexity

Pallas, J. and Fredriksson, M. 2013. "Corporate Media Work and Micro-dynamics of Mediatization", *European Journal of Communication*, 28(4): 420–35.

Pallas, J., Fredriksson, M., and Wedlin, L. 2016. "Translating Institutional Logics: When the Media Logic Meets Professions". *Organization Studies*. 37(11): 1661–1684.

Parsons, T. 1956a. "Suggestions for a Sociological Approach to the Theory of Organizations I", *Administrative Science Quarterly*, 1(1): 63–85.

Parsons, T. 1956b. "Suggestions for a Sociological Approach to the Theory of Organizations II", *Administrative Science Quarterly*, 1(2): 225–39.

Pattek, S., Moorehead, M., and Abele, J. 2016. *The Evolved Chief Marketing Officer: CMOs Broaden Their Influence and Leadership*. Heidrick and Struggles in collaboration with Forrester. https://www.heidrick.com/Knowledge-Center/Publication/The-evolved-CMO-in-2016-CMOs-broaden-their-influence-and-leadership.

Peppard, J. 2010. "Unlocking the Performance of the Chief Information Officer (CIO)", *California Management Review*, 52(4): 73–99.

Pernell, K., Jung, J., and Dobbin, F. 2017. "The Hazards of Expert Control: Chief Risk Officers and Risky Derivatives", *American Sociological Review*, 82(3): 511–41.

Perrow, Ch. 1961. "The Analysis of Goals in Complex Organizations". *American Sociological Review*, 26(6): 854–866.

Perrow, Ch. 1986. *Complex Organizations: A Critical Essay*. Third edition. New York: Random House.

Pettigrew, A. 1973. "Occupational Specialization as an Emergent Process", *Sociological Review*, 21(2): 255–78.

Pettigrew, A. 1992. "On Studying Management Elites", *Strategic Management Journal*, 13: 163–82.

Pfeffer, J. and Salancik, G. 1978. *The External Control of Organizations: A Resource Dependence Perspective*. New York: Harper & Row.

Pihakis, J., Shah Paikeday, T., Armstrong, K., and Meneer, E. 2019. "The Emergence of the Chief Diversity Officer Role in Higher Education", *Russell Reynolds*

Associates. 19 July; retrieved from https://www.russellreynolds.com/insights/thought-leadership/the-emergence-of-the-chief-diversity-officer-role-in-higher-education on, 19 Jan 2020.

Powell, T. and Angwin, D. 2012, "The Role of the CSO", *MIT Sloan Management Review*, 54(1): 15–16.

Powell, W. and Sandholtz, K. 2012. "Amphibious Entrepreneurs and the Emergence of Organizational Forms", *Strategic Entrepreneurship Journal*, 6(2): 94–115.

Power, M. 1997. *The Audit Society.* Oxford: Oxford University Press.

Power, M. 2004. *The Risk Management of Everything: Rethinking the Politics of Uncertainty.* London: Demos.

Power, M. 2005. "Organizational Responses to Risk: The Rise of the Chief Risk Officer". In Hutter, B. and Power, M. (eds), *Organizational Encounters with Risk* (pp. 132–48). Cambridge: Cambridge University Press.

Power, M. 2007. *Organized Uncertainty: Designing a World of Risk Management.* Oxford: Oxford University Press.

PricewaterhouseCoopers. 2008. *I for Innovation: The Next-generation CIO.* Center for Technology and Innovation, PricewaterhouseCoopers LLP.

Puranam, P. 2018. *The Microstructures of Organizations.* Oxford: Oxford University Press.

Radek, E. and Menz, M. 2020. Top Management Teams: Structure and Review: A Research Agenda. Working Paper. Retrieved from: https://www.alexandria.unisg.ch/publications/260735.

Raffaelli, R. and Glynn, M.A. 2015. "What is so Institutional about Leadership: Leadership Mechanisms of Value Infusion", *Research in the Sociology of Organizations*, 44: 283–316, Bingley: Emerald Group Publishing Limited.

Rao, H., Monin, P. and Durand, R. 2003. "Institutional Change in Toque Ville: Nouvelle Cuisine as an Identity Movement in French Gastronomy", *American Journal of Sociology*, 108(4): 795–843.

Raskino, M. 2015. CEOs Must Reappraise the Role of Chief Strategy Officers, Gartner, Inc.

Rassam, A. 2018. The Keys to Successful CEO–CHRO Partnerships. https://www.heidrick.com/Knowledge-Center/Article/The_keys_to_successful_CEO_CHRO_partnerships

Raymond, A. 2021. The Chief People Officer Vs Chief Talent Officer—What is the difference? Redline Group Recruitment News and Blogs. https://www.redlinegroup.com/insights/the-chief-people-officer-vs-chief-talent-officer-what-is-the-difference-81843919254

Raynard, M. 2016. "Deconstructing complexity: Configurations of Institutional Complexity and Structural Hybridity", *Strategic Organization*, 14(4): 310–35.

Reay, T, Golden-Biddle, K., and Germann, K. 2006. "Legitimizing a New Role: Small Wins and Microprocesses of Change", *Academy of Management Journal*, 49(5): 977–98.

Rickards, T., Smaje, K., and Sohoni, V. 2015. Transformer in Chief: The New Digital Officer, *McKinsey Digital*, September. Retrieved from: https://www.mckinsey.

com/business-functions/organization/our-insights/transformer-in-chief-the-new-chief-digital-officer

Rivero, J. and Spencer, J. 1998. "Designing CEO and COO Roles". In Nadler, D., Spencer, J., & Associates (eds.), *Executive Teams* (pp. 60–80). San Francisco, CA: Jossey-Bass.

Roberto, M. 2003. "The Stable Core and Dynamic Periphery in Top Management Teams", *Management Decision*, 41(2): 120–31.

Roberto, M. 2005. *Why Great Leaders Don't Take Yes for an Answer: Managing for Conflict and Consensus*. Philadelphia, PA: Wharton School Publishing.

Roberts, D. and Watson, B.P. 2014. *Confessions of a Successful CIO: How the Best CIOs Tackle Their Toughest Business Challenges*. Hoboken, NJ: John Wiley & Sons, Inc.

Rockart, J., Ball, L., and Bullen, C. 1982. "Future Role of the Information Systems Executive", *MIS Quarterly*, 6(4): 1–14.

Rogish, A., Sandler, S., and Shemluck, N. 2020. "Women in the C-suite: Growth in Emerging Leadership Roles Creates New Opportunities in Financial Services". *Deloitte Insights*. 4 March. Retrieved from: https://www2.deloitte.com/us/en/insights/industry/financial-services/women-in-the-c-suite.html

Rovnick, N. 2018. "EasyJet Revenues Boosted by Struggles at Rival Airlines", *The Financial Times*, 23 Jan, https://www.ft.com/content/f8d70cf2-000f-11e8-9650-9c0ad2d7c5b5

Russell 3000 Index. 2021. FTSE Russell. https://research.ftserussell.com/Analytics/FactSheets/temp/5e5164de-077a-4abd-b2ec-dc380d993677.pdf, 31 July.

Russell Reynolds. 2009. CIO Leadership Diagnostic, p 4.

Russell Reynolds. 2012a. Leadership and Talent, "The Rise of the CDO", p. 3.

Russell Reynolds. 2012b. The Evolution of the Chief Procurement Officer, p. 2.

Russell Reynolds. 2017. Inside the Mind of the CHRO, p. 7.

Russell Reynolds. 2020a. "The End of Expertise? Rethinking the C-suite", *Thought Leadership*.

Russell Reynolds. 2020b. The Rise of the Chief Content Officer in non-Media Companies, 18 February.

Sahlin, K. and Wedlin, L. 2008. "Circulating Ideas: Imitation, Translation and Editing". In Greenwood, R., Oliver, C., Sahlin, K., and Suddaby, R. (eds), *The SAGE Handbook of Organizational Institutionalism* (pp: 218–42). London: Sage.

Sahlin-Andersson, K. and Engwall, L. (eds.). 2002. *The Expansion of Management Knowledge: Carriers, Flows, and Sources*. Stanford, CA: Stanford University Press.

Sandhu, S. and Kulik, C. 2019. "Shaping and Being Shaped: How Organizational Structure and Managerial Discretion Co-Evolve in New Managerial Roles", *Administrative Science Quarterly*, 64(3): 619–58.

Schick, S. 2019. The Man Who Founded CDO Club Is Ready to Scale His Community of Digital Leaders. B2B News Network, 21 June. Retrieved from: https://www.b2bnn.com/2019/06/cdo-club/

Schjeldahl, P. 2018. "Hilma af Klint's Visionary Paintings", *The New Yorker*, 15 October, https://www.newyorker.com/magazine/2018/10/22/hilma-af-klints-visionary-paintings.

Schotter, A., Mudambi, R., Doz, Y., and Gaur, A. 2017. "Boundary Spanning in Global Organizations", *Journal of Management Studies*, 54(4): 403–21.

Schultz, M. and Hernes, T. 2020. "Temporal Interplay between Strategy and Identity: Punctuated, Subsumed, and Sustained Modes", *Strategic Organization*, 18(1): 106–35.

Schüßler, E. and Sydow, J. 2015. "Organizing Events for Configuring and Maintaining Creative Fields". In Jones, C., Lorenzen, M., and Sapsed, J. (eds), *The Oxford Handbook of Creative Industries* (pp. 284–300). Oxford: Oxford University Press.

Scoblic, J. 2020. "Learning from the Future: How to Make Robust Strategy in Times of Deep Uncertainty", *Harvard Business Review*, 98(4): 37–47.

Seabrooke, L. and Henriksen, L. (eds). 2017. *Professional Networks in Transnational Governance*. Cambridge: Cambridge University Press.

Selznick, P. 1957. *Leadership in Administration: A Sociological Interpretation*. Los Angeles: University of California Press.

Selznick, P. 1969. *Law, Society and Industrial Justice*. New York, NY: Russell Sage Foundation.

Selznick, P. 2005. "American Society and the Rule of Law", *Syracuse Journal of International Law and Commerce*, 33(1): 29–39.

Sehgal, S. 2020. "What Do Successful Chief Digital Officers Do?" Capgemini. Retrieved from: https://www.capgemini.com/2020/03/what-do-successful-chief-digital-officers-do/.

Seo, M.-G. and Creed, W. 2002. "Institutional Contradictions, Praxis, and Institutional Change: A Dialectical Perspective", *Academy of Management Review*, 27(2): 222–47.

Shah, B., Hartman, G., and Whipple, B. 2014. CMOs: Time for Digital Transformation. Accenture Interactive. Accenture. Retrieved from: https://www.accenture.com/t20150523T022804__w__/usen/_acnmedia/Accenture/Conversion-Assets/DotCom/Documents/Global/PDF/Dualpub_10/Accenture-CMO-Insights-2014-pdf.pdf

Shepherd, D., McMullen, J., and Ocasio, W. 2017. "Is that an Opportunity? An Attention Model of Top Managers' Opportunity Beliefs for Strategic Action", *Strategic Management Journal*, 38(3): 626–44.

Show, M. 2016. The CPO Is dead. LinkedIn post, retrieved from: https://www.linkedin.com/pulse/cpo-dead-michael-shaw/

Simon, H. 1962. "The Architecture of Complexity," *Proceedings of the American Philosophical Society*, 106(6): 467–482.

Singh, A. and Hess, T. 2017. "How Chief Digital Officers Promote the Digital Transformation of Their Companies". *MIS Quarterly Executive*, 16(1): 1–17.

Slavich, B., Svejenova, S., Opazo, P., and Patriotta, G. 2020. "Politics of Meaning in Categorizing Innovation: How Chefs Advanced Molecular Gastronomy by Resisting the Label", *Organization Studies*, 41(2): 267–90.

Smircich, L. and Morgan G. 1982. "Leadership: The Management of Meaning", *Journal of Applied Behavioral Science*, 3: 257–73.

Snyder, M. 1974. "Self-Monitoring of Expressive Behaviour", *Journal of Personality and Social Psychology*, 30: 526–37.

Soderstrom, S. and Weber, K. 2020. "Organizational Structure from Interaction: Evidence from Corporate Sustainability Efforts", *Administrative Science Quarterly*, 65(1): 226–71.

Spencer Stuart. 2015. From Chief Marketing Officer to CEO: The Route to the Top. Spencer Stuart. Retrieved from: https://www.spencerstuart.com/-/media/pdf%20files/research%20and%20insight%20pdfs/cmotoceo_09jun2015.pdf

Spencer Stuart. 2017a. Human Resources, Staying on the Leading Edge, Five Important Qualities for Aspiring Chief Human Resources Officers, pp. 2–3.

Spencer Stuart. 2017b. License to Thrive: Next Generation Sustainability Leaders, p. 9.

Spencer Stuart. 2018a. The Rise of the Learning Culture. Point of View. Spencer Stuart. Retrieved from: https://www.spencerstuart.com/-/media/2018/pov/pov2018-the-rise-of-the-learning-culture.pdf

Spencer Stuart. 2018b. The Technology Officer. "The CIO and Digital Transformation", p. 3.

Spencer Stuart and Weber Shandwick. 2012. The Rising CCO IV. Retrieved from: https://www.webershandwick.com/uploads/news/files/Rising_CCO_IV.pdf

Stephenson, C. and Olson, N. 2017. "Why CIOs Make Great Board Directors", *Harvard Business Review*, 15 March, https://hbr.org/2017/03/why-cios-make-great-board-directors, accessed on 12 July 2020.

Stern, I. and Westphal, J. 2010. "Stealthy Footsteps to the Boardroom: Executive Backgrounds, Sophisticated Influence Behavior, and Board Appointments", *Administrative Science Quarterly* 55(2), June: 278–319.

Stets, J. and Burke, P. 2000. "Identity Theory and Social Identity Theory", *Social Psychological Quarterly* 63(3): 224–37.

Stjerne, I. and Svejenova, S. 2016. "Connecting Temporary and Permanent Organizing: Tensions and Boundary Work in Sequential Film Projects". *Organization Studies*, 37(12): 1771–1792.

Strand, R. 2014. "Strategic Leadership of Corporate Sustainability", *Journal of Business Ethics*, 123: 687–706.

Strang, D. and Baron, N. 1990. "Categorical Imperatives: The Structure of Job Titles in California State Agencies", *American Sociological Review*, 55: 479–95.

Strang, D. and Meyer, J.W. 1993. "Institutional Conditions for Diffusion". *Theory and Society*, 22: 487–511.

Study.com. 2020. Chief Listening Officer: Job Description & Salary, 30 May. Retrieved from: https://study.com/articles/chief_listening_officer_job_description_salary.html

Svejenova, S. and Alvarez, J.L. 2017. "Changing the C-suite: New Chief Officer Roles as Strategic Responses to Institutional Complexity". In Krücken, G., Mazza, C., Meyer, R. E., and Walgenbach, P. (eds), *New Themes in Institutional Analysis:*

Topics and Issues from European Research (pp. 135–61). Cheltenham: Edward Elgar.

Swidler, A. 1986. "Culture in Action: Symbols and Strategies". *American Sociological Review*, 51(2): 273–286.

Talman, K. 2020. "Does a Sustainability Leader Add Value at Board Level?", *The Financial Times*, 7 December.

Thompson, J. 1967. *Organizations in Action. Social Science Bases of Administrative Theory*. New York: McGraw Hill.

Thompson, J. 2020. "Big Investors' Sustainability Push Drives Demand for Environmental Expertise", *Financial Times*, 2 March.

Thornton, P., Ocasio, W., and Lounsbury, M. 2012. *The Institutional Logics Perspective: A New Approach to Culture, Structure and Process*. Oxford: Oxford University Press.

Tinker, A. and Lowe, E. 1978. "Some Empirical Evidence as to the Case of the Superordinate Integrator". *Journal of Management Studies*, 15(1): 91–108.

Tobak, S. 2009. "The Chief Everything Officer Phenomenon", *CBS Money Watch*, 17 June.

Tolbert, P. and Zucker, L. 1983. "Institutional Sources of Change in Formal Structures of Organizations: The Diffusion of Civil Service Reform: 1880–1935", *Administrative Science Quarterly*, 28: 22–39.

Tolbert, P. and Zucker, L. 2020. "What Are Microfoundations? Why and How to Study Them?". Research in the Sociology of Organizations, 65A: 3–8, Bingley: Emerald Group Publishing Limited.

Tricker, B. 2015. *Corporate Governance: Principles, Policies, and Practices*. Oxford: Oxford University Press.

Tulimieri, P. and Banai, M. 2010. "The CEO and CFO—A Partnership of Equals", *Organizational Dynamics*, 39(3): 240–7.

Tushman, M. 1977a. "A Political Approach to Organizations: A Review and Rationale". *Academy of Management Review*, 2(2): 206–216.

Tushman, M. 1977b. "Special Boundary Roles in the Innovation Processes", *Administrative Science Quarterly*, 22(4): 587–605.

Tushman, M. and Scanlan, T. 1981a. "Characteristics and External Orientations of Boundary Spanning Individuals", *Academy of Management Journal*, 24(1): 83–98.

Tushman, M. and Scanlan, T. 1981b. "Boundary Spanning Individuals: Their Role in Information Transfer and Their Antecedents", *Academy of Management Journal*, 24(2): 289–305.

Ulrich, D. and Filler, E. 2014. *CEOs and CHROs: Crucial Allies and Potential Successors*. Los Angeles, CA: Korn Ferry Institute.

Ulrich, D. and Filler, E. 2015. "CEOs and CHROs: Expectation, Connection, and Succession", *Leader to Leader*, 77: 33–41.

Ulrich, D. and Wilson Burns, E. 2018. How Do HR Influence Others? The RBL Group, 16 November.

Ulrich, D., Schiemann, B., and Sartain, L. 2015. *The Rise of HR: Wisdom from 75 Thought Leaders*. Alexandria, VA: HR Certification Institute.

Uyterhoeven, H. 1972. "General Managers in the Middle", *Harvard Business Review*, 50(2): 75–86.

Vaara, E., Sorsa, V., and Pälli, P. 2010. "On the Force Potential of Strategy Texts: A Critical Discourse Analysis of a Strategic Plan and Its Power Effects in a City Organization", *Organization*, 17(6): 685–702.

Van de Ven, A.H., Ganco, M., and Hinings, C.R. 2013. "Returning to the Frontier of Contingency Theory of Organizational and Institutional Designs", *The Academy of Management Annals*, 7(1): 393–440.

Van Dijk, T. 1995. "Aims of Critical Discourse Analysis", *Japanese Discourse*, 1(1): 17–28.

Vancil, R. 1978. *Decentralization: Managerial Ambiguity by Design*. Homewood, IL.: Dow Jones-Irwin.

Vancil, R. 1987. *Passing the Baton: Managing the Process of CEO Succession*. Boston, MA: Harvard Business School Press.

Vancil, R. and Green, C. 1984. "How CEOs Use Top Management Teams", *Harvard Business Review*, January–February: 65–73.

Vermeulen, P.A.M., Zietsma, C, Greenwood, R., and Langley, A. 2016. "Strategic Responses to Institutional Complexity", *Strategic Organization*, 14(4): 277–86.

Waeger, D. and Weber, K. 2019. "Institutional Complexity and Organizational Change: An Open Polity Perspective", *Academy of Management Review*, 44(2): 336–59.

Wageman, R., Nunes, D., Burruss, J. and Hackman, R. 2008. *Senior Leadership Teams: What It Takes to Make Them Great*. Boston, MA: Harvard Business School Press.

Watson, T. 1977. *The Personnel Managers: A Study in the Sociology of Work and Employment*. New York: Routledge.

Weber, K. and Waeger, D. 2017. "Organizations as Polities: An Open Systems Perspective", *Academy of Management Annals*, 11(2): 886–918.

Weber, M. 1978. *Economy and Society. An Outline of Interpretive Sociology*. Edited by Roth, G. and Wittich, C., Berkeley, CA: The University of California Press.

Weiss, R. and Miller, L. 1987. "The Concept of Ideology in Organizational Analysis: The Sociology of Knowledge or the Social Psychology of Beliefs?" *Academy of Management Review*, 12(1): 104–16.

Westphal, J. and Graeber, M. 2010. "A Matter of Appearances: How Corporate Leaders Manage the Impressions of Financial Analysts about the Conduct of Their Boards", *Academy of Management Journal*, 53(1): 15–44.

Westphal, J. and Zajac, E. 2001. "Decoupling Policy from Practice: The Case of Stock Repurchase Program", *Administrative Science Quarterly*, 46(2): 202–28.

White, H. 1992. *Identity and Control: A Structural Theory of Social Action*. Princeton, NJ: Princeton University Press.

White, H. 2008. *Identity and Control: How Social Formations Emerge*. Princeton, NJ: Princeton University Press.

Whitley, R. 1989. "On the Natural of Managerial Tasks and Skills: Their Distinguishing Characteristics and Organization", *Journal of Management Studies*, 26(3): 209–24.

Whittington, R. 2019. *Opening Strategy: Professional Strategists and Practice Change, 1960 to Today*. Oxford: Oxford University Press.

Whittington, R. and Yakis-Douglas, B. 2020. "The Grand Challenge of Corporate Control: Opening Strategy to the Normative Pressures of Networked Professionals", *Organization Theory*, 1: 1–19.

Whittington, R., Caillvet, L., and Yakis-Douglas, B. 2011. "Opening Strategy: Evolution of a Precarious Profession", *British Journal of Management*, 22: 531–44.

Wilensky, H.L. 1964. "The Professionalization of Everyone?", *American Journal of Sociology*, 70(2): 137–58.

Willmott, H. 2015. "Why Institutional Theory Cannot Be Critical". *Journal of Management Inquiry*, 24: 105–111.

Willmott, H. 2019. "Can it? On Expanding Institutional Theory by Disarming Critique". *Journal of Management Inquiry*, 28: 350–353.

Williams, P. 2002. "The Competent Boundary Spanner?", *Public Administration*, 80(1): 103–24.

Williams, P. 2013. "We Are All Boundary Spanners Now?", *International Journal of Public Sector Management*, 26(1): 17–32.

Woodward, J. 1965. *Industrial Organization: Theory and Practice*, Oxford: Oxford University Press.

Woolbridge, B. and Floyd, S. 1990. "The Strategic Process, Middle Management Involvement, and Organizational Performance", *Strategic Management Journal*, 11(3): 231–41.

Wright, P., Boudreau, J., Pace, D., Sartain, E., McKinnon, P., and Antoine, R. 2011. *The Chief HR Officer: Defining the New Role of Human Resource Leaders*. San Francisco, CA: Jossey-Bass.

Wrzesniewski, A. and Dutton, J. 2001. "Crafting a Job: Revisioning Employees as Active Crafters of Their Work". *Academy of Management Review*, 26(2): 179–201.

Yagi, N. and Klienberg, J. 2011. "Boundary Work: An Interpretative Ethnographic Perspective on Negotiating and Leveraging Cross-Cultural Identity", *Journal of International Business Studies*, 42: 629–53.

Zald, M. and Lounsbury, M. 2010. "The Wizards of Oz: Towards an Institutional Approach to Elites, Expertise and Command Posts". *Organization Studies*, 31(7): 963–96.

Zealley, J., El-Warraky, N., and McGrath, M. 2019. Way beyond Marketing: The Rise of the Hyper-relevant CMO. #CMOInsights, Accenture. Retrieved from: https://www.accenture.com/_acnmedia/PDF-97/Accenture-CMO-Long-Report.pdf#zoom=50

Zielinsky, D. 2019. Can CHROs and Chief Digital Officers Get Along? SHRM, 8 April. Retrieved from: https://www.shrm.org/resourcesandtools/hr-topics/technology/pages/can-chros-and-chief-digital-officers-get-along.aspx

Zorn, D. 2004. "Here a Chief, There a Chief: The Rise of the CFO in the American Firm", *American Sociological Review*, 69(3): 345–64.

Zorn, D., Dobbin, F., Dierkes, J., and Kwok, M. 2004. "Managing Investors: How Financial Markets Reshaped the American Firm". In Knorr Cetrina, K. and

Preda, A. (eds), *The Sociology of Financial Markets* (pp. 269–89). Oxford: Oxford University Press.

Zuboff, S. 2019. *The Age of Surveillance Capitalism*. London: Profile Books.

Zucker, L. 1987. "Institutional Theories of Organizations", *Annual Review of Sociology*, 13: 443–64.

Index

Note: Tables and figures are indicated by an italic *t* and *f* following the page number.